The Word in Motion
New Testament

Rachael Carman
Illustrated by Anderson Carman

Contributing Authors:
Davis Carman, MS
Bonnie Newell, PhD Religious Studies
Doug Powell, MA Apologetics
David Webb

apologia

The Word in Motion
Volume 2: New Testament

Published by
Apologia Educational Ministries, Inc.
P.O. Box 896844
Charlotte, NC, 28289-6844
www.apologia.com

Published in partnership with
Walk Thru the Bible Ministries

ISBN: 978-1-946506-65-8

Cover and Book Design: Doug Powell
Illustrations: Anderson Carman

Printed by Asia Printing Co., Ltd, Seoul, South Korea
April 2021

10 9 8 7 6 5 4 3 2 1

To the glory of God and His Kingdom.

To the families who seek to know and serve the Lord.

To my grandchildren and those yet to be born.

Table of Contents

PART I: THE NEW TESTAMENT IN 40 POINTS

PART 2: THE 27 BOOKS OF THE NEW TESTAMENT

Acknowledgments

There's nothing like a great story. And although this curriculum is about the best story of all time, the backstory of how this curriculum came to be is pretty good in its own right. From the first time I attended a Walk Thru the Bible live seminar to when this textbook arrived in the Apologia warehouse was a total of twenty-five years. I know, right? That's a long time from concept to publication by any industry standard.

During this lengthy incubation period, God was at work teaching me perseverance, patience, diligence, and faith. The Word in Motion was always God's project, for God's people, based on God's Word. And it finally came together in His perfect timing, which was much later than I'd originally hoped but which I can now say, without hesitation, was indeed the right time. Through twenty-five years of writing, wrestling, and waiting, nothing has been wasted. Nothing. I'm as grateful for everything that was left on the editing room floor as I am for what made it to print in these two volumes.

It was my mom, Nancy McCaghren, who first suggested that our young family attend a Walk Thru the Bible live seminar. The event was held at Calvary Church in Charlotte, North Carolina. Phil Tuttle was the presenter that weekend, and his enthusiasm for God and His Word was inspiring.

Then an idea flickered in my mom brain. Although we were still new to homeschooling at that time, it occurred to me that the Walk Thru the Bible motions and outline might be adapted into a wonderful curriculum that parents could use at home with their children. I successfully arranged a meeting with Phil at the Walk Thru the Bible offices in the Atlanta area. I walked in full of energy and passion and with a baby on my hip. Phil listened to my idea and then kindly advised me to fan the flame and keep him posted. I really appreciated how encouraging you were that day, Phil. Thanks for not laughing out loud and for sincerely listening. I felt heard.

Fast-forward to 2011, and I was back in Phil's office. This time I had a speaking ministry and publishing platform in Apologia Educational Ministries. We actually signed a contract and got to work. My team put in a great many hours of writing, development, discussions, and meetings. Unfortunately, it proved to be the wrong time yet again, as the project ran into a series of speed bumps, detours, and roadblocks. Phil did leave the door open for future discussions, though it seemed to me that this project was on life support and flatlining, if not already dead and buried.

Fast-forward again, this time to 2017. That year, I kept crossing paths with Phil Tuttle and Walk Thru the Bible. To be honest, this irritated me. I didn't want to be reminded of my failure, my dead dream, the never-finished project. Yet I could sense the Holy Spirit was moving. So Davis called Phil—again—and to say their discussion went well would be an understatement. Phil moved The Word in Motion from his list of "woulda-coulda-shoulda" projects to Walk Thru's "ongoing partnerships" file, and it seemed this might finally be the right time. We met with Walk Thru's Genny Baxley, who clearly believed in my dream. Thank you, Genny, for trusting me with this project and supporting us through its development. And thank you, Maggie Eldridge, who helped me register for Walk Thru training and consistently prayed for me. I love your heart!

The motions for the Bible story lines were provided by Walk Thru the Bible. I want to thank Jane O'Conner for helping me put together hand signs to go with the key words for each book.

Thanks to Lisa Nance and the moms at the HELP co-op who field-tested some of the curriculum content. You and your children provided me excellent feedback and reminded me each week of the many families I was working to help. I miss you all and think of you often.

David Webb, my editor, you and I have worked together on several writing projects. Thank you for staying true to my voice and yet editing it all in a way that others can read and enjoy! Thank you, Doug Powell, for the beautiful layout of the book and for your apologetic and doctrinal expertise. You both advised me and contributed to the development of each lesson, helping me to avoid errors along the way.

Thank you, Anderson Carman, for the spot-on illustrations, especially those of the real and raw characters and events of the Bible. It's been a particular pleasure to work with you on this project from the time you were only three years old and learning the original Walk Thru the Bible outline.

Thank you, Matt Barclay, for the multiple roles you played on this project. You were video master, audio recording expert and editor, and general apologetic and doctrine fact-checker. Thank you for your patience and honesty with me in the studio and for our various discussions of Scripture and God. Kamilah Peebles, you were the perfect onsite assistant for the video shoot, organizing the props, the scripts, and me—no small task. I also appreciate your work in the marketing of this curriculum. Thanks for your passion for the families and for all of the ways you challenge me to get the message out there. Thanks for your professionalism as well as your friendship.

Thank you, Michelle Moody, for leading the marketing team at Apologia. Ladd Lesh, thanks for steering the ship so ably and for shouldering the day-to-day operations. I am also grateful for the proofreading team of Lori Jaworski and Gerri Smith. It's good to know you have such keen eyes. The team at Apologia is the best!

Thanks to the women who hold up my weary arms—my prayer team: Jane Blythe, Jan Critz, Nita Erlien, and Kamilah Peebles. Each of you provided me words of encouragement at just the right time. You challenged and inspired me by your own spiritual diligence and perseverance. You faithfully and boldly took me, this project, and the families who would use this curriculum before the throne of grace. I'm so grateful.

Davis, you walked with me through all of this—a project that has occupied my thoughts during almost three-fourths of our thirty-four years of marriage. You're my man. You listened to my dream, my drafts, and my discouragement. Even when I thought the project was dead, you held on to hope. And you dared to call Phil and knock on the door one more time. Thanks for heading up this project and making it a priority at Apologia.

And thanks to my children—my original focus group—Charles, Anderson, Savannah Anne, Molly, Lilly, Joseph, and Benjamin. Thanks also to my daughters-in law, Tessa and Laura, and my three grandchildren (so far)—Cosette, Atticus, and Vincent. Thank you all for your encouragement and support as I've worked to complete this curriculum. You inspire me as you seek to honor God in word and deed. May God and His Word guard your hearts and guide your steps.

Introduction to the NEW TESTAMENT

Welcome to The Word in Motion! Whether you were raised going to church, you're new to the Christian faith, or you're just curious about the Bible, you're in for an amazing adventure. The Bible is the story of God's love for mankind and all of creation. But it's not just any story. It's the most important story ever told.

So we gathered a team of award-winning scholars, teachers, authors, and artists to develop an engaging and colorful resource that makes the Bible clear, understandable, and meaningful for the whole family. The Word in Motion is published by Apologia in partnership with Walk Thru the Bible Ministries. The curriculum is based on Walk Thru the Bible's updated forty-point Old Testament and New Testament outlines with accompanying motions and Bible book key word flash cards.

Just like the Bible, the Word in Motion curriculum is divided into two volumes: the Old Testament and the New Testament. In this second volume, we will study the New Testament. Here, God's story of love continues as the promised Messiah appears and walks among us, healing the sick, setting free the oppressed, and proclaiming the coming of His kingdom. We'll discover who Jesus is and what He's done. We'll learn about His earthly ministry, His death, and His resurrection. We will meet the men and women who followed Him and see how they turned the known world upside down with their testimony, faith, and Spirit-filled teaching.

The Bible can be intimidating no matter what your background, and the sixty-six books that make up the entire text loom large. Although the New Testament contains fewer books than the Old Testament, it still manages to include four different accounts of the life of Christ, the persecution and spread of the early church, the sermons and travels of major apostolic figures, and a powerful vision of the final struggle between good and evil. It can be a little overwhelming.

Yet it's in the New Testament that the main character of God's story is at last revealed, and we realize that everything that came before and everything that comes after is centered on this one individual—the only begotten Son of God. The birth of Jesus, the Christ, changes everything to the point that all of human history is measured relative to this moment. And it's only by reading and studying His teaching, and that of His apostles, that we come to understand the deeper meaning of prophecies, offerings, feasts, the law, and events of the Old Testament. Only with this hindsight can we begin to comprehend, for example, why God commanded Abraham to sacrifice his son Isaac yet stayed his hand at the last moment.

A Supporting Cast of Imperfect Characters

Earlier, I welcomed you to an adventure. Maybe you've never thought of Bible study as an adventure. But why not approach it that way as a family? Adventures take us to unknown places where we meet new people, gain new perspectives, and learn new things about ourselves and the world we live in.

The pages of Scripture offer all this and more.

Through this study, we'll visit some ancient locations and learn about cultures and practices that are foreign to us today. There we will meet some ordinary people who found themselves in extraordinary circumstances—people who were just living their lives when the Creator of the universe appeared and walked among them.

Throughout the Old Testament, the people, events, and prophets all pointed to the birth of Christ. In the New Testament, we get to meet Immanuel, "God with us." Think about that. God Himself stepped down from His throne to live among us as a man. His life, death, and (spoiler alert) resurrection from the dead—this is the climax of God's story.

Here, as in the Old Testament, we meet many people who are very much like you and me. Flawed, imperfect people. Moms, dads, and children. The rich and the poor. Patricians and the working class. Religious authorities and humble seekers. Celebrants, worshipers, and mourners. The rejected, oppressed, and broken. There are even a couple of people whom Jesus raises from the dead. You'll notice that some of these people are named and some go unnamed, but most are just ordinary people whom He calls to an extraordinary life.

Jesus consistently meets these flawed people right where they are, seeing them and their need through eyes of compassion, ready and able to forgive their sin. He knows the hearts of men and women, yet He came to save the world, not to condemn it. Even His miracles aren't intimidating displays of His infinite power but, rather, significant demonstrations of His love.

In the Gospels, Jesus calls, teaches, heals, leads, challenges, prays, answers, declares, prophesizes, talks, and fulfills. We will find a variety of responses from a variety of witnesses to these events. We will see Jesus interact with large crowds, small groups, families, and individuals. Yet in each instance His message is the same—a declaration of God's love and an invitation to live in the light of that love, to trust and obey and walk in a manner worthy. Some people respond in faith, some with criticism, some with disbelief, some with rejection, some with jealous hatred. Nothing new here. These kinds of responses are still in evidence today. Although Jesus came to declare and display the love of the Father, some still choose to reject that love.

What will *you* do with Jesus?

What Makes This Curriculum Unique?

There are plenty of Bible studies and curricula out there, as well as books and resources designed as guides to the people, places, and books of Scripture. So what sets The Word in Motion apart, making it the right choice for you and your family?

It's Engaging

The Word in Motion will engage a student's head, heart, and hands. During this study, you and your children will be encouraged to listen, see, talk, and move. Isn't that awesome? What's more, integrating auditory, visual, verbal, and kinesthetic learning styles reinforces fundamental biblical truths. That is, we're supposed to use our ears to hear, eyes to see, mouths to speak, and our hands and feet to serve while loving God with all our strength and living worthy of the light to which we've been called. The Christian faith isn't meant to be a passive, sit-still faith but, rather, an active, growing, and thriving faith. Hence the title, The Word in Motion.

Auditory learners will benefit from the video and narrative components (especially with a parent reading to them). Visual learners will engage with the videos and the beautiful illustrations. Verbal learners will thrive during discussions and, if they're ready, when reading to younger siblings. Kinesthetic learners will love the all-new, whole-body motions designed to help them remember the forty-point New Testament outline and the hand signs that help them remember the key word for each book of the New Testament.

In other words, this curriculum is designed to meet each of your children right where they are and in the way they learn best. The companion notebooking journal also includes a variety of activities for children to express themselves and build their understanding through writing, memorizing, presenting, analyzing, and creating. Your whole family will love it!

It's Foundational

The study of God's Word is essential for all of God's people, and as parents, we're charged with the discipleship of our children (Deuteronomy 6:7; Ephesians 6:4). It is important, therefore, that we know and teach what the Bible teaches. The Word in Motion provides the whole family with tools for learning and remembering the people, places, events, and teachings of the New Testament and how they are connected to the bigger picture of God's story. Thus, you and your family will be equipped with an outline of the New Testament that enhances your understanding of Scripture while offering opportunities for more in-depth study.

In addition, your family will also learn the major theme, a key word, and a hand sign for each book of the New Testament. There are twenty-seven books, which might sound like too many to study in detail, but it is actually possible for you and your students to know and quickly recall the messages contained in every one of them. If someone were to ask, would you be able to tell them what the book of James or Jude or Philemon is all about? By the end of this course, you'll be able to answer with a confident "Yes!"

Knowing the key people, places, and events of the New Testament narrative and the theme of all twenty-seven New Testament books will also give you new insight and clearer understanding of the events recorded in the Old Testament.

It's Timely

We know that a smaller percentage of people now attend church than in times past. And research has revealed that among those who claim to believe, biblical knowledge is marginal, as more and more Christians are being conformed to the world's belief system. Now is the time for families of faith to take a stand and become more biblically literate. As the people of God, we need to know what the Bible says and what it doesn't say. We need to know who the God of the Bible is, so that we can worship Him alone and not the gods of this world. We need to know how to pursue a right relationship with God and how to live as His children. And we need to place our hope in Jesus, not the world, for He is the One who will never fail us.

As parents raising the next generation, we need to know these truths ourselves and teach them diligently to our children. We are charged with the responsibility of training our children in the fear and admonition of the Lord. This means that we must intentionally instruct them in the ways of the Lord, His love, His commandments, His grace, and His truth. We cannot give what we do not have, but we can lead our families on a journey to learn these important truths together.

This curriculum has been developed with specific tools to help you and your family remember God's story, respond to His invitation, and rejoice in the hope of heaven that we have through Jesus Christ.

Preparing for Adventure

So what can you do to prepare yourself and your family for this adventure?

First, pray. Thank God for the revelation of His Word, the Bible, and the opportunity to learn from its truth. Ask Him to open your eyes and ears and heart—and those of your family—for all that He wants to teach you through this study. Ask Him to bless you as you lead your family in this study of the New Testament, and thank Him in advance for all He is going to show you.

Second, prioritize this study. The truths you and your kids will learn in this study hold the potential for significant life change. Together, you will discover that the time you spend seeking God in His Word is never wasted time. He always blesses it.

Third, prepare your mind. Know that like any other worthwhile endeavor, this is going to be challenging. Determine now that you will stay the course and see it through. When you come to a topic that is difficult or unclear, instead of giving up, dare to dig deeper. Dare to exercise faith and persevere, and encourage your family to do the same.

And finally, enjoy! This is an adventure, remember? Most adventures include risk, unforeseen roadblocks, imposing trails, and dangerous crossings. But they also come with awesome views, lifelong memories, and exhilarating discoveries! Lean into the journey. Whether or not this road is familiar to you, breathe it all in and enjoy a new perspective as you learn to stand on the rock-solid truth of the Bible.

Once again, welcome to The Word in Motion curriculum!

Rachael Carman

How to Use This Curriculum

The best way to work through *The Word in Motion: New Testament* curriculum is as a family—specifically, read by Mom and/or Dad with their children gathered around them, perhaps even snuggled together on the sofa. Just as seeking God through prayer and studying the Bible is a great way to begin the day, starting each school day with Bible class sets a positive tone for the rest of the day while cultivating a high view of God by making His Word a priority in your family.

Over the next few pages, we will walk you through how to use this curriculum. We will also introduce you to its primary components and then break down the parts of a lesson and show you how they reinforce the teaching. We will also suggest a general weekly rhythm for doing The Word in Motion, one that will allow you to complete a full lesson each week, for a total course time of thirty weeks. For more detailed course scheduling recommendations, we have included a lesson plan in the notebooking journal that suggests specific pages to read each day and identifies the corresponding activities to complete in the notebooking journal.

Before we get started, it is important that you remember to embrace and encourage the joy of learning, especially when it comes to studying the Bible. You are helping your children to establish healthy spiritual habits that will serve them well throughout their lives. To that end, The Word in Motion is not a curriculum to grit your teeth and grind through just to get it done. No, this is an adventure to enjoy together as you explore the magnificent wonders of God's story and the eternal truths of His Word.

Now, without further ado, here's what you need to know to get the most out of this curriculum.

Your Guide on This Journey

Meet Wyatt. He will be your tour guide as you take this journey through the Bible. Wyatt wears a blue hat and white T-shirt with the Word in Motion logo. You'll see him at the start of each video and textbook lesson, and he found his way into several pages of the notebooking journal. Wyatt will help you learn the motions, and you'll see him in most of the video lessons and Bible book key word flash cards.

The Tools You Will Use

The Word in Motion curriculum comes with three primary tools you will use to guide your family through this Bible study. These tools are the teaching videos, textbook, and the companion notebooking journal.

In addition, you will want to keep your Bible close at hand. You will be encouraged throughout this course to read directly from God's holy Word. Your children need to see and understand that it's important to always go to the original source and seek out what Scripture says directly instead of just taking someone else's word for it. Please note that this curriculum uses the ESV as the default translation. However, be assured that this curriculum will work just as well with your family's preferred translation.

Now let's take a look at each of the tools you will use to teach from The Word in Motion.

Videos

Each lesson begins with a four- or five-minute video you will stream online through Apologia's Book Extras site. Your family should watch the video together. In it, I'll teach the first half of the lesson. (In other words, the combination of the video and the textbook narrative comprise the entire lesson.) I will present some background, context, and a related Bible story. I will then teach you one or more motions or hand signs that go with that week's lesson.

In Lessons 1–15, you will learn forty motions that will help you remember the people and events of the New Testament. Developed by Apologia's publishing partners Walk Thru the Bible, these motions are key to learning and remembering the story line of the Scriptures. The motions incrementally build on one another as you progress through the course. During the week, there will be several opportunities to review the motions so that by the end of the course, your family will be able to master a complete forty-point outline of the entire New Testament.

Similarly, in Lessons 16–30, I will teach you a hand sign to remember a key word and theme for each of the twenty-seven books of the New Testament.

Textbook

In addition to the Bible, your textbook for this course is *The Word in Motion: New Testament*. Beginning at the literal beginning, the textbook will enable you and your family to explore the key people, places, and events of the New Testament. Along the journey, you will gain a deeper understanding of how all the parts of the Bible fit together to form the glorious story of God's love for humanity and His plan for our redemption.

The textbook contains a total of thirty lessons, each of which is designed to be completed in a week. Thus the course may be completed in thirty weeks. The textbook is divided into two parts. Part 1 includes Lessons 1–15 and covers the history revealed in the New Testament. Here you will find biblical narratives that tell the storyline of God and His people, along with discussion questions. Part 2 includes Lessons 16–30 and provides an overview and summary of all twenty-seven books of the New Testament with full-color visual aids.

Notebooking Journal

Notebooking is a creative way for kids to personalize and capture what they have learned in an artful keepsake. As kids do the activities in *The Word in Motion: New Testament Notebooking Journal* and think about their lives in light of each lesson, spiritual truths will come alive for them and make real-life application engaging. Everything they learn in this course will be processed and documented somewhere in the notebooking journal pages. Therefore, each student will need to have his or her own notebooking journal. Please keep in mind that the pages may not be reproduced.

Audiobook and Book Extras

Two other resources are available to help you on your journey through the New Testament and The Word in Motion. The first is the free Book Extras website. Here you will find not only the course videos but also useful links to sites and materials for supplementing your studies. The Book Extras have been selected to help you take this study deeper and are most appropriate for, though not limited to, parents and older students.

The other resource, *The Word in Motion: New Testament Audiobook* is available for purchase as an MP3 download exclusively through Apologia. I recorded the audiobook as a teaching supplement. It is best utilized as a repeat of the textbook lessons, not as a substitute for the family reading the textbook together. Listening to the audiobook while running errands in the car or at bedtime would be an excellent use of this resource.

What's in a Lesson? – Part 1, Lessons 1–15

As I mentioned, the New Testament course is divided into two parts. Part 1 includes Lessons 1–15 and covers the historical events revealed in the New Testament narrative. Each of these lessons contains the following elements.

Video

Begin each lesson by watching the online video teaching together. Each video opens with a brief teaching to introduce the lesson's content. This is followed by a demonstration of one or more motions that correspond to the forty-point outline. These motions will help you remember key people and events from the lesson.

Motions

Each week, you will learn one or more new motions and practice the motions you've already learned. The motions for the week's lesson are sequentially numbered and listed on the first page of the lesson. You will want to review these motions often. If you need to refresh your memory about the motions you've already learned, turn to the "Quick Reference to the New Testament 40-Point Outline" provided in the textbook. You can also review the motions by watching the summary video on the Book Extras website.

Passage

This is a reference to the Bible passage you can read for more details of the story covered in the lesson. Again, it's important to stress that the primary source for this curriculum is God's Word, the Bible.

Take It to Heart

This is a memory verse that goes with the key theme of the lesson. There is a page in the notebooking journal where students will be able to practice the memory verse by copying it in their best handwriting. Memorizing God's words and hiding them in our hearts is a great way for us to guard our hearts.

Narrative

This is a three- to four-page illustrated narrative of the biblical story line, including key people, places, and events of the New Testament. This is not a repeat of the video, so make sure you watch the video *and* read the narrative. The narrative picks up where the video lesson left off; think of it as the rest of the story. Conversational in tone, the narrative also covers important biblical themes and places them within the context of the overarching story of Bible. Mom or Dad can read the story aloud from the textbook, or you may choose to have other family members take turns reading to the group. The motions you learn from the video will go along with this story.

Let's Talk About It

Each lesson includes five review questions for the family to discuss together. This is an opportunity for everyone to reflect on what they remember from the video teaching and the narrative reading. There's also a place in your notebooking journal to write down your answers to these questions. In the textbook, this section is designated by a red "question mark" icon.

Sidebar Articles

These brief articles were written to provide context and a fuller understanding of the Bible story. Many of the subjects were selected to help students better understand and relate to what it must have been like to live in Bible times. Topics include tent making, Roman citizenship, armor, hospitality, scrolls, and more. These articles are designated by a green "light bulb" icon.

Doctrine

The content of this course is nondenominational. However, each lesson includes discussion of a Christian doctrine historically agreed upon by the church. Among the doctrines discussed in this course are the angels, water baptism, temptation, miracles, salvation, the Holy Spirit, mission work, fasting, righteousness, trials, grace, and more. These articles are indicated by a blue "shield with a cross" icon.

Character Sketch

Each lesson includes a profile of a Bible character told from that person's perspective. Some of these profiles are humorous in tone or language, while others are dramatic or even tragic. All of the people in the Bible were real people, and we sometimes forget that. These readings will help students to consider what it might have been like to be that person—and to remember that God uses all kinds of people to accomplish His purposes. These profiles are indicated by a purple "human face" icon.

Exploring the Miracles and Parables

Each lesson includes a suggested reading from Scripture in which a parable is told or a miracle is documented. The apostle John noted that Jesus did far more than could be contained in the four Gospels (John 21:25). This means that we know only a small portion of His actions and His teaching. But it also underscores the importance of studying what is available to us in the biblical narrative. You will be asked to seriously consider each of these readings in the notebooking journal. These readings are indicated by a yellow-and-black "magnifying glass" icon.

Prayer

Every lesson concludes with a prayer that touches on the themes discussed in the lesson. You can pray this together and add to it as the Spirit leads. These prayers are indicated by an orange "praying hands" icon.

Weekly Rhythm for Lessons in Part 1

In order to complete *The Word in Motion: New Testament* course in a single school year, you'll want to set a goal to complete one lesson each week. To help you successfully realize this goal and still enjoy margin in your family life, we suggest a four-day schedule that looks something like this:

Day 1
Watch the video
Practice the motions
Read the sidebar article
Read the character sketch
Read the memory verse
Write the memory verse in your notebooking journal

Day 2
Read the narrative and note the biblical text references
Review the memory verse
Review the motions
Discuss the Let's Talk About It questions
Answer the review questions in your notebooking journal

Day 3
Read the doctrine article
Review the memory verse
Review the motions
Do the additional activities in your notebooking journal

Day 4
Read the assigned parable or miracle
Read the prayer and pray together
Review the memory verse
Review the motions
Do any remaining activities in your notebooking journal

What's in a Lesson? – Part 2, Lessons 16–30

Part 2 of this course includes Lessons 16–30 and covers all thirty-nine books of the Old Testament. Each of these lessons contains the following elements.

Video

Again, you will begin each lesson by watching the online video teaching together. Each video lesson in Part 2 of the course opens with a brief teaching to introduce one or more books of the Old Testament. Students will learn a key word for each book and a hand sign to help them remember the key word. They will also learn how Jesus can be found in every book of the Bible.

Book-About Cards

Each Book-About Card is an overview of a book in the New Testament. In other words, this card is about the book. The information on each card includes the human writer of the book, approximate dates when it was written, the book's intended audience, the genre of the book, key characters, highlights of the content, a memory verse, and a statement of what we can learn about Jesus from this book of the Bible.

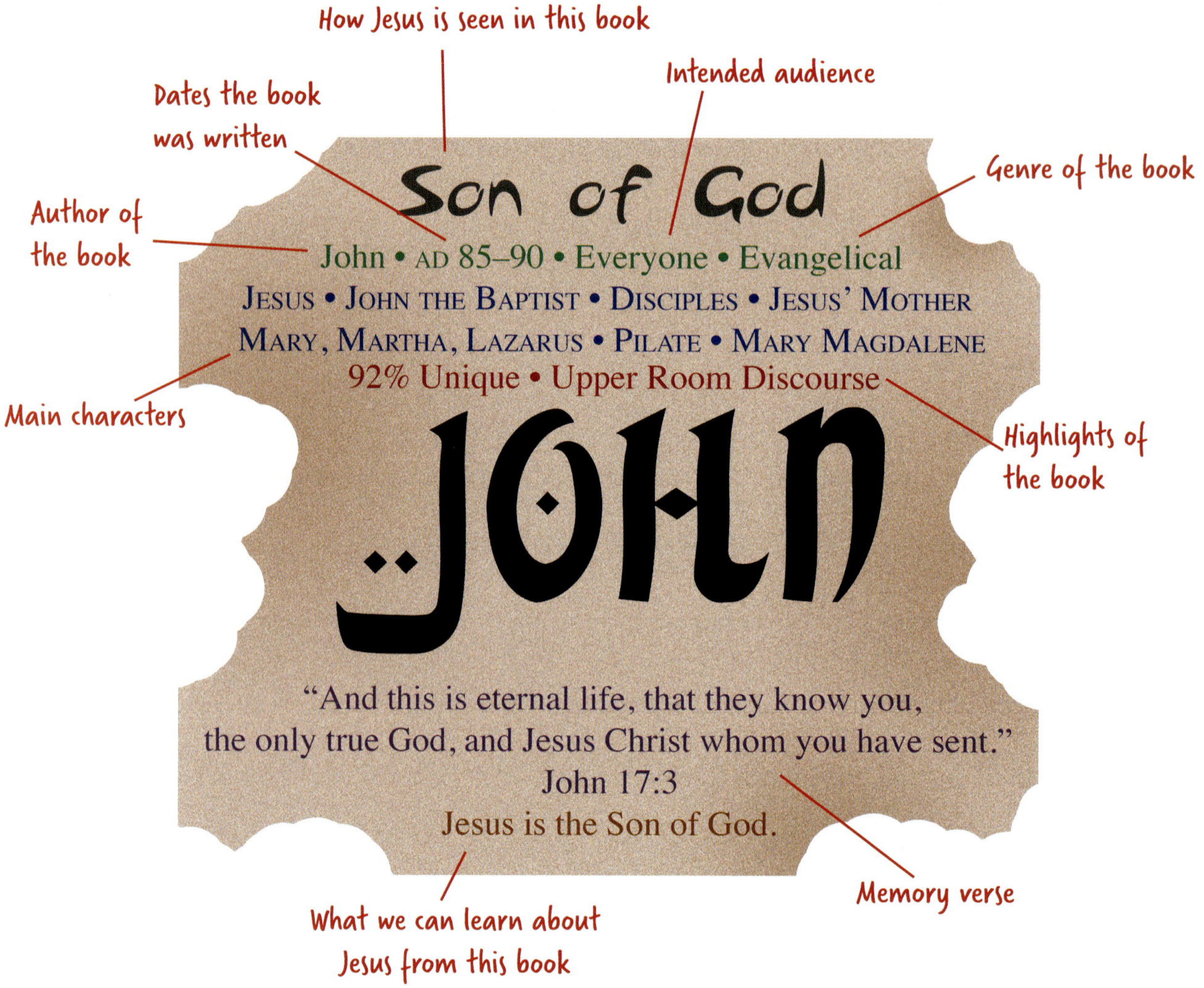

Key Word Card

These illustrations "show" the major theme of each book. In the "Quick Reference to the 39 Books of the Old Testament" found immediately after Lesson 30, you will find all of the Key Word Cards along with explanations of how to interpret each image. These images are sometimes goofy and corny, but that's the point. The purpose is to help you recognize and remember the key word and theme of each book. These illustrations, most of which feature our friend Wyatt, are designed to make the content unforgettable.

Key Chain
The key word is written on a key chain, making it easier to find than your car keys.

Take It to Heart
The memory verse goes with the key theme of each book of the Bible. There is a page in the notebooking journal where students will be able to practice the memory verse by copying it in their best handwriting. Memorizing God's words and hiding them in our hearts is a great way for parents and children alike to guard their hearts.

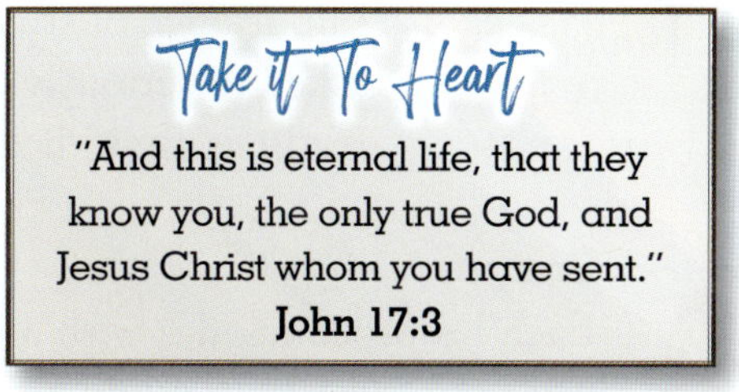

Bible Reading
Instead of a narrative that I wrote, like those you read in Part 1, in Part 2 you will be reading directly from God's Word. Take the Bible, find the assigned passages, and read them together. Don't skip this part—it's a powerful exercise. These readings represent key passages from each book of the Old Testament.

Sidebar Articles
These brief articles were written to provide context and a fuller understanding of the Bible story. Many of the subjects were selected to help students better relate to what it must have been like to live in Bible times. Topics include altars, the harvest, gleaning, the walls of Jericho, anointing kings, and more. These articles are designated by a green "light bulb" icon.

Doctrine
The content of this course is nondenominational. However, each lesson includes discussion of a Christian doctrine historically agreed upon by the church. Among the doctrines discussed in this course are the fall of mankind, sin nature, worship, idolatry, sabbath rest, miracles, repentance, God's sovereignty, giving, the problem of evil, prophecy, redemption, and more. These articles are indicated by a blue "shield with a cross" icon.

Character Sketch
Each lesson includes a profile of a Bible character told from that person's perspective. Some of these profiles are humorous in tone or language, while others are dramatic or even tragic. All of the people in the Bible were real people, and we sometimes forget that. These readings will help students to consider what it might have been like to be that person—and to remember that God uses all kinds of people to accomplish His purposes. These profiles are indicated by a purple "human face" icon.

Exploring the Miracles and Parables

Each lesson includes a suggested reading from Scripture in which a parable is told or a miracle is documented. The apostle John noted that Jesus did far more than could be contained in the four Gospels (John 21:25). This means that we know only a small portion of His actions and His teaching. But it also underscores the importance of studying what is available to us in the biblical narrative. You will be asked to seriously consider each of these readings in the notebooking journal. These readings are indicated by a yellow-and-black "magnifying glass" icon.

Prayer

Each lesson concludes with a prayer that touches on the themes discussed in the lesson. You can pray this together and add to it as the Spirit leads. These prayers are indicated by an orange "praying hands" icon.

Weekly Rhythm for Lessons in Part 2

To help you successfully realize your goal of completing one lesson per week and enjoy margin in your family life, we suggest a four-day schedule that looks something like this:

Day 1
Watch the video
Practice the lesson's key words and hand signs
Read the Book-About card
Read the character sketch
Read the memory verse(s)
Write the memory verse(s) in the notebooking journal

Day 2
Read the Bible passage
Review the memory verse(s)
Discuss and answer the review questions in the notebooking journal
Review the key words and hand signs

Day 3
Continue reading the Bible passage, if necessary
Read the sidebar article
Read the doctrine article
Review the key words and hand signs
Review the memory verse(s)
Do the additional activities in your notebooking journal

Day 4
Read the assigned parable or miracle
Read the prayer and pray together
Review all key words
Review the memory verse(s)
Review all hand signs
Complete the remaining activities in your notebooking journal

Accessing the Videos

As I mentioned, each of the thirty lessons in *The Word in Motion: New Testament* is accompanied by a four- to five-minute video teaching segment. These videos are available to stream online at Apologia's Book Extras website. To access this popular page, you will need to log in to your Apologia account or create one if you haven't done so yet.

Start by 1) going to www.Apologia.com, then 2) click on "My Account." If you already have an account, enter your username or your email and password to enter the Book Extras website. If you don't have an account yet, you can register to create one.

Once you have logged in, enter the following course password in the box and click the "Submit" button:

WordinMotionNTthecross

Under the column header "Your Book Extras Subscriptions," you should see a link for *The Word in Motion: New Testament*. Click on the title and you will be taken to a list of all thirty video lessons. Then simply click the link for the lesson you wish to view.

Please note, these instructions are subject to change as we update the Book Extras website.

PART 1

NEW TESTAMENT Outline

Lesson 1

GREECE, ISRAEL & ROME

Motions

1. Greece–Language
2. Israel–Hopes
3. Rome–Roads

Passage

Daniel 2

Take it To Heart

**But when the fullness of time had come, God sent forth his Son, born of woman.
Galatians 4:4**

So God's story continues. The Old Testament began with these words from the book of Genesis: "In the beginning, God. . . ." Those are four foundational words. Read them again slowly. *In the beginning, God.* Before history, before creation, before time, there was only God. Even then He knew you. He knew you would sin, and He knew the terrible price He would have to pay to save you. Yet He already loved you so much that He was willing to make that sacrifice. And so He created the heavens and the earth, and the story began.

Thinking back on our study of the Old Testament, it's amazing to think about all we've already learned about God. For one thing, He spoke to His chosen people, the Israelites, through His prophets. For a thousand years, the Lord had been sending His prophets to remind the people what was expected of them: to serve their God and worship only Him. There had always been at least one prophet in the land during this time—until Malachi died around 400 BC. Suddenly, there were no more prophets. Why? Because God didn't send any! The Jewish people heard only silence from heaven for the next four hundred years.

Now four hundred years may seem like a long time to you and me, but it's no more than a blink of an eye to God. And just because there were no prophets delivering messages from God, that doesn't mean He wasn't busy working behind the scenes. In fact, He was preparing the world for something huge: the BIGGEST event in history!

This huge event is what the New Testament is all about. But to truly understand the meaning and importance of this event, we must be familiar with the events leading up to this moment. Remember, the Bible is the story of God's love for mankind. The New Testament is part two of the story, which began in the Old Testament.

Like all good stories, this story has a setting, characters, plot, conflict, and resolution. Most of the story takes place in an area that today we call the Middle East. This region includes a special place we call the Promised Land because it was the land God promised to Abraham, Isaac, and Jacob and their descendants, the Jewish people.

The Jews—also called Hebrews or Israelites—are important characters in God's story because they are His chosen people. The Old Testament characters we usually think of as "bad guys" are those who openly defy God, including Goliath, Jezebel, and the Egyptian pharaoh who enslaves God's people and refuses to let them go. The characters we usually think of as the "good guys" in the story are those who try to honor God with their lives and their choices: Noah, Abraham, Joseph, Moses, Joshua, Gideon, Ruth, David, Esther, Elijah, and others.

Because the Old Testament includes a great many characters and events, the plot can seem complicated at times. But it's really pretty straightforward. Over and over God shows His love for His people. He provides for their every need. He is patient with them. He forgives their sins. And He is faithful to keep His promises to them. Sometimes, His people choose to obey. More often, they do not obey and then find themselves in an awful fix. Then they cry out to God, and in His mercy He answers them. And for a while, the people seek God and worship only Him. But their tendency is to eventually wander away from His hand of protection.

To kindle hope among the faithful, God promises to send a Messiah, a King who will destroy evil and restore righteousness on the earth. This Messiah will be the resolution to the story's conflict. He will rescue humanity from enslavement to sin and make a way for people to be reconciled with God. God's prophets tell of many signs that will mark the Messiah's coming.

By the time the Old Testament comes to a close, the kingdom of Israel has been divided in two, and both nations have been displaced from God's Promised Land. Israel has been scattered to the winds and Judah exiled to captivity in Babylon. Although some have decided to return and rebuild under the leadership of Ezra, Zerubbabel, and Nehemiah, many choose to stay in the nations where they have settled.

And then God goes silent.

There are no new prophets, and God's people can only wait.

So what happened in the world during the next 400 years, prior to the events of the New Testament? During this time, God allowed three political powers to rise up. The first was Greece. In 336 BC, Alexander the Great began the greatest military campaign the world has ever known. He built a massive army and proceeded to conquer most of the known world, including the Persian Empire that had once conquered God's people. And so Jerusalem was now ruled by the Greeks.

Each time Alexander conquered a new land—he was never defeated in battle—he instituted a program of Hellenization, meaning that the people he defeated were required to adopt the Greeks' language and culture. Greek society had made many admirable advances in science, technology, architecture, philosophy, and the arts, and Alexander was determined to spread these achievements around the world.

In order to achieve this goal, he established community education centers in every conquered land, including Judah, or *Judea* as it was called in the Greek language. This led to Greek becoming the dominant language in the region. As fewer and fewer young people were able to read the Scrip-

tures in the original Hebrew, a Greek translation of the Scriptures known as the Septuagint was written. Later, the New Testament would be written mostly in Greek. Thanks to Alexander's schools, this common language would be key in the future spread of the gospel and God's message of love.

When Alexander lay dying, he summoned his officers and divided his kingdom among them. And so Judea fell under the rule of first one Greek kingdom and then another, and it seemed the Jews would never again control their own homeland. But in 167 BC, after a foreign king had desecrated the temple and issued a decree forbidding practice of the Jewish religion, Judah Maccabee and his brothers led a revolt of the people that succeeded in making Judea an independent kingdom once more—the second political power I mentioned earlier. The Maccabees cleansed the temple in Jerusalem and restored traditional Jewish worship. This rekindled the people's longing for the promised Messiah. They expected Him to come as a victorious warrior and powerful ruler who would restore Israel to the glory it had known under King David and King Solomon. They didn't expect a Prince of Peace.

About this same time, a third power arose in the Mediterranean region: Rome. Because the Greek forces were widely scattered to maintain their hold over the many lands conquered by Alexander, Rome was able to march on Athens and defeat Greece rather easily. Then in 63 BC, Rome captured Jerusalem and its army occupied Judea.

The Romans were also builders. Some of the most significant structures they built were roads. In fact, if you travel to Europe today you can still see the remains of some of these roads. The Romans constructed these roads as routes for moving their armies and transporting trade goods. But after establishing the church, God would use these same roads for spreading His message of love and redemption to the nations.

As you can see, the time period between the Old and New Testaments was not a time of inactivity. I like to think of it as a time of preparation. If your Bible is like mine, only one page separates the Old Testament from the New Testament. But we would need many, many more if we were to write down all that God was doing during this time. He was working behind the scenes, setting the stage for the entrance of this story's central character, Jesus Christ, and the proclamation of the gospel.

EXPLORING THE MIRACLES
Read about the creation of the heavens and earth in Genesis 1:1–2:3.

ALEXANDER THE GREAT

Do you want to know your future? Would you change how you live your life each day if you knew what the future has in store for you?

During his thirteen-year reign, Alexander the Great conquered most of the known world, including the Persian Empire, Asia Minor, and Egypt. Before Alexander was born, the prophet Daniel interpreted King Nebuchadnezzar's dream about a large statue. (You can read about the dream in Daniel 2, our Bible reference for this lesson.) Although never mentioned by name, one part of the statue represented Alexander's empire. Later, Daniel had another vision that prophesied Alexander's conquests 180 years before his birth (Daniel 11:2–4).

As Alexander approached Jerusalem, the high priest and other Jews met him outside the city's walls. They accompanied Alexander to the temple, where he read Daniel's prophesy about a mighty king from Greece. Alexander not only believed that he was the king in the prophecy, but he also showed great favor to the Jewish people. He allowed the Jews to keep the laws of their ancestors and pay no taxes every seventh year. Alexander destroyed many other cities but spared Jerusalem.

God knew Alexander's purpose before he was born. God knew you and your purpose before you were born (Psalm 139:13–16; Jeremiah 1:5; Ephesians 2:10). Have you asked God what His purpose is for your life?

? LET'S TALK ABOUT IT

1. When you think of the Bible as a single, epic story, what would you say is the story's main theme, the big idea that the Bible returns to over and over? Looking back at what you read in the Old Testament, what was one of your favorite stories within the bigger story?
2. Why are the 400 years between the Old Testament and New Testament thought of as a time of silence?
3. Which nations became world powers during this 400-year period? What major contribution did each of them bring to God's story as it was continuing to unfold?
4. Why do you think it is important to know that the Hebrew Scriptures were translated into Greek during this time and came to be commonly read in this language?
5. Are you learning any foreign languages? Which ones? Do you think you might want to study Hebrew, Greek, or Latin?

Hope

Hope is an expectation of good things to come. Our culture tends to use the word hope to mean wishing for something that, more often than not, is unrealistic, as in "I hope the Great Pumpkin brings me a real, live penguin for my birthday!" But hope is only an irrational belief if the person or thing you place your trust in either doesn't exist or is incapable of giving you what you hope for.

The fact is, hoping is not very valuable all by itself. Your hope is only as good as the person or thing you are trusting. Another way of saying this is that you can hope for something with all your heart, but it will never happen if you have placed your faith in a god that does not exist.

When we say we have hope as Christians, it means we are trusting in God because He has shown Himself to be completely trustworthy and good. Therefore, we believe that what He has said will come to pass.

This is extremely important for us because we will have to wait—sometimes far longer than we want to—for the good things that God has promised. For example, we have hope that God will ultimately punish evil and bring justice, but that won't happen until Christ's return. We also have hope for eternal life with Jesus, but again, we will not experience it as soon as we would like.

But just because we must wait does not mean we are any less certain about these things. God has given us every reason to hope in the promises He has made, and He will not fail us.

The Maccabees Speak

My name is Judah, and I lived a day's walk west of Jerusalem. My father served as a priest in the holy temple in Jerusalem. He was Mattathias the Hasmonean, a direct descendant of Aaron, the first High Priest and brother of Moses.

Judea had been ruled by Greek kings for more than a century and a half, and so I grew up speaking both Greek and Hebrew. Otherwise, the Greeks left the Jews in peace, and we were allowed to walk in the ways of our God and worship Him. But some of Judea's wealthier families preferred to do away with Jewish law and adopt the worldlier lifestyle of the Greeks. This led to intrigues and power struggles that caught the attention of a new king, Antiochus IV. In response, Antiochus and his soldiers stormed Jerusalem and slaughtered 40,000 men, women, and children. Another 40,000 were sold into slavery.

The wicked king desecrated God's temple and plundered its wealth. He then outlawed our beliefs and rituals and decreed that all Jews must worship Zeus as the supreme god. But my father, Mattathias, refused. When a Greek official commanded him to make a sacrifice to the Greek gods, Mattathias killed both the Greek and the Jew who had stepped forward to obey the order. My father then fled to the wilderness with me and my four brothers. From there he called upon all Jews to stand by their covenant with the God of Abraham, Isaac, and Jacob and join him in battle to take back Jerusalem. Soon after, my father took ill, but before he died, he chose me to lead the people in revolt.

For the next several years, my brothers and I waged war against the Greeks. Although we possessed few arms and even fewer trained fighters, God was with us, and we won battle after battle using unconventional tactics. At some point, the people began calling me Judah Maccabee. Some said this new name meant "the Hammer," while others said it meant "chosen by God." Whatever its origin, the name stuck and was taken up by my brothers as well.

Within three years, we drove the Greek forces out of Jerusalem and set about purging the city of statues of false gods and goddesses. We then purified the temple and rededicated it to the Lord—an occasion still celebrated on the autumn holiday you call Hanukkah. Although Judea would not win independence for several more years, the taking of Jerusalem helped to revive the Jewish people's faith in God and rekindled our longing for the promised Messiah.

NOTE: The story of the Maccabees-led revolt is told in two history books written between the time of the Old and New Testaments. Although the Jews themselves never considered the books to be scripture inspired by God, events recorded in the books of the Maccabees are so important to Jewish history that they—along with about a dozen other historical books—are sometimes included as additional study material in published Bibles. Collectively, these books are called the Apocrypha, which literally means "hidden things." Most Protestant Bibles do not include the books, but when they do, they are placed in their own section like an appendix. On the other hand, Roman Catholic and Eastern Orthodox churches accept the Apocrypha as scripture, which means that they base some of their doctrines and beliefs on these books.

Prayer

Dear God in Heaven,

You are sovereign over all of creation, including history. You spoke through Your prophets to foretell of people, kingdoms, and events to come. You have raised up heroes and villains alike and made the nations rise and fall according to Your perfect will. As I learn the history of the world, I can see that You were preparing people to recognize and believe in Your one Son, Jesus Christ. Although I was born long after these events, I know that You are at work even now in the world. I know that Your desire is for every person to know Jesus and accept Your gift of salvation. Help me to have confident hope in Your plans for me and for all who believe in Your Son.

In the precious name of Jesus. Amen.

Lesson 2

THE BIRTH OF CHRIST

Motions

4. Birth

Passages

Matthew 1–2
Luke 2

Take it To Heart

And she gave birth to her firstborn son and wrapped him in swaddling cloths and laid him in a manger, because there was no place for them in the inn.
Luke 2:7

Let's look at what is arguably one of the climaxes of the Bible story. It's not the main high point, but it is a huge one on the way to the ultimate crescendo. We'll get there soon, but let's enjoy this one for all it's worth. God sent His only begotten Son to be born to a young virgin named Mary. I mean, seriously, did any of you see that one coming? What kind of plan was this? Let's find out.

The birth of Jesus of Nazareth was greatly anticipated, or at least it should have been. In the video, we talked about how the prophets had long foretold of the Messiah's birth, including where and how it would happen. In fact, all the events of Scripture have been leading up to this one night in Bethlehem.

It's a huge moment in the history of the world. Of course, you have probably heard the story so many times that you've become kind of ho-hum about it. If that's the case, you're missing the thrill, the wonder, the mystery of it all. I want you to try and hear the tale with fresh ears and an open heart because the Christmas story is central to understanding everything that happens before and after. It's the story that splits time—literally! It's a story that must be told and retold, because this story changes everything.

Strangely, movies have had a hard time telling it well, and yet it has so many cinematic elements. A young couple in love. Miracles, angels, and heavenly visions. Magnificent songs, glorious spectacle, and mysterious visitors from exotic lands. Political intrigue, a dastardly crime, and a daring midnight escape.

And there's a baby too!

Nothing about this story is predictable. Nothing about this story is easy or simple. But God's love and faithfulness are evident on every single line.

When babies are born these days, their arrival tends to generate a bunch of mail, usually in the form of birth announcements and shower invitations. Today, I'd like to focus on the invitations from God, specifically those He sent to Zechariah, Mary, Joseph, and some unnamed shepherds keeping watch over their flock by night. As we consider the varying nature of their RSVPs, we will stop to read selections from the biblical account of the story.

The first four books of the New Testament are called the Gospels because the word *gospel* means "good news." These four books tell the story of the life of Jesus, who is also called Messiah, or "Christ" in the Greek language. The Gospels of Matthew and Luke tell us about His birth, but let's start with Luke whose account begins with a priest called Zechariah and his wife, Elizabeth.

Elizabeth and Zechariah believe they will never have children because they are already much too old. But God has other plans: He will bless them with a son—John the Baptist—who will be great before God and prepare people's hearts for the coming Messiah. One day, as Zechariah is serving in the temple, the angel Gabriel appears and gives him the glorious news that he is to be a father. Zechariah is so flabbergasted that he dares to ask, "How can I be sure this will happen?" His unbelief doesn't go over too well with the angel. Stop here and take a few minutes to read the actual account in Luke 1:5–25.

A few months later, in the village of Nazareth, the angel Gabriel visits Mary, a young woman engaged to be married to the carpenter Joseph. Gabriel has come to deliver what might be the strangest—and certainly most wonderful—invitation and birth announcement in all of history. Now read Luke 1:26–38.

The angel tells Mary, "The power of the Most High will overshadow you," meaning she is to miraculously become pregnant and God is the Father! Unlike Zechariah, Mary does not doubt the angel despite her amazement. But she does wonder aloud how this marvelous thing is possible. We all need to remember the angel's response: "Nothing will be impossible with God." So Mary accepted God's invitation, remained pure, and carried the Son of God.

(*Pause for effect.*)

Think about this for a moment. Mary has agreed to *be* a mom before she is supposed to be able to be a mom. Think of the scandal once Mary begins sporting a baby bump at the village well! Naturally, people will assume that Mary has given herself to a man outside of marriage.

This situation is problematic for Mary's fiancé, Joseph. He is reeling and doesn't know what to think other than, *I loved and trusted this woman!* In accordance with Jewish tradition, their engagement involves a legally binding contract, so it's not really possible to simply "call off" the wedding.

Worse, a woman found guilty of adultery could be sentenced to death by stoning! But Joseph is a good man and a just man. He has no desire to humiliate Mary, so he decides to divorce her quietly.

Enter another angel. This part of the story is particularly tender to me. Just as Joseph's head is spinning, God sends an angel to visit him in a dream and "get him in the loop." This is all to fulfill the prophecy that the Messiah must be born of a virgin. "Do not be afraid to take Mary as your wife," the angel says. "She will give birth to a son, and you shall call His name Jesus, for He will save His people from their sins." Well, that's good enough for Joseph. He obeys and weds Mary. You can read the details in Matthew 1:18–25.

Fast-forward several months to when Mary is "great with child." The Roman emperor has decreed that a census be taken of the whole empire for the purpose of taxing the people. Because Joseph's ancestors come from Bethlehem, he and Mary must travel there to be registered and counted.

Lean in now and let the story come alive in your mind. Imagine Joseph and Mary packing for a weeklong journey, then saying goodbye to family and friends. See them traveling the long, dusty road to Bethlehem with no air conditioning, no Ramada Inn, no fast-food drive-thru. (Do you picture Mary on foot or riding a donkey? The Bible is not specific on this point, but walking is said to be good for inducing labor.) Look up and gaze at the stars as they sleep under the open sky each night. Tune in to the birdsong waking them at dawn. Sense the excitement build as they near the village of Bethlehem. Hear the anxious tone in their voices as the time draws near for Mary to give birth. Smell the animals and the straw as Joseph prepares a makeshift cradle in a feeding trough. Feel the anticipation in the air as the Messiah's arrival draws closer and closer. Listen for the child's first cry to break the silence and then see the gift of God in His mother's arms.

Now read Luke 2:1–20. Yeah, I know. Simply, "Wow!"

Thus far, we have seen God's angels deliver messages to three separate individuals, inviting them to participate to varying degrees in the arrival of His only begotten Son, the long-awaited Messiah. But someone is missing—a witness. A witness is a person who can testify that a particular event, such as a birth or a wedding, has taken place. To witness the birth of the King of kings, God sends His angels to invite some shepherds.

Did you see that coming? Me neither.

Let's take a quick look down a side road.

During the holidays, our family often finds time to watch the classic animated TV special *A Charlie Brown Christmas*. In it, bossy Lucy sends Charlie Brown on an errand to buy a Christmas tree for the gang's pageant—a great big, shiny aluminum tree that captures the season's modern spirit.

But when he returns with a small, unimpressive tree that leans to one side, everyone makes fun of him.

Charlie Brown was already feeling depressed. Now he hangs his head in shame and wonders why it seems that the most important thing about Christmas is the tree. In frustration he cries out, "Isn't there anyone who knows what Christmas is all about?"

His closest friend, Linus, who has been cast as a shepherd in the pageant, says, "Sure, Charlie Brown. I can tell you what Christmas is all about." And he proceeds to tell the story of the birth of the Savior of the world:

And there were in the same country shepherds abiding in the field, keeping watch over their flock by night. And, lo, the angel of the Lord came upon them, and the glory of the Lord shone round about them, and they were sore afraid. And the angel said unto them, "Fear not! For, behold, I bring you tidings of great joy, which shall be to all people. For unto you is born this day in the City of David a Savior, which is Christ the Lord. And this shall be a sign unto you: Ye shall find the babe wrapped in swaddling clothes, lying in a manger." And suddenly, there was with the angel a multitude of the heavenly host praising God and saying, "Glory to God in the highest, and on earth peace, good will toward men."

When asked for the true meaning of Christmas, Linus quotes directly from the King James Bible, Luke chapter 2, verses 8–14.

Well done, Linus.

CENSUS

"Pack a small bag. We are walking to New York City today," Mom said.

"That's a hundred miles!" I said. "Why are we walking that far?"

"It is time to take the census, and even though we live in Philadelphia, we must return to where your dad was born."

When Quirinius was governor of Syria, a decree went out that everyone had to be registered or counted in his own city. Joseph is a descendant of King David, whose family lived in Bethlehem, so Joseph and Mary must go there to be counted. They would have walked or rode a donkey from Nazareth to Bethlehem—about a hundred miles—even though Mary was expecting a child. It was prophesied that the Messiah would be born in Bethlehem (Micah 5:2), so it was no accident that this census was called for. God's plan for the birth of the Messiah was being fulfilled.

In the United States, a census is taken every ten years. The information collected in the census is used to determine the number of representatives each state will send to Congress. The data will also be used to distribute federal funds for things like educational programs, healthcare, highways, and law enforcement. Everyone is important, so everyone is counted.

EXPLORING THE MIRACLES
Read about the virgin birth in Luke 1:26–38.

LET'S TALK ABOUT IT

1. How do you think Mary felt when the angel told her that she was chosen to be the mother of God's Son?
2. Why was it hard for Joseph to believe Mary's story about a miraculous conception?
3. What are some of the specific details in the story that tell you that God was at work in everything that happened?
4. Why is the birth of Jesus such a big deal? Why is it so important to God's whole, big, complete story?
5. We use the letters BC to refer to the years "before Christ" and the letters AD to refer to years after the birth of Christ. What do you think the letters "AD" stand for? And why is this a big deal?

Angels

Angels are spiritual beings created by God. They are part of the world that is invisible to human beings. Although angels do not have physical bodies, they can appear to people when God commands them to. Angels worship the Lord, serve God, act as His messengers, protect and encourage His people, fight against demons, and sometimes carry out God's judgments. We don't know how many angels were created, but we do know there are a huge number of them.

Some people speculate that the cherubim (Ezekiel 1:4–25 and 10:3–14) and seraphim (Isaiah 6:1–7) described by the prophets are two types of angels, although the description of these beings bears little resemblance to the way we usually think of angels. Others think that a cherub and seraph are not angels but are different creatures altogether.

Given that Christmas decorations so often depict angels as females, you might be surprised to learn that every time angels appear in the Bible, they are said to be masculine. In fact, there exists no feminine form of the Greek word for angels.

Like human beings, angels think, feel emotions, make choices, and know the difference between right and wrong. At some point after God rested on the seventh day, some angels rebelled against God and were cast out of heaven. These angels are now called demons, and they serve Satan. Rather than a plan of salvation, these fallen angels received judgment from God. This should give us some idea of just how precious human lives are to God: He loves us so much, He sent His Son to die for us but not for the fallen angels.

God does not need angels to work out His plan, but He does use them to carry out His plans. By sending angels to protect His children, God not only reveals His astounding love for us but also gives us glimpses of the invisible world we will one day see for ourselves. They also model for us the importance of obedience and show that our primary purpose—the meaning of life—is to worship and glorify the Lord.

Mary Speaks

Although I sincerely believed the angel who told me that I would conceive by the Holy Spirit, there were moments afterward when I wondered if it was all a dream. Most days I awoke thrilled to have been chosen by God. But then there were days when it just didn't make sense. I mean, the Son of God was being formed in my womb. Experiencing this miracle firsthand took my breath away.

Of course, I thought about the ramifications and wondered how others would react. My mother and father loved me and knew that I had been with no man, but would they still trust me after they learned I was pregnant? And poor, dear Joseph—I could not ask him to raise a son who was not his own. And yet somehow I knew he would choose to do so.

And then there were the neighbors. Nothing could stem the tide of gossip once the women started talking. To give myself space and to prepare for the unknown of what I was about to face, I decided to visit my older cousin Elizabeth. We had received remarkable news that she was pregnant in her old age. Surely I could talk to *her* about what was happening in me. And I knew she would be glad for the extra pair of hands around the house as her delivery date drew nearer.

After a long, uncomfortable journey on foot, I finally arrived. As I entered the humble home of Elizabeth and Zechariah, I was welcomed by the heavenly aroma of hot bread. My cousin was carrying a fresh loaf in her apron and setting it on the table when I greeted her cheerfully. She dropped the bread and, hands on her tummy, turned and locked eyes with mine. Then she said the most extraordinary things!

I've heard that some women glow when they're pregnant, but this was especially true of Elizabeth. She was quite beautiful, tears of joy rolling down her face as she spoke. She said the baby in her womb had leaped for joy when he heard my voice. And she spoke with authority, saying that I was blessed for believing that the words spoken to me from God would indeed be fulfilled.

Yes, I believed when the angel spoke to me. But now my faith became unshakeable: I was the mother of God's Son, and I knew God's will would be done in my life.

Prayer

Dear Heavenly Father,

I don't think I'll ever fully understand how Jesus, the Son of God, took on human flesh. But I do believe it's true. Thank You for choosing an obedient young woman who let Your will be done in her life. I pray that I will be open to doing my part in Your big story. Help me not to question my role—no matter how big or small, easy or hard, extraordinary or mundane it may be. And each time I think of the mystery of the Incarnation, keep me in awe of Your glory, Your power, Your majesty, and Your amazing love!

In Jesus' name I pray. Amen.

I hope that learning about John the Baptist inspires you. Sure, he wore uncomfortable clothes, and his diet plan wouldn't sell many books these days. But John lived a life of meaning and purpose. He called people to repent and prepare for the coming of Jesus.

What about you? How is God using you to draw others to Himself? What are some ways you live differently from the world because of your devotion to God? Where do you point people who are unhappy with their lives?

John the Baptist pointed his listeners to Jesus. Remember how before he was born, John leapt in the womb when he heard Mary's voice, and immediately his own mother, Elizabeth, knew that Mary was the mother of the Messiah? Even then, John was calling people's attention to the coming of the Lord.

Thirty years later, the scene shifts to the region around the Jordan River, the same river the Jews had crossed to enter the Promised Land. There, John is drawing large crowds with his preaching. What is he preaching that's so popular? Prosperity? Tolerance? Feel-good spirituality? No, John is teaching repentance. Hardcore, turn-from-your-sins-and-get-right-with-God repentance. And his fiery sermons are attracting Jews from all over Jerusalem and Judea.

Meanwhile, the temple priests are hearing all kinds of wild rumors about the oddly dressed man preaching with authority in the wilderness, and they decide they'd better scurry down to the river and find out for themselves what's going on.

What's going on is something they've never seen before: John is standing in the river, baptizing people. Of course, the Jews had cleansing rituals for purifying the body, but this was something else. Something *more*.

Then one day, Jesus comes to John to be baptized. John recognizes Him not as his cousin but as his Lord. He is reluctant at first, but Jesus assures him that it's the right thing to do. So John obeys and baptizes Him. As Jesus comes up out of the water, John sees the Holy Spirit descend from heaven like a dove and rest upon Jesus. Then he hears a voice from heaven say, "This is my beloved Son, with whom I am well pleased."

So Jesus has been baptized and empowered by the Spirit. So what does He do next after what might be considered headline news? The answer: He goes to the wilderness. Does that sound strange to you? It does to me. After I was baptized, we celebrated with some friends at our house.

Does Jesus hire an agent? After all, the hottest preacher in the land has just declared Him to be the Christ, the Son of the Most High. You can't buy that kind of publicity! A good agent would say, "You've got to strike while the iron's hot!" At the very least, He should demand a sit-down with the high priest of the temple, right?

But Jesus doesn't do any of these things. Instead, He is led into the wilderness alone and fasts for forty days. I don't see this becoming a new diet fad anytime soon. First of all, forty days is a long time. Most of us can barely make it till four o'clock before we start to whine that we're "starving." And fasting is quite different from just looking forward to our next meal or hinting to Mom that a nice snack would be appreciated right about now.

Biblical fasting means making an intentional choice to go without food for a time to help us focus on God's Word and discipline our minds and bodies to pursue the things of God. Sometimes we fast to seek God's direction or help with a problem. Sometimes, if we are having trouble letting go of a particular sin, repentance might be our motivation for fasting. But here we see Jesus fasting in preparation for being tempted by Satan himself.

Forty days without food would deplete anyone physically, not to mention emotionally and intellectually. There's no doubt that the body of Jesus, who was fully man *and* fully God, is in a weakened state when the devil shows up on that last day to tempt Him. Yet even in this condition, Jesus doesn't waver, doesn't negotiate, and doesn't falter. He answers each temptation with clarity and confidence, relying on God's Word as the foundation for each rebuttal.

For his first temptation, Satan calls attention to Jesus' deep physical hunger while also mocking His identity as God in human flesh. "If you are the Son of God," he says, "command this stone to become bread."

Many temptations come to us as promises to satisfy our physical desires. Hunger is just one example of a physical craving, but we have others too. Instead of controlling our cravings, we often give in to them. But sometimes it is better to deny our physical wants as a way of disciplining our bodies and minds and devoting them to the things of God. We would do well to remember Jesus' response. Quoting Moses, He says, "It is written, 'Man shall not live by bread alone, but by every word that comes from the mouth of God.'" In other words, we need more than just food to truly live.

Next, the devil dares Jesus to jump from the highest point of the temple, saying that if He truly is the Son of God, angels will rescue Him. At least, that's what the Scriptures say. In essence, Satan is saying, "Let's see if God will really do what He said He would." Once again, Jesus answers by quoting Moses: "It is written, 'You shall not put the Lord your God to the test.'"

Satan has one last shot, so he entices Jesus with power. All of us wish sometimes we could tell others what to do and boss them around a bit, if only to feel better about ourselves. Here the devil offers to give Jesus all the world's kingdoms and their glory if Jesus will just kneel down and worship him. This sounds like a once-in-a-millennium offer—that is, until we realize it's pretty much the same temptation the devil floats by us every day, luring us with promises of popularity or fame if we will just compromise our principles a little. Jesus knows this, and He's not going to stand for it. "Be gone, Satan!" He commands. "For it is written, 'You shall worship the Lord your God and Him only shall you serve.'" At this point, the devil leaves Jesus, and angels arrive to take care of Him.

Jesus boldly faced temptation while hungry, alone, and tired, setting for us an example of how to respond to the temptations we face. Through this encounter, He also showed us how to prepare ourselves to resist the temptations we will inevitably face. The secret? Build resolve by keeping your focus on God and His Word. Jesus did this through the discipline of fasting and studying the Scriptures.

In stepping down from His throne in heaven to take on human form, Jesus experienced the same discomforts we do—hunger and exhaustion, tears on His checks and grit between His toes, rain pouring on His head and the sun beating on His shoulders. But He also faced every temptation we deal with. Every one! The devil wants you to believe that the temptations you face are unique, but they're not. As Solomon wrote in Ecclesiastes 1:9, "There is nothing new under the sun." The devil is still working with the same old bag of tricks.

Jesus can empathize with your weaknesses because He was tempted in all the ways you are. You can look it up in Hebrews 4:15. He understands, so don't be afraid to confess your sins to Him. The best news of all is that Jesus never gave in to temptation. He never sinned.

Not long after these events, John the Baptist is preaching again when he sees Jesus walking toward him. Instead of keeping the focus on himself and his ministry, John directs the crowd's attention to Jesus and says, "Behold, the Lamb of God, who takes away the sin of the world!" He then tells them the story of Jesus' baptism and proclaims, "I have seen and have borne witness that this is the Son of God." Now *that's* pointing people to Jesus!

The next day, John the Baptist is standing with two of his followers when Jesus passes by again. This time, John all but orders these two young men to switch teachers and follow Jesus. One of the young men is Andrew, a fisherman by trade. After spending the rest of the day with Jesus, Andrew rushes off to find his brother Simon—whom Jesus will call Peter—and tells him, "We have found the Messiah!"

And suddenly, the whole focus of the story has shifted.

The central character, now an adult, has made His entrance.

SCROLLS

Luke 4:16–30 tells of Jesus attending synagogue in His home town. He stood up to read from the Scriptures and was handed a scroll containing the book written by the prophet Isaiah. In biblical times, a scroll was a long strip of papyrus, parchment, or leather pages attached to one another.

The original Bible was not a book, but a series of scrolls made of parchment using the skin of kosher animals, such as cows, sheep, goats, and deer. The scrolls weighed twenty to twenty-five pounds and could be as large as two feet tall. The Old Testament as Jesus knew it consisted of twelve to twenty scrolls of different sizes. Sheets of parchment often were sewn together with sinew (a tendon from an animal) into one long scroll.

Black ink for the scroll was made from boiling oil, tar, and wax. Then tree sap and honey were added to the mixture and allowed to dry. Later, gallnut juice was mixed with the dried ink. The scribe used a feather or reed pen and dipped it into the black ink before writing. The writing appeared on only one side of the scroll most of the time.

Two wooden shafts were attached on either end of the scroll. Each shaft extended beyond the top and bottom of the scroll to serve as handles to hold the scroll as it was read. A sash was used to tie the scroll closed. A mantel—made from velvet and embroidered with golden thread, silk, and beads—was placed over the scroll to protect it.

Compare the book you're reading with a scroll. What materials are used for the pages in your book? What about the cover? What kind of ink is used for the writing and graphics? How do the book and a scroll compare in terms of weight and size? Which would you prefer to read?

EXPLORING THE MIRACLES
Read about Jesus casting out demons from a wild man in Mark 5:1–14.

LET'S TALK ABOUT IT

1. What admirable character qualities do you see in John the Baptist?
2. Name some of the sacrifices John made to fulfill God's call on his life.
3. What are some of the things you're tempted to do? How do you respond to temptation?
4. Jesus showed us that one of the best ways to respond to temptation is with Scripture. What are some passages you could memorize to help you fight against temptation?
5. Andrew and the first disciples dropped everything right away to follow Jesus. Why should you—or anyone, for that matter—make a decision quickly to follow Jesus?

Water baptism

Just before Jesus ascended into heaven, He left some final instructions with His disciples. We call these instructions the Great Commission. Jesus said, "Go therefore and *make disciples* of all nations, *baptizing them* in the name of the Father and of the Son and of the Holy Spirit, *teaching them* to observe all that I have commanded you" (Matthew 28:19–20, authors' emphasis).

What is baptism? The very first thing you need to know about baptism is that Jesus commanded it as something all Christians must do to follow Him. However, Christians through the centuries have had disagreements about what baptism means, who should receive it, and how it should be done.

To John the Baptist, this act symbolized cleansing and purification for those who had confessed their sins to God and repented. Jesus was baptized by John, even though He had no sins to confess. So not only was baptism commanded by Jesus, but He Himself was also baptized.

Some Christians see baptism as an initiation into the church. Some see it as the sign of the New Covenant, replacing the circumcision that was required of the Jews under the Old Covenant. Some have said that baptism is absolutely necessary for a person to be saved from his or her sins, but most Christians reject this view because it makes baptism a kind of work we do to help "earn" salvation, which is not possible.

Another thing Christians disagree on is how to baptize someone. Many believe that baptism can only be done properly by full immersion. They often point to the Greek word baptidzo, which literally means "to dip" or "to immerse." However, this view has developed primarily in the last few hundred years. Historically, baptism has been done either by immersion or by sprinkling water over the head of the believer. Variations on the Greek root are used in Scripture to refer to sprinkling and "washings" (Hebrews 6:2; 9:10).

What nearly all Christians do agree on is that baptism is an important step in becoming a disciple, meaning that you are committing yourself to learn to think and feel and act as Jesus does.

John the Baptist Speaks

When a man learns he is to be a father, it is understandable that he wants to run to and fro, shouting the news. But when my father heard I was coming, he was speechless! That's a little joke my mother likes to tell. My parents told me many times the story of how I came to be called John, how the neighbors and relatives were confused at my naming because none of our family had been called John. I confounded people's expectations ever after.

My father was a priest, and both my father and mother are descended from the high priest Aaron. Thus, I was expected to be a priest, but God had other plans for me. I did not serve in the temple in Jerusalem; the rock and the river were my synagogue, a simple coat of camel's hair and a leather belt my priestly raiment. I never tasted wine or hard drink, and I ate mostly locusts and wild honey, yet I was satisfied. I was not weighed down by the cares of this world, and my only desire was to ready the hearts of the people for the Christ, who even then walked among them.

At one time, I would have been called a navi, or prophet. The Lord gave me a message, and I delivered that message to those who needed to hear it. But the priests and scribes of my time believed there would be no new prophets until Elijah returned, as Malachi said he would. Yet they came and demanded to know who I was. They asked if I was the Christ. I was not. "Are you Elijah?" they asked. I said only, "I am the voice of one crying in the wilderness, 'Make straight the way of the Lord!' as Isaiah said."

You see, the faith of the people was dry and dead like the desert where I preached. This was especially true of their religious leaders, who required piety of the people while their own hearts were far from the Lord. And so I called them to repent, for another was coming, the strap of whose sandal I was not worthy to untie.

When He came to me to be baptized, I saw the skies open and the Spirit descend upon Him, and I heard the voice of God thunder His approval. And yet the crowd did not react. The ears and eyes of their hearts had been dulled by unbelief and years of worldly living. Had they seen and heard as I, they would have seized Him and declared Him King that very moment. But His time had not yet come. A different destiny lay ahead for Jesus of Nazareth.

Prayer

Dear Heavenly Father,

You called John the Baptist to make ready a people for the Lord. Thank You for his courage and bold preaching. I can only imagine how excited he must have been to announce that Jesus was the Lamb of God. I would have loved to be in the crowd that day when Jesus was baptized and You proclaimed that He was Your one and only Son!

Thank You that Jesus rejected the devil's temptations and ultimately lived a perfectly sinless life. Help me to follow Him all the days of my life.

in Jesus' name. Amen.

The third chapter of the Gospel of John contains the account of a nighttime meeting between Jesus and Nicodemus, a Pharisee. In the next chapter, Jesus meets the Samaritan woman at the well. John is the only one of the four Gospels that tells of these two encounters. As you read these stories, pay close attention to the details. Think about the time of day each meeting takes place, who is present, and the questions that are asked.

Before we talk about one of my favorite Bible stories, here's a quick history lesson about the animosity between the Jews and Samaritans. These two cultures have been squabbling for more than seven centuries by the time Jesus meets the woman at the well. For example, when Nehemiah led the effort to rebuild the temple walls in Jerusalem, a few prominent Samaritans did everything in their power to block his progress. Around that same time, the Samaritans built their own temple on a mountain thirty miles from Jerusalem, claiming *it* was the only proper site for worshiping God.

More recently, the Samaritans had made a practice of giving safe harbor to Judean criminals and fugitives from justice. So as you can see, the two sides had a long history of despising one another. Therefore, Jews would travel well out of their way to avoid any contact with the Samaritan people.

But Jesus does not go the long way around to avoid Samaria. In fact, He goes there on purpose. He knows there is a woman there who is spiritually thirsty, and He makes it His business to be where she will be that day. This is a pattern that emerges throughout the Gospels—Jesus meeting people where they are, or in this case, where they are going to be.

By this time, Jesus has gathered a group of followers called "disciples," and upon arriving at the woman's village, Jesus sends them into town to buy food. After they have gone, He sits down by the town's well and waits. He knows she is coming.

Try to imagine that you are watching the encounter from a nearby window. Feel the heat of the midday sun on your face as you see Jesus sitting by the well. He is clearly tired from walking all morning. Now notice the woman who comes to draw water from the well. There is something about her that tells you she is thirsty for more than this well can provide.

Jesus speaks to her. He asks for a drink from the well. This may not sound like a big deal, but it is highly unusual for a Jewish man to speak to a Samaritan woman. It just isn't done. But Jesus doesn't seem to mind breaking with tradition and cultural norms.

The woman, however, is rather shocked.

Her reaction doesn't surprise Jesus. But then, nothing does. Instead, He says, "If you only knew the gift God has for you and who you are speaking to, *you* would ask *me*, and I would give you living water." Now He has her attention.

Living water? She isn't sure what that is, but it sounds wonderful.

Jesus tells her that the water He has will quench her thirst so that she will never thirst again. Ever.

I love her response: "Sir, give me this water." If the offer is genuine, not only will she never thirst, but she will no longer need to make these painful trips to and from the well.

Jesus then tells the woman to go and bring her husband to Him. This probably startles her as much as His offer of living water. You see, she isn't married at the moment, although she is living with a man. Jesus tells her that she has already had five husbands. He doesn't have to say that she also has some deep wounds and hurts or that she knows what it's like to be disappointed again and again. She is lonely. She is tired. She is thirsty.

His revelation of these few facts prove to the woman that He is a prophet. But it also means that Jesus knows this woman. He knows about her past. He knows about her hurts. He knows her reputation and yet is still talking with her. This makes her a little uncomfortable, so she shifts the conversation to the ongoing dispute between their peoples regarding where they are supposed to worship. Jesus goes along with it and explains to her the importance of worshiping the Father in spirit and truth. At this point, the woman says that she knows the Messiah is coming and will tell them "all things."

Jesus says, "I who speak to you am He."

Speechless, the woman leaves her water jar and runs into the city. She never does get around to drawing water from the well. Instead, she tells anyone who will listen that she has met the Messiah, and He offered her more than she could imagine. He knew all about her but still cared for her.

Just then the disciples return, and there's an awkward silence. They clearly wonder why Jesus was talking with a woman, but no one asks. They offer Him some food they've brought with them, but He declines, saying, "My food is to do the will of Him who sent Me and to accomplish His work."

As a result of this intentional, out-of-the-way meeting at a well outside a small town in Samaria, Jesus stays two days teaching and many believe in Him.

Whatever your needs are, God knows. He knows where you are on your faith journey. He knows you, flaws and all, and still He loves you and cares deeply about your joys and sorrows and dreams. He knows how much you long to know Him and to be held by Him. And it's at this intersection of your need and your seeking that He will meet you.

EXPLORING THE PARABLES

Read the parable of the pearl of great value in Matthew 13:45–46.

JACOB'S WELL

Have you ever been surprised when someone you didn't know spoke to you, especially if that person was someone you considered to be popular, important, or different from you?

Jesus met the Samaritan woman at Jacob's well. Jacob was the son of Isaac and the grandson of Abraham and Sarah. According to Genesis 33:18–20, Jacob "pitched his tent" outside the city of Shechem, and he later purchased this plot of land. It is believed that this is where Jacob dug his well, which exists to this day about forty miles north of Jerusalem.

In the time of Jesus, this area was part of Samaria, and Jews and Samaritans did not associate with each other. In fact, they disliked one another intensely. So you can imagine the Samaritan woman's surprise when Jesus, a Jewish man, struck up a conversation with her. He was breaking a cultural taboo, and she didn't know what to think at first.

Jacob had dug this well to provide water for his household and his livestock, as this was a very dry land. But Jesus offered the woman "living water," which John 7:39 tells us is the Holy Spirit. Jesus explained to her that everyone who drank from the well in the ground would thirst again, but those who accepted the "living water" would have eternal life.

In her confusion, she asked Jesus if He was more important than her ancestor Jacob. When Jesus told her He was the promised Messiah, she dropped her water jar and ran back to town to share the news. Her witness resulted in many believing in Him. Jesus then stayed in town with the Samaritans for two days, and many more believed (John 4:39–40).

Jesus' message of God's love and His gift of salvation is for all people who will receive it. Do you know someone who needs to hear this message? Will you go today and share the message?

LET'S TALK ABOUT IT

1. Why didn't the Jews and Samaritans like each other? How do you think they treated one another?
2. Are you nervous to talk to people who aren't very popular or likable? What are some ways you can make an unpopular person feel loved and accepted?
3. Do you think you would recognize Jesus if He introduced Himself to you? What could He do to convince you that He is the Son of God?
4. How thirsty are you for the living water that Jesus makes available to you?
5. Why do you think the disciples were so anxious for Jesus to announce Himself to the world?

faith & belief

Modern culture often uses the word *faith* very differently from how the Bible uses it. Many today speak of faith as a kind of wishing or hoping, meaning that it is little more than a preference or opinion. But the Greek word that is translated as faith in the New Testament means "being persuaded" or "having a firm conviction."

What do you need to be persuaded that something is true? Reasons.

What do you need to be convinced? Evidence.

A biblical understanding of faith is that faith is like a container—it's only as valuable as the thing you put in it. If you put trash in a box, then the box is worthless. But if you put diamonds in that same box, then the box becomes valuable. Faith is only as valuable as the thing you believe in.

Many people believe in things that aren't true. They point to *how many* believe the same thing or how much they believe it as evidence that what they believe is true. But the number of believers and the sincerity of their belief doesn't tell us anything about whether what they believe is true. After all, if you sincerely believe a lie, it is still a lie—even if the whole world believes it.

Biblical faith goes beyond mere belief. Faith that the Bible speaks of means trusting in something you have good reasons to believe is true. And in order to know whether something is true, it must be backed by reasons and evidence.

Some people think that reasons and evidence are contrary to faith. However, without reasons and evidence, you cannot have biblical faith. God did not merely give us something to believe; He gave us ways of investigating and testing what He says so that we will know we can trust Him with our very lives.

Nicodemus Speaks

I was a Pharisee and a member of the Sanhedrin, the ruling body of the Jews. My position was one of prestige, and I commanded great respect among God's people. Indeed, I considered myself an educated man worthy of honor. Yet as I look back on the events concerning Jesus of Nazareth, I see that I was a fool and a man most to be pitied.

News had reached me of strange events at a wedding in the village of Cana, and there were rumors of other signs and wonders performed by the one called Jesus. I had known nothing of the man only weeks before, and yet in recent days a number of Jews had left their work and their families to follow Him. Miracles had long been in short supply in Israel, and I wondered: Could this man be the promised Messiah? I knew the ruling council would not easily be swayed and might even see this man as a threat to their authority. So I took it upon myself to question Jesus alone.

Under the circumstances, I felt it would be prudent to meet Him at night. This would mean fewer witnesses and therefore fewer wagging tongues come daylight. I greeted Jesus with respect, knowing that if the rumors of signs were true, God must be with Him. But His response bewildered me! He said that unless one is born again, he cannot see the kingdom of God. I asked how a man could be born a second time, and Jesus marveled that a teacher of Israel did not understand these things.

He then spoke with authority of the Spirit of God and eternal life and of the light that has come into the world. He spoke of God's Son, saying, "Whoever believes in him is not condemned, but whoever does not believe is condemned already, because he has not believed in the name of the only Son of God." I so wanted to believe! But I had too much to lose.

The English poet Henry Vaughn would later write of that moonlit encounter, "Wise Nicodemus saw such light / As made him know his God by night." But was I wise? Had I looked upon Him with the eyes of faith, surely I would have recognized my Savior and forsaken all to follow Him. But my sight had become dulled by the trappings of power and the prestige of my position, for I loved the glory that comes from man more than the glory that comes from God.

Prayer

Dear Heavenly Father,

Thank You that I am one of Your children. I know that You love me completely, more than any earthly person could ever love me. I feel like I'm Your favorite child, and yet I know You love everyone the most. Help me to love everyone in my family equally and deeply.

Father, teach me about forgiveness. You have forgiven me of so much. So many times I have let You down, so many times I have disobeyed, yet You forgive me every time! Forgiveness is not always easy for me, but I can do all things through You in Your strength. When I forgive other people, You are glorified, and I want my life to glorify You!

In Jesus' name, I pray. Amen.

Lesson 5

Rejection, Selection, Parables, Miracles

Motions

9. Rejection–Selection
10. Parables–Miracles

Passage

Matthew 5–7
Mark 3
Luke 4–5, 8

Take it To Heart

Blessed are the...
Matthew 5:3–12

Jesus' ministry was off and running. Already He commanded the attention of crowds to the frustration of the Jewish leaders. Wherever He went, whether teaching in a synagogue or preaching on a mountainside, Jesus caused quite a stir. He mingled with the people, observed their sad situation, and took compassion on them.

The Sermon on the Mount is perhaps the most recognized of His teachings. For this lesson, Jesus chose creation as His venue, speaking on a hillside somewhere near the Sea of Galilee. I just love that He taught the people outdoors, surrounded by the beauty of God's handiwork! Matthew recorded this sermon in chapters 5–7 of his Gospel.

On this day, Jesus talked about what blesses a person's life. He told the people why it's important to be dependent on God, be humble, seek justice, keep their hearts pure, be merciful, make peace with others, and do what is right even if they are persecuted for doing it. We call this set of teachings the Beatitudes. The word beatitude comes from a Latin word that means both "happy" and "blessed."

Jesus challenged His listeners to accept and embrace suffering when they are persecuted for their love of God. His listeners lived under Roman oppression, so they knew all about persecution.

He also encouraged the people to live in a way that brings glory to God and points others to His Son. To make His point in a way the people would understand, Jesus used salt as an example. Like salt, a Christian's life should add flavor to the world and help to preserve godliness in our culture. Then He used light as another example. Jesus said our lives should be like a light high on a hill that shines for everyone to see. In the darkness of night, a light can guide people who are lost and give

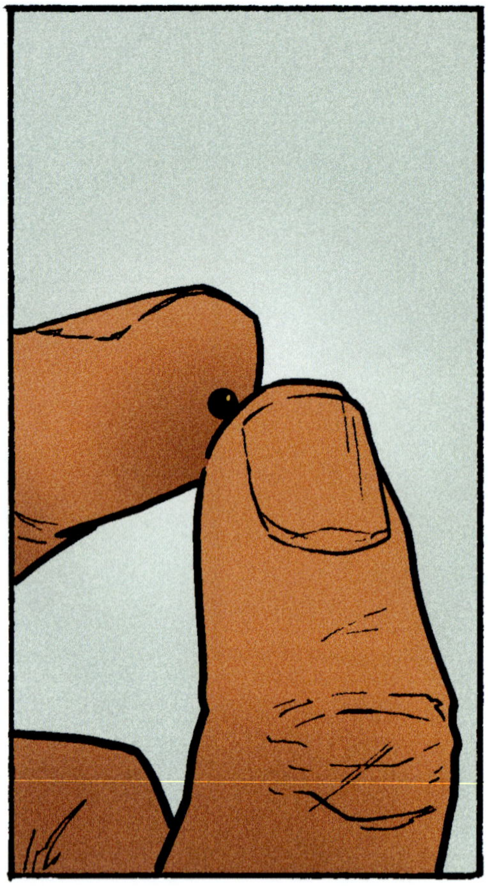

them hope. Jesus also taught them not to give in to hate or anger or lust, because He knew these attitudes only bring a person pain and heartache. Instead, He said, we should pray for those who hate us.

In this sermon, Jesus also taught the people how to pray and even gave them an example to follow (Matthew 6:9–13). We call this the Lord's Prayer, and it is a model for our own personal prayers. The prayer begins by declaring that God is the sovereign ruler of the universe and asking Him to reveal His holiness and glory to everybody: "Our Father in heaven, hallowed be your name."

This is followed by telling God how we long to see Him establish His kingdom on the earth so that people everywhere would seek Him and obey Him as the angels do in the spiritual realm: "Your kingdom come, your will be done on earth as it is in heaven."

The next line speaks of two of our greatest needs—God's daily provision and forgiveness of our sins—and our need to forgive those who have wronged us: "Give us this day our daily bread, and forgive us our debts, as we also have forgiven our debtors."

The prayer ends by asking God to help us recognize when we are being tempted and for the strength to resist: "And lead us not into temptation, but deliver us from evil."

Remember that prayer is a conversation between you and your heavenly Father. God wants you to speak from your heart when you talk with Him. Studying the Lord's Prayer is a great way to remind yourself who God is and why He is to be "feared," but God is far more interested in hearing you open your heart to Him than in the specific words you say.

The Sermon on the Mount ends with a parable. Jesus often taught using parables, which are sometimes called "earthly stories with heavenly meanings." Jesus told stories that used places and situations that common people understood and knew well. For example, some of His parables involved farming, and many of His listeners were farmers. So Jesus spoke of sowing a crop, bringing in the harvest, and separating the wheat from the chaff. His stories almost always involved everyday objects that people would be familiar with, such as seeds, lamps, coins, yeast, and fishing nets.

Jesus finished His sermon by telling the parable of the wise man, the foolish man, and the houses they built. Take a moment to read about it in Matthew 7:24–27. This story is about the importance of a house's foundation. The wise man builds his home on a rock, and so when storms beat against the house, it remains sturdy and secure. But the foolish man builds his home on sand, and so when storms beat against his house, it comes crashing down around him. With this parable, Jesus said to build our lives on the right and firm foundation—God and His Word. He was forecasting storms in our future and warning us that when the rain falls and the wind roars, a life built on a weak foundation such as money, power, or popularity is doomed to failure, and the destruction will be great.

After reading the Sermon on the Mount, what do you think God is most concerned about in the lives of His people? Their salt supply? Their daily bread? Their knowledge of sound construction principles? The correct answer is the condition of their hearts. So much of Christ's teaching is about who we are on the inside. In Proverbs 4:23, Solomon instructs us that, above all, we must guard our hearts because everything we do—the way we think, feel, speak, choose, act—flows from the heart. That's why God looks at a person's heart and not his or her outward appearance.

Nearly all the parables of Christ deal in some way with the human heart. But only those who had eyes to see and ears to hear could understand the parable's meanings. Many hearts among God's people had become so hardened that they were unable or unwilling to understand or humble themselves before the Lord so that they might experience God's "kingdom come." Only a few were willing to see, hear, and obey. What about you? Do you have eyes to see and ears to hear?

In addition to the many sermons and parables Jesus presented, He also performed miracles that demonstrated His authority over creation and His power over sickness and death. Jesus healed lepers, restored sight to the blind, caused the lame to walk, and brought the dead back to life. He multiplied five loaves and two fish to satisfy the hunger of more than 5,000 men—with twelve baskets of leftovers. He walked on water, and He calmed the stormy seas. Jesus did these miracles to show He is our Healer, our Provider, and Lord of all creation.

EXPLORING THE MIRACLES
Read about Jesus healing Peter's mother-in-law in Luke 4:38–39.

PARABLES

Some people talk about the Bible as if God's Word were little more than a list of rules and facts about God and religion. They forget that the Bible is full of stories, songs, and history. In fact, Jesus often taught the people by telling stories called parables.

A parable is a picture painted with words. Jesus used these word pictures to help explain a principle He was teaching. Most of the time, the parables of Jesus revealed something about the kingdom of God and how it works very differently from the way the world does things. He also used parables to reveal to those who listened carefully that He was the promised Messiah.

Jesus constructed His parables around everyday experiences and common-sense examples that anyone could understand, whether they were workers in a field, wealthy landowners, or priests in the temple. He could have chosen to impress people by speaking in lofty phrases and five-denarius words like a philosopher or a highly educated scribe. Instead, Jesus used stories to speak to all the people in a way that they could understand instantly, making the stories engaging and memorable.

Yet many who heard the parables did not always comprehend their meaning. Sometimes Jesus used a parable to teach a lesson that would only be understood later, after His death and resurrection. He explained the meaning of these parables in private to His disciples, who would later teach the parables to others and put them in writing for us to read.

LET'S TALK ABOUT IT

1. The memory verse for this lesson is longer than most. But some people think it is one of the most important sections of Scripture to know by heart. Were you able to memorize it?
2. If you had to tell someone in one or two sentences what Jesus said in the Sermon on the Mount, how would you sum it up?
3. Do you have a favorite parable? If so, which one? Try to retell it in your own words.
4. How important do you think it was that Jesus did miracles? Which of His miracles seems the most amazing and supernatural to you? Why?
5. What was Jesus telling us when He spoke about those who have eyes to see and ears to hear?

Miracles

We often use the word "miracle" to describe something that amazes us, like an unusually effective stain remover, or something that happens despite being highly unlikely, as when the United States hockey team defeated the heavily favored Russians at the 1980 Winter Olympics. Both aspirin and penicillin were called "a miracle drug" when introduced to the world. But a true miracle is more than an impressive product, a spectacular achievement, or a medical breakthrough. A miracle is an unusual work of God that calls attention to His power and majesty and fulfills His purposes for creation.

God is at work in His creation at all times, and the ways in which He acts bring reliability and consistency to creation. But sometimes God chooses to take action in a very unusual way. And when He does, it is a kind of communication meant to reveal something about Himself. Miracles are never meaningless or just for show.

In the Bible, miracles always come from God, reveal something about Him, and accomplish something good. Often miracles were given to prophets as a sign. A prophet had to be able to show he had the authority to speak for God, and miracles were the sign that he should be listened to. The prophets never claimed to have the ability to do miracles by their own power; the source was always God.

Because God is always at work in the world, miracles are not a violation of the laws of nature such as gravity. The laws of nature describe one of the ways God upholds and governs the world. But God makes choices about how He acts, and sometimes He acts in a way that is different from His normal way. So miracles are not scientifically "impossible," because science observes and describes the world as it normally works. Miracles don't contradict science; they are breaks from the norm. Both describe how God works in the world, just in different ways.

Andrew Speaks

I was born to be a fisherman. Surely this is what my Jewish parents intended when they gave me a Greek name meaning "manly." My brother, Simon, and I were raised in the fishing village of Bethsaida on the Sea of Galilee. We later made our home in Capernaum, where we continued in the trade taught to us by our father. Fishing is all we knew, but we were doing all right for a couple of uneducated seamen. We owned both our boat and a home in the city, despite much of our profit going to the Romans and their tax collectors.

The work was difficult, but fish were always in demand. Summer or winter, we toiled long hours, casting our nets on the waters and dragging them up again and then repeating the process. We often fished at night because the night made our nets almost invisible to the fish in the water. We caught mostly musht (a kind of tilapia) and biny (a kind of carp) and sold them in town. Much of our time, however, was spent on the shore mending our nets. It was tedious work but necessary if we hoped to catch more fish.

Simon was married, which kept him occupied outside of work. But I spent my free time learning from the man you know as John the Baptist. He spoke passionately about repenting of our worldly ways and preparing our hearts for the coming Messiah, who he claimed was among us already. I was hungry to know more about this One who would bring with Him the salvation of God.

One of our partners in the fishing business, John (the brother of James and son of Zebedee), was also a disciple of the Baptist. One day, we were speaking with our teacher when he pointed to a man walking past us and said, "Behold, the Lamb of God!" Neither of us hesitated; we simply turned and followed this man, knowing and trusting that He would be our teacher now. We spent the rest of the daylight listening to Jesus of Nazareth, and I knew in my heart He was the Promised One.

At the first opportunity, I found Simon and practically dragged him with me to meet Jesus, saying, "We have found the Messiah!" Upon meeting Him, my brother asked Him bluntly, "Are you the Messiah?" Jesus did not answer but instead gave him a new name: Peter, which means "the rock." After that, we needled him about being hard-headed, calling him "Simon Peter," and the name stuck.

Not long after, Jesus came to us as we were fishing. Simon Peter and I were casting our net just off shore, while John and his brother James mended nets on the beach. Jesus beckoned to us and said, "Come, follow Me, and I will make you fishers of men." At once, we set down our nets and left them behind to follow our Lord.

Yes, I was born to be a fisherman.

Prayer

Dear Heavenly Father,

You created the heavens and the earth by Your word. There is nothing that You can't do. I know that Jesus is Your divine Son, equal with You in every way—holy, sovereign, all-powerful. He demonstrated Your power over all creation with His many miracles, and He showed Your perfect love for us by healing many who were in need. Even though all have sinned against You, Jesus had compassion for us in our sinful state. Thank You for recording His teaching and parables so that I will know Your ways and learn to walk in them. Help me to love You with a pure heart and build my life on the solid rock of Your Word.

In Jesus' name, I pray. Amen.

Lesson 6

Testimony of Peter & Transfiguration

Motions

11. Testimony of Peter
12. Transfiguration

Passage

Matthew 16:13–17:13
Luke 9:18–36

Take it To Heart

He said to them, "But who do you say that I am?" Simon Peter replied, "You are the Christ, the Son of the living God."
Matthew 16:15–16

The question we discussed in the video is one we all must face. It's a question every person must answer. It is one you must answer. Who do you say that Jesus is? Jesus claimed to be God's Son. Do you believe Him?

Jesus asked His disciples, "Who do the crowds say that I am?" They told Him that some people were saying He was John the Baptist, who had recently been beheaded by King Herod. Others were speculating that He was Elijah or one of the other prophets of old.

The Pharisees, Sadducees, and scribes did not believe. They rejected Jesus. Despite the Old Testament prophecies, which they were surely familiar with, they didn't know Jesus for who He was and is. They professed to have knowledge and wisdom, yet they didn't recognize their God when He was standing right in front of them. They rejected His teaching and ignored His many miracles because they had neither eyes to see nor ears to hear. Their hearts were cold, hard, and lifeless as empty tombs.

Jesus then asked His disciples, "But who do you say that I am?" They believed that Jesus was the Messiah, although it's clear from reading the Gospels that they didn't fully comprehend what it meant that He was the Son of God. Still, they had left their homes, their families, and their jobs to walk with Jesus and learn from Him. They were committed to this path. Even when many of His followers turned away and left Him because they couldn't understand some of His more difficult teachings, the main group of twelve disciples remained with Him until His final days.

Jesus had selected these men to be apostles, or "sent ones." He trained the twelve to preach the Good News and then sent them into the towns and villages, giving them authority to cast out demons and heal every kind of disease and illness. However, three of the men—Simon Peter and the brothers James and John—were closer to Jesus than the others, forming something of an inner circle. He took them to places where He didn't take the others.

About a week after Jesus asked them, "Who do you say I am?," He took Peter, James, and John up on a mountain to pray. The Bible doesn't specify which mountain it was, but what happened next is so significant that the event is recorded in three of the four Gospels.

As Jesus prayed on the mountain, He became "transfigured." This means that His face and clothes began to glow. His clothes were gleaming white, as though made of light, and His face shone like the sun. In Isaiah 53, the prophet said of the Messiah that there would be nothing in His everyday appearance that would make us think He was the Son of God, and indeed, Jesus usually looked like an ordinary man. But on this mountaintop, His appearance was transformed so that His glory shone brightly.

Then two other men appeared and spoke with Jesus. Together they talked of how Jesus would soon depart from the earth, for the time of His death was drawing near. One of the men was Moses, through whom the law had been given to God's people. The other was Elijah, among the greatest of the Old Testament prophets.

Where were the three disciples during all this? Snoozing. They had dozed off while Jesus was praying and almost missed the whole thing! They awoke to find Him transfigured and speaking with Moses and Elijah. Cue Peter to speak without thinking, as was his habit. He said, "Master, it is good that we are here. Let us make three tents, one for you and one for Moses and one for Elijah." In essence, Peter was saying, "Let's all stay right here. This is awesome! I'll build us some tents, and we can all just hang out on this mountain."

At that very moment, a bright cloud overshadowed them, and a voice spoke from the cloud, saying, "This is My beloved Son, with whom I am well pleased. Listen to Him!" Wow! God the Father just spoke out loud to confirm that Jesus was His Son. When the disciples heard this, they fell on

their faces, terrified. But Jesus bent down and touched them, saying, "Get up. Don't be afraid." And when they lifted their heads, they saw only Jesus. The cloud had gone, and Moses and Elijah had disappeared. The disciples were once again alone on the mountain with their Master.

This is an important moment in history. This startling event, which we call the Transfiguration, is powerful to picture in our minds, but it might seem kind of random if we don't read what came before it. In the days leading up to this moment, Jesus had taught His disciples that soon He must suffer much and be put to death but would be resurrected on the third day. This had to be very confusing for the disciples. They had not expected the Messiah to be rejected by the Jews, who had long looked forward to His coming. In fact, they probably thought Jesus had come to free them from Roman oppression and take His rightful place as King. So how did His death fit into the picture? And what was this talk about a resurrection?

The Transfiguration was a bold exclamation in answer to their questions. Jesus had revealed Himself in glory as the One who came to fulfill both the law and the prophets, represented on the mountain by Moses and Elijah. And God the Father had spoken from heaven, identifying Jesus as His Son. There could be no doubt about it. Jesus was the Christ, the Son of the living God. Wow!

I enjoy hiking in God's creation, and one of my favorite things to do is to climb a mountain trail to its peak. No, I don't have dreams of conquering Everest. In fact, with a few exceptions, the "mountains" I've climbed were more like tall hills. But every time out, I can't help but get more and more excited as I climb higher and higher. I wonder what the view at the top will be like; anticipation builds as every step takes me closer and closer. Finally and suddenly, I break into a clearing, and I am there—the summit. The air is fresher and the view exhilarating. A new wave of energy strengthens me as I marvel at the beauty from on high. I can only imagine what it must have been like for Peter, James, and John to stand on a mountain with the very One who made the mountain!

Returning from my own mountaintop experiences, I often become quiet and introspective. I begin to rethink my priorities, my challenges, my victories. Everything looks different from the mountaintop. And so it was for Peter, James, and John. Coming down off the mountain, they had much to think about. If they thought they knew who Jesus was on the way up the mountain, now there could be no doubt. They no longer had to wonder if this man was the Messiah. God Himself had confirmed it: Jesus was His Son, the Christ. But what did that mean? And what would it mean for their lives and the lives of all mankind that God walked among them?

And so we come full circle to the question we faced at the start of the lesson: Who do you say Jesus is? Was He just a good man and a good teacher? Just a prophet? Just a miracle worker? Or was He—is He—who He claimed to be: the Messiah, our Savior? And if He is Lord and Master, Savior and Friend . . . well, that changes everything.

EXPLORING THE MIRACLES
Read about Jesus healing the centurion's servant in Matthew 8:5–13.

WHO WERE THE PHARISEES & SADDUCEES?

The Gospels depict the Sadducees and Pharisees as some kind of religious authorities who were nearly always in conflict with Jesus during His earthly ministry. So who were these men, and what did they have against Jesus?

The Sadducees and Pharisees were similar to today's political parties in that they controlled much of the power in Jewish society while often clashing over their beliefs. Both had a strong presence on the Sanhedrin, the seventy-member ruling council and authority over religious matters in Judea, although the Sadducees held a majority on the council.

The Pharisees were mostly middle-class businessmen and educators who taught strict obedience to God's laws in daily life. The Pharisees were zealous for the law but were legalistic about how to follow it. Jesus said they got so wrapped up in the minutiae of rules that they missed the more important matters of the heart like "justice and mercy and faithfulness" (Matthew 23:23). Thus, they were hypocrites because they did not practice what they preached. The Pharisees also believed that traditional Jewish teachings were just as important as the written law, sometimes even more so, leading Jesus to accuse them of ignoring God's commandments for the sake of their traditions (Mark 7:1–13).

Whereas the Pharisees controlled the synagogues and were closer to the common man, the Sadducees were the wealthy elite who controlled both the temple and the Sanhedrin, the two most important institutions in Jewish society. The chief priests and high priests in the time of Christ were Sadducees. They cooperated with their Roman rulers, collecting taxes and accommodating Roman laws, thus making the Sadducees unpopular with the working class.

The Sadducees rejected man-made religious rules and even the prophets, believing that only the Torah—the five books written by Moses—contained the inspired words of God. The Sadducees also disagreed with the Pharisees about the supernatural. The Pharisees taught the existence of angels and demons, the resurrection of the dead, and an afterlife with rewards and punishments for individuals, but the Sadducees believed in none of these things (Acts 23:8). Jesus told them, "You are wrong, because you know neither the Scriptures nor the power of God" (Matthew 22:29).

Both parties considered Jesus to be a threat. The Pharisees feared that His teaching and miracles would undermine their position with the people. The Sadducees were afraid that His increasing popularity might attract unwanted Roman attention. And so the two groups set aside their differences and plotted together to have Jesus killed (John 11:45–53).

LET'S TALK ABOUT IT

1. Who do you say Jesus is? Why do you say that? What evidence can you point to that proves who He is?
2. Someone in the Old Testament asked to see God's glory. Do you remember who it was? Where did it happen?
3. What are some other biblical events you have read about that took place on mountains?
4. Do you remember another time when God the Father spoke from heaven about His Son? What was the occasion? What did God say?
5. How do you think the disciples knew the two other men on the mountain were Moses and Elijah? And why do you think these two men of old were chosen to join Jesus at the transfiguration?

the deity of christ

Some people think that Jesus never claimed to be God. Although He is never quoted as saying the words "I am God," that doesn't mean He didn't teach that He was in fact God incarnate. Jesus knew that merely saying "I am God" wouldn't mean much in a pagan society where there were lots of so-called gods. Instead, He claimed to be a very specific God in a very specific way to a very specific people (the Jews) who would not misunderstand what He was saying.

Jesus claimed to be God in three ways. First, He forgave sins. This is something only God can do. Think of Mark 2:1–12, in which Jesus healed the paralytic man whose friends lowered him through the roof. Before addressing the man's obvious physical need, Jesus forgave the man's sins. The scribes who were in attendance were appalled that He was claiming to do what only God can do and, therefore, was proclaiming Himself to be God. In answer to their unspoken objections, Jesus then healed the man to prove that He had the authority to forgive sins.

Second, Jesus claimed to be God by accepting the worship of others. For example, after He walked on water, the disciples responded by worshiping Him (Matthew 14:33). When Jesus rode into Jerusalem on a donkey a few days before His arrest and crucifixion, the crowd greeted Him with palm branches and shouts of praise and worship (John 12:12–13). In these instances and others, Jesus did not correct those who worshiped Him. He accepted what was only proper for God to accept.

Third, Jesus said many things that would be blasphemous unless He truly was God. One of the best ways to show that Jesus claimed to be God is by pointing out how the Pharisees reacted to Him in the Scriptures. He often said things that made Himself equal with God, leading the Pharisees to cry out against Him. In some cases, they picked up rocks to stone Him (John 8:58–59; 10:30–33), for according to God's law, blasphemy was a capital crime punishable by stoning (Leviticus 24:13–16). These attempts to stone Jesus showed that they understood His claims correctly, even if they didn't believe He was God.

Simon Peter Speaks

I was a coarse man with fisherman's hands, and I was not afraid to speak my mind. Like it or not, you knew where you stood with me. Sure, I had a bad habit of putting my foot in my mouth, but I expected my friends to stand by me as I stood by them. I thought I knew my place in the world.

And then I met Jesus of Nazareth. My brother came to me one night, all out of breath, claiming he had found the Messiah and insisting that I come and meet Him. So I did, and I liked Him immediately. But was He truly the Messiah?

Well, it was true that He was no ordinary wandering teacher. He spoke with such authority, and He knew the holy Scriptures like no one I had ever heard speak in the synagogue. And when Jesus looked at me, I saw that He knew me in ways that frightened me.

Then there were the signs. Jesus made the blind see and the lame walk. He healed lepers and cast tormenting spirits out of crazed men and women. He even cured my bedridden mother-in-law!

Then there was that time we were on the lake and a furious storm blew in over the eastern mountains. I'd seen some rough weather in my time, but this sudden tempest had me worried we might not make it. Yet while the rest of us worked furiously to regain control of the boat and keep us afloat, Jesus lay in the stern, sleeping like a baby. I was about to rouse Him myself when one of the others woke Him, shouting over the howling winds and crashing waves, "Teacher, don't you care that we're about to drown?!" But Jesus didn't get angry or scared. He didn't even seem surprised to wake to such conditions. He simply stood up, looked out over the wind and the waves, and said, "Peace! Be still!" And just like that, the sea was completely calm. You wouldn't know there had been a breeze, let alone a life-threatening storm.

Some of the others were asking one another, "Who is this guy that even the winds and waves obey Him? But I knew. If I wasn't convinced before, I was now. When the day came that Jesus asked us, "Who do you say that I am?," I didn't hesitate. I blurted out, "You are the Christ, the Son of the living God."

I was never a very humble man, and I was often overeager to get things done. But I learned humility and patience at the feet of my Lord, and I experienced His forgiveness and unearned grace after I denied even knowing Him the night He was arrested. I can't take any credit for it, but when I was filled with the Holy Spirit on the day of Pentecost, I never felt more alive and energized to preach the gospel to as many people as possible. Anything worthy I ever accomplished was because Christ lived in me.

Prayer

God Almighty,

I believe with my whole heart that Jesus is Your only Son, eternally begotten, not made. I believe that for our sake He came down from heaven, was conceived of the Holy Spirit, took on human flesh, and was born of the virgin Mary. I believe that He suffered under Pontius Pilate, died on the cross, was buried, and rose again on the third day according to the Scriptures. I believe that Jesus is the Christ, the Son of the living God.

In His name I pray. Amen.

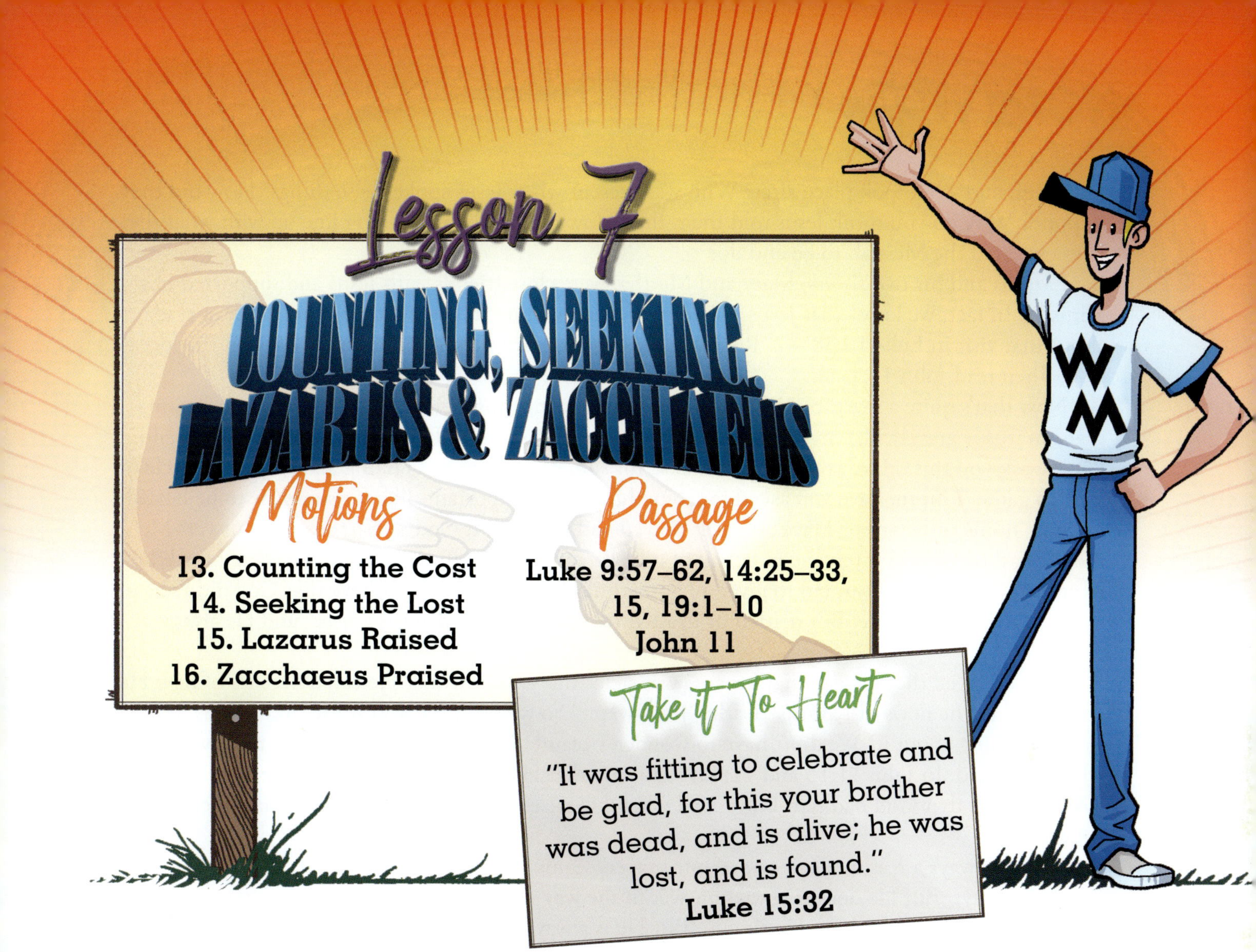

In lesson four, where we discussed Nicodemus and the woman at the well, the notebooking journal contained an activity asking you to compare and contrast the two figures. At the end of the activity, you were asked to consider which of them you related to most. Today we will look at another pair of people, Lazarus and Zacchaeus. Once again, I'd like you to take time to look at them closely.

When you read the Bible, remember that you are reading about actual events that happened to real people. These are not myths or make-believe tales. Of course, the Bible doesn't tell us *all* the events that took place in the history of God and His people. The apostle John said that if he were to record all the things Jesus did on earth and nothing else, "the world itself could not contain the books that would be written."

The sixty-six books of the Bible are really just the highlights of God's greater story. But He calls our attention to the people featured in these stories because He wants us to learn from them. You may already be familiar with the stories we're going to talk about today. If you are, resist the urge to tune out and hear only "blah, blah, blah." These stories and characters deserve your special attention because God chose to put them in His holy Word. He wants to teach you something through all of the Bible, even the stories you've heard many times before.

As we discuss the story of Lazarus, keep in mind that Jesus has already told His followers three times that He must suffer and die. Take a moment and read about these three occasions in Mark 8:31–38, 9:30–32, and 10:45, paying attention to the details. What took place just before these teachings, and what took place after? Who was present when Jesus spoke these things? How did they respond? Why do you think Jesus told them this? How did this hard teaching line up with what the Jews expected the Messiah to be and do?

Lazarus and his two sisters, Mary and Martha, were close friends with Jesus and supported His ministry. In fact, we know that Jesus visited their house before this story took place. You can read about that visit in Luke 10:38–42. Remember what you learn about Martha and Mary on that occasion. Then read John 11:1–46.

Now that's quite a story, but it's not without some confusing points. For example, after hearing that Lazarus is gravely ill, why does Jesus wait instead of rushing to Bethany to heal His sick friend? Let me ask you this: Have you ever asked God for something? I'm not talking about a new bicycle or a video game. I mean, have you asked for something really important, like for someone to be healed or come home or be saved? Have you ever prayed and prayed but God doesn't seem to answer? Me too. I've asked God to intervene in behalf of other people or myself and waited and waited for Him to answer. Sometimes I wanted to give up. Sometimes I was tempted to believe that God didn't hear me or that He didn't care. But neither of those things was true. God always hears, and He always cares.

Jesus received the message that Lazarus was sick. And we know that He cared because of how He responded to the news of Lazarus' death: "Jesus wept." So why did He wait until Lazarus was dead to do anything about it? We don't have to wonder, because Jesus comes right out and tells everyone why He waited. In John 11:15 and 11:42, Jesus says that He waited for Lazarus to die so that people would believe that God had sent Him. And when He raises Lazarus from the dead, many people believe.

There's always a reason when one of our prayers seems to go unanswered. God always hears our prayers. Always. But He doesn't always answer in the way we want, hope, or expect. Often, God doesn't answer when we think He should. But He is always right on time—His time. In this story, Jesus seemed to be late, but He wasn't. He was right on time to glorify the Father. And that's true for every answer He gives to prayer. He is using the time we wait to grow us, grow our faith, and glorify God.

So what are you asking God for today? What does your heart desire? Things of this world? Or more of Him? Prayer is for your benefit. It helps you learn to wait on the Lord. Prayer is where you practice trusting Him with your hurts and your desires, remembering who He is and that He is able to do infinitely more than you can ask or imagine. Prayer helps you rest in His presence, enjoy His peace which passes understanding, feel the goodness of His love, and experience His mercies which are new every morning.

The second character we meet in today's lesson is Zacchaeus. We only know a few things about him, but they are notable. Take a moment to read the story in Luke 19:1–10. Write down in your notebooking journal some of the character qualities you see in Zacchaeus.

Once again, we have a story of Jesus meeting a person exactly where he is. It must have been startling to be called out in front of a crowd while perched in a tree, but Zacchaeus had nothing to lose. True, he was a wealthy man and a Jew, but his neighbors despised him for collecting heavy taxes from them on behalf of the Romans.

Zacchaeus thought he had climbed the sycamore tree that day in order to see Jesus, but it turned out he was there to be seen *by* Jesus. And when Jesus saw Zacchaeus, He didn't just see a short man in a tree; He saw Zacchaeus like He saw the Samaritan woman at the well. For Jesus, seeing meant

knowing. He knew Zacchaeus. He knew his heart and that Zacchaeus was open to receiving His teaching.

In Luke 19:10, Jesus says that He came to seek and save the lost. In this week's reading assignment, Luke 15, Jesus tells three parables about a shepherd who searches for a lost sheep, a woman who turns her house upside down looking for a lost coin, and a father who waits for his lost son to return home. All of these stories should give you confidence that God cares deeply about you, His child, and will go to great lengths to keep you close and safe at His loving side.

EXPLORING THE PARABLES
Read the parables of the lost coin and the lost sheep in Luke 15:1–10.

DEATH

God created the world without death. It was only after Adam sinned that death became something everyone has to deal with and experience. In fact, it's such a big part of our lives that the Bible speaks of three different kinds of death.

Physical death is when our bodies no longer work. Whether from disease, accident, or old age, at some point each person's heart will stop and his or her brain will no longer function. When this happens, that person's soul will continue to exist in the spiritual realm until the resurrection on the last day. At that time, every follower of Jesus will be given a glorified body that cannot die.

Spiritual death is our inheritance from Adam. Since he sinned, every person has been born with a sinful nature. (Jesus is the only exception.) This fallen nature means that although we are physically alive, we are spiritually dead. We do not naturally desire God or choose His ways. Instead, we rebel against Him and reject Him. It takes a work of the Holy Spirit to make us spiritually alive so that we may be reconciled to God.

Eternal death is how the Bible describes the way people who reject Jesus will spend the rest of their existence. Even though we tend to think of death as when we stop existing, that's not what happens. Every single person will exist forever. The only question is whether we exist in God's favor, which is called eternal life, or we exist in God's wrath and punishment.

LET'S TALK ABOUT IT

1. Why is it significant that Jesus wept at the news of Lazarus' death?
2. What are you praying about today? Whom are you praying for?
3. How does God ask you to wait in prayer?
4. Why do you know you can trust God to hear and answer your prayers?
5. Are you curious about who Jesus is? What are you willing to do to see Him? To know Him? Is Jesus welcome in your heart?

SALVATION

Salvation is a word that means to be rescued from danger or difficulty or even death. Who needs to be rescued or saved? Everyone! All people need to be saved from the power and effects of sin. Sin causes suffering and destruction, and the wages, or reward, for sinning is death (Romans 6:23). All people have sinned, and so all people need saving.

Couldn't we just decide not to sin? No. Because of Adam's sin, each of us is born with a sinful nature, making us slaves to sin. There is no part of us that wants to choose, or has the ability to choose, to obey God. We are born God's enemies, and because of our sin we deserve eternal punishment. And there's absolutely nothing we can do about it. We all desperately need a savior because we cannot save ourselves.

In His mercy, God sent His only Son, Jesus, to provide a way of salvation. Jesus lived a sinless life on earth as the spotless Lamb of God, and His death on the cross paid for the sins of all those who believe in Him. When we believe, His life of perfect obedience is credited to our accounts so that we can stand before God clothed in the righteousness of Christ. Jesus is our Savior because He did for us what we cannot do for ourselves. And the only way to receive salvation is through faith in Him.

Old Testament believers were also saved through Christ. How was this possible before the life, death, and resurrection of Jesus? Romans 4 makes it clear that the way of salvation has always been through faith. In the Old Testament, it was faith in the promise that the Messiah would come and fulfill all the requirements of the law once and for all. For those who believed God's promise, their faith was credited to them as righteousness. Thus, both Old Testament and New Testament believers are saved through the work of the Messiah.

Sometimes we think of salvation as merely being rescued from our sin. But when we are saved, we are rescued to something as well: the kingdom of God. Our salvation not only removes us from danger of destruction, but it also places us in the eternal safety of God's favor!

Martha Speaks

I confess, I was always a worrier and a bit of a scold. And I was quick to let my frustration be known when things weren't going precisely the way I thought they should. You may have heard the story of how I foolishly scolded Jesus because I was frustrated with my sister, Mary.

The Son of God Himself had come to visit our home, and I was determined to make a good impression. As Jesus sat down and began talking to Mary, I got busy being a good hostess. I brought Him refreshment and then excused myself to prepare the big dinner I had planned. I dropped a couple of hints that I could use my sister's help, but she either didn't hear or didn't care. As I grew more impatient, I banged a few pots around to get her attention, but Mary didn't respond.

Finally, my frustration boiled over, and I said to Jesus, "Lord, doesn't it seem unfair that my sister just sits there while I do all the work? Tell her to come and help me." I'm ashamed now to think of how I behaved. Jesus told me that "only one thing is needed," and I realize now that knowing Him is far more important than any selfish concern.

And so it was that I didn't hesitate to send for Jesus when our brother, Lazarus, became gravely ill. I knew the Son of God could—and would—heal him. But He didn't arrive in time, and Lazarus died. I was sorely tempted to chide Jesus again when He arrived four days later as we were mourning. And yet I trusted Him as I trusted no other. So I ran out to meet Him and said, "Lord, if you had been here, my brother would not have died. But even now I know that God will give you whatever you ask." My faith was rewarded as Jesus awakened Lazarus, even though my brother was dead and in the tomb for four days.

You see, it is foolish to be frustrated with the Lord. Not only is He capable of far greater wonders than we could ever hope or imagine, but He loves us with a perfect love and intends only the best for us. In fact, He is perfect in all His ways—including His perfect timing.

Prayer

Dear Heavenly Father,

It's great to read about people and things that were lost but eventually found. I know that I am not much different—I was lost and couldn't find my way to You. But Your grace is amazing. You pursued me, and I couldn't resist responding to Your love. I believe that Jesus is Your Son. I believe He died on the cross as a sacrifice for my sins. I believe He was buried and was raised again on the third day, proving that He is victorious over death and Satan. I love to be in Your presence, and I long to spend eternity with You!

In Jesus' name. Amen!

Lesson 8

Triumphal Entry, Temple Cleansing & Last Supper

Motions

17. Triumphal Entry
18. Temple Cleansing
19. Last Supper

Passage

Luke 19:28–48, 22:7–38

Take it To Heart

"Blessed is the King who comes in the name of the Lord! Peace in heaven and glory in the highest!"
Luke 19:38

We're nearing the climax of God's story. We have come far since the book of Genesis, yet all the stories and people we've met along the way have all been pointing to Jesus as the Lamb of God come to save His people from their sins.

Remember, Jesus told His disciples what had to happen. Three times in Mark's Gospel He foretold of His suffering and death and how it was a necessary part of God's plan. But they just didn't understand. The disciples, like many Jews, were expecting the Messiah to be a warrior king who would lead them to victory over their Roman oppressors. But that's not what Jesus came to do. He came to seek and save the lost and give His life for them.

And yet He did nothing to silence the people at the gates of Jerusalem where they greeted Him as a king, laying their cloaks and palm branches in His path and shouting, "Hosanna to God in the highest!" and "Blessed is the King who comes in the name of the Lord!" These people recognized the majesty of Jesus even if they didn't understand His mission. Some Pharisees in the crowd chided Jesus to rebuke His followers for their riotous behavior. He answered, "If these were silent, the very stones would cry out instead!"

On this day, Jesus was returning to Jerusalem for the Feast of Passover. You'll remember from your Old Testament study that the Passover feast was a time to remember how God delivered His people from slavery to the Egyptians. On the night of the very first Passover, God instructed His people to sacrifice a spotless lamb and smear some of its blood on the doorframes of their houses. This blood was a sign for the angel of death to "pass over" their homes as he brought death to the firstborn of Egypt. In this way, God saved His people.

The first Passover, and every one after, pointed to the coming Messiah and the life He would give to save God's people once and for all. And now Jesus had come to fulfill the Passover. This time the Lamb of God, born in Bethlehem and unblemished by sin, would be the sacrifice.

For their last meal together, Jesus and His disciples gathered in a large, furnished guest room. They probably followed the traditional pattern for the celebration of the Passover, including lighting candles and reading a psalm. But before they could get started, their feet needed washing.

In the first century, people walked everywhere on dirt roads, wearing nothing on their feet but sandals of rope and leather. So it was common courtesy to welcome guests to your home by washing their dusty, sweaty feet, although this task was usually given to the lowliest servant in the house. On this evening, the owner of the room had provided a towel and a bowl for water but no servant to wash their feet.

Think about it. These were the sweaty, stinky feet of grown men. Thirteen pairs. Gross! It wouldn't have been a fun job, but it was probably nice to have your feet washed after a long day of walking on dusty roads.

When no one else volunteered, Jesus took it upon Himself to do this dirty job. He didn't ask any of the disciples to help. He simply took off His outer robe, poured some water in a bowl, and began washing His disciples' feet and wiping them with the towel. He didn't huff or sigh or slosh the water in frustration. He just got to it.

Can you imagine the King of the universe kneeling before you and washing your feet? Peter couldn't. He strenuously objected to his Master doing this filthy work (although you'll notice Peter didn't volunteer to take over and finish the job). But Jesus insisted. He said that either He washed Peter's feet or Peter wasn't one of His disciples. "Then don't stop with my feet," Peter replied, "wash my hands and my head too!"

After putting His robe back on, Jesus sat down and taught the disciples, using the foot washing as an example of how He wanted His disciples to serve one another. He then gave them a new commandment: Love one another. "Just as I have loved you," He said, "love one another. By this all people will know that you are my disciples."

The time had almost come for Jesus to write a new chapter in the story of the Passover feast. But before He lay down His life, He showed us how we are to remember His sacrifice. During the meal,

Jesus blessed the unleavened bread and broke it and gave it to the disciples, telling them that the bread represented His body, which would be given for them. Jesus also took a cup of wine, and after giving thanks, He told His disciples to drink from it. "Drink of it, all of you, for this is my blood of the covenant, which is poured out for many for the forgiveness of sins." The sacrifice Jesus was about to make would restore the relationship between God and those who chose to believe.

This event is recorded in three of the Gospels: Matthew 26:26–29, Mark 14:22–25, and Luke 22:14–20. Whenever Christians come together to remember His sacrifice by eating the bread and drinking the fruit of the vine, we call it "communion," the Eucharist, or the Lord's Supper.

At this point in the meal, Jesus grew troubled and then surprised everyone by announcing that one of them was about to betray Him. Yet no one seemed to understand His meaning when He told Judas Iscariot, "What you are going to do, do quickly." Judas had arranged with the Sadducees and scribes to hand Jesus over to them when the crowds weren't around to prevent His arrest. Judas, having been possessed by Satan, barely protested His innocence but rose and departed into the night.

EXPLORING THE PARABLES
Read the parable of the two sons in Matthew 21:28–32.

PRAYER

Prayer is conversation in which we speak to God and listen for what He has to say to us. This is not the only way He speaks to us—He communicates with us through Scripture, for example—but it is the only way we speak to Him. Every person's faith is about an ongoing relationship with God, and every relationship requires good communication. That's what prayer is.

Prayer is how we give God thanks for all the blessings He graciously gives us. It is how we offer up worship and confess that we need Him. It's also how we ask things of Him. All of these prayers proclaim that God is good, sovereign, and righteous.

Because God is all-knowing, He doesn't need us to tell Him about our situations or requests in order for Him to know about them. But by praying, we acknowledge that God is in control of those things. He has given us the gift of prayer not because our prayers change His mind but because it changes our hearts. God is not only sovereign over all the situations and concerns we bring Him, but He also controls how these things will be dealt with. And oftentimes He chooses to work through our prayers in order to change us to be more like Jesus.

Of course, we must avoid the temptation of treating God like a wishing well and asking for things out of selfishness. It's also possible to ask for good things that are not within God's will, and it's tempting to become frustrated when God has other plans. How we pray says something about the condition of our hearts. How we respond to God's answers also says something about our hearts. Prayer is a tool that's constantly at work, shaping us as we use it.

LET'S TALK ABOUT IT

1. What is Jesus teaching us by washing His disciples' feet? What are some acts of service you could do to follow His example? Whose feet are you willing to wash?
2. Why do you think Peter was so resistant to having Jesus wash his feet? Why did his attitude change so quickly to the other extreme of wanting Jesus to wash his whole body?
3. Why is it important for us to often remember Jesus' death, burial, and resurrection by taking part in the Lord's Supper?
4. In communion, what does the bread represent? What does the wine represent?
5. Sometimes our worldly desires and selfish ambitions get in the way of our following Jesus. What distracts you from remembering Jesus' sacrifice?

Blood Sacrifice

In the Bible, blood is a very important symbol. Blood is used to speak of both death and life, and it takes on particular importance in Scripture because it is through blood that sacrifice is made for sin.

We have seen that the penalty for sin is death. Because life is in the blood, the shedding of blood is how payment for sin—that is, atonement—is made. In the Old Testament, God's law required that animals be ceremonially sacrificed as sin offerings. The blood of these animals became a substitute for the death of those who made the sacrifices. However, the principle of an animal's blood paying for a person's sins existed long before the law was handed down through Moses. In the Garden of Eden, after Adam and Eve ate the forbidden fruit and realized they were naked, God clothed them with animal skins. The skins that covered them could only be gotten by sacrificing the animals and shedding their blood.

But the sacrifices required by the law were themselves a symbol that pointed to a time when payment for a person's sins would be made once and for all, rather than being offered at specified times of the year. The system of sacrifices pointed to the person and work of Jesus Christ, who paid for the sins of all who believe in Him by the shedding of His blood on the cross.

The word *communion* comes from a Latin word meaning "mutual participation." It is through the shedding of Christ's blood that we become united to Him, and it is this spiritual union that we celebrate at the Lord's Supper when we drink from the cup.

Judas Speaks

My soul screams in anguish, for I have done an unspeakable evil! An innocent man is sentenced to die come morning, and I am the foul wretch who sold him out for a pittance of thirty silver pieces.

Why did I do it? This morning, as I stood before the chief priests and offered up Jesus of Nazareth to them, I told myself that this was the right move, the smart move. Yet now I barely remember saying the words or taking their money.

For three years I followed this man, convinced he was the Messiah raised up by God to drive the Romans from our land. Think about it. Crowds followed us everywhere, ready-made armies who would rise up against our Roman oppressors if he commanded them. The people hung on his every word—well, except for those times when he spoke in riddles, telling tales of lost sheep and scattered seeds. But there were also the signs. I saw him do such works that would make a fighting zealot out of the most hardened cynic. With this man leading the way, we could not fail.

Did I believe he was God? Of course not. That was Peter's foolishness, although I knew the others believed it; they had taken to calling him "Lord" instead of "teacher." But why would God alienate his own priests, men with the kind of wealth and resources it would take to finance a revolution? And what about the Pharisees and scribes? They have the ear of the people, and yet Jesus took every opportunity to berate and provoke them! Why should they believe he was the Messiah?

I wanted to counsel him to negotiate a deal with these influential leaders, but I couldn't get him alone for two minutes. The Galileans were always there, blocking access to him as if they were his bodyguards. If Jesus had other plans, another agenda, why wouldn't he take me into his confidence? He chose me to be one of the twelve, so he must have recognized my passion, my savvy, my vision. I could have been a major asset in the new kingdom. What could these fishermen ever hope to do for him?

Okay, so I was angry and frustrated when I made the deal with the chief priests. I don't know what I was hoping would happen. Maybe this would force the Messiah to reveal himself openly with a show of power. Maybe his arrest would galvanize the people to rise up against their oppressors. Or maybe I wanted nothing more than a glint of recognition in the eyes of my teacher as I betrayed him with a kiss.

Jesus did not strike down his enemies. He stood silent as the council condemned him to death in spite of his innocence. Why couldn't they see him for who he is?

Why couldn't I see him for who he is?

There can be no hope for me now.

Prayer

Dear Heavenly Father,

Jesus came into this world as a humble babe born in a stable, and yet wise men brought gifts to honor Him as King. And when He rode into Jerusalem on a donkey, the crowds acknowledged Him as the King who comes in Your name. Yet Jesus humbled Himself and washed the dirty feet of His disciples. I really want this lesson to sink into my heart. Help me to consider others before myself. Remove the worldly thoughts and selfish ambitions that compete with my love for You. Help me to fall in love with You and to love my neighbor as myself.

I pray this in the name of Jesus. Amen.

Lesson 9

Betrayed, Denied, Crucified, Resurrected

Motions

20. Prayed–Betrayed
21. Tried–Denied
22. Crucified
23. Resurrection

Passage

Luke 22–24

Take it To Heart

And he [Jesus] withdrew from them about a stone's throw, and knelt down and prayed, saying, "Father, if you are willing, remove this cup from me. Nevertheless, not my will, but yours, be done."
Luke 22:41–42

We have come to what appears to be a really sad ending to this story. Jesus—who came in love, who taught and healed and changed the lives of many, who obeyed the Father and pointed others to Him—is sentenced to death. And not just any death. He is sentenced to die on a cross. Death by crucifixion was considered to be the most brutal and torturous of deaths.

The Sanhedrin condemned Jesus for a variety of offenses, including violating the Sabbath, threatening to destroy the temple, and speaking blasphemy by claiming to be the Messiah and Son of God. But under Roman law, the council had no authority to execute anyone, so they brought Him to Pontius Pilate, the Roman governor over Judea. There they accused Jesus of stirring up rebellion against Caesar, forbidding the people from paying their taxes, and proclaiming Himself to be a king. They knew that treason against Rome was punishable by death.

So Pilate questioned Jesus in his quarters, sparking a fascinating exchange recorded in John 18:33–38. Jesus did not defend Himself against the charges but made it clear that His kingdom was not of this world. When Pilate asked Him to explain, Jesus said that He was born to testify to the truth and that those who love the truth listen to Him. You can almost hear the world-weariness in Pilate's voice when he replies, "What is truth?"

When Pilate went out to deliver his verdict, he found a crowd gathered outside with the council members. He announced that he had found no fault with Jesus yet was willing to punish Him before setting Him free. This did not satisfy the council or the crowd, and they insisted that Pilate crucify Him. He replied, "Why? What evil has He done?" But they shouted all the more, "Crucify Him! Crucify Him!"

Pilate knew that Jesus was innocent, but he feared that a riot might break out any minute. So he called for a bowl of water and, in view of the crowd, washed his hands of the matter, saying, "I am innocent of this man's blood. See to it yourselves." Then he ordered that Jesus be scourged and delivered Him to be crucified.

Scourging was such a horrific act, so terrible and vicious and painful, that I cannot bring myself to describe it here. Suffice to say that this punishment killed some men before they could be crucified. The Gospels don't provide us a detailed description of Jesus' condition after scourging, but the

Old Testament prophet Isaiah described it this way: "His appearance was so disfigured beyond that of any human being and his form marred beyond human likeness" (Isaiah 52:14, NIV).

Then they bound Jesus and led Him to the place of crucifixion like a Lamb to the slaughter. He was forced to carry His cross through the streets. The weight of the beams became unbearable as Jesus was suffering from exhaustion, dehydration, and a tremendous loss of blood. So the soldiers pulled a man from the crowd—Simeon of Cyrene—to carry the cross for Him. Their destination was just outside the city—a hill called Golgotha, Greek for "place of the skull." In English, we call it Calvary. There Jesus laid down His life willingly. The soldiers didn't have to wrestle Him or hold Him down. This was the moment for which He had come.

When Jesus was nailed to the cross, our sins were nailed there with Him. He wasn't guilty. He was utterly innocent and completely blameless. The spotless Lamb of God. Yet He took upon Himself all of the sin of the world. Every sin—past, present, or future. The weight must have been crushing. And with His blood He paid our debt, the death we deserved for our sin. Yet even on the cross Jesus was interceding for those who put Him there: "Father, forgive them, for they don't know what they are doing."

There's another aspect of the cross that we need to at least try to understand. Nailed to the wood with the sin of the world on His shoulders, Jesus was profoundly separated from God the Father in a way He had never known. Living a sinless life qualified Jesus to serve as the spotless Lamb of God, but it also meant He had perfect fellowship with His Father. But when He took on the sin of the world, He became separated from the Father, just like us. It was from this place of separation that Jesus cried out, "My God, My God, why have You forsaken Me?"

The Gospels record a few interactions Jesus had with people while hanging on the cross. One of these was an exchange with the two thieves who were crucified on either side of Him. One mocked Jesus and said that if He was really the Christ, He should save all three of them. The other thief rebuked His fellow criminal, saying, "Do you not fear God? We deserve this death for the crimes we've committed, but this man has done nothing wrong." He then looked at Jesus and said, "Remember me when you come into Your kingdom." And Jesus promised him they would be together in paradise.

As the end came, Jesus cried out, "I am thirsty." After receiving some sour wine, He said, "It is finished." With these words Jesus summarized all that He had done to glorify the Father: He was born of a virgin, lived a sinless life, pointed others to the Father, and paid the price for our sins. Now He had finished the work the Father had given Him to do.

Finally, Jesus called out with a loud voice, "Father, into Your hands I commit My Spirit!" He bowed His head, breathed His last breath, and died.

Jesus freely gave Himself to die on the cross. Then He was buried in a tomb, and a large stone was rolled in front of the entrance. But there is good news. Really good news. He was raised on the third day! This is the climax of God's story. According to 1 Corinthians 15:6, Jesus appeared to more than five hundred witnesses after His resurrection, so we know it really happened. Today, we celebrate His resurrection every year on Easter Sunday.

EXPLORING THE MIRACLES
Read about Jesus healing the servant's ear in Luke 22:47–51.

BURIAL CUSTOMS

If you have ever attended a graveside service at a cemetery, you probably heard a pastor read a Scripture passage and pray. After the family and friends went home, did you wonder what happened to the casket and the body of the deceased? The workers at the cemetery placed the casket in a cement vault and buried it in the ground. Later, a marker or headstone with the person's name, birthdate, and the date of death was placed over the grave to help visitors remember the person who was buried there.

Today, when a person dies, the body is usually embalmed to preserve it so that people who come to the funeral can see the deceased as they remember him or her. The embalming process is important in part because funerals often don't take place until several days after the death.

First-century Jews believed that, out of respect for the dead, a body needed to be buried before sundown on the day the person died. The body was anointed with oil and washed with warm water. Then it was wrapped with linen cloth along with spices, probably to mask the odor.

Jews believed that contact with a dead body made a person unclean spiritually and physically, so bodies were buried in tombs outside the city walls. Tombs were often natural caves or sections carved out of rock on a hillside. People carried the deceased to the tomb on a wooden platform or stand called a bier (pronounced BEER). A procession of family and friends followed. They mourned for seven days near the entrance of the tomb. A year after the death, the family gathered the decayed bones from inside the tomb and placed them in an ossuary, or bone box, for a secondary burial.

Family members from many generations were often buried in the same tomb. How do you remember your great-great-great grandparents? You might have a few very old pictures of them or remember stories told to you by your family members. The Jews remembered their ancestors because they were buried in one place near their village.

LET'S TALK ABOUT IT

1. Can you imagine what it must have been like to witness Jesus stumbling through the streets and carrying His cross? Can you imagine standing with Mary and John and watching Jesus die on the cross? How do you think these events would have affected you?
2. What lessons can we learn from the interaction Jesus had with the two thieves?
3. Jesus was clearly in agony being forsaken by His Father. How much do you desire a closer relationship with God? How does it feel when you know that you've sinned and your sin has put up a kind of wall between you and God?
4. Mary, the mother of Jesus, was a thoughtful person. On a few occasions, Luke speaks of Mary pondering or reflecting on events in the life of Christ. Do you think she understood any more or less about the life and death of Jesus than His disciples?
5. The last sayings of Jesus from the cross seem quite intentional. Which one stands out to you? Why?

propitiation

Because God is perfectly holy, just, and righteous, He hates sin and must punish it. If He didn't punish it, He would not be just and righteous. Because God's standard is absolute perfection and the penalty for sin is death, we are hopelessly lost as sinners. The only way to turn away God's wrath is for a sacrifice to be made in our place. Jesus offered Himself as a sacrifice to satisfy God so that we could be reconciled to Him. The payment for sin that satisfies God is called *propitiation*.

To satisfy God, propitiation has two parts. One part involves taking on the punishment for sin. As a perfect and sinless human being, Jesus did not deserve to be punished for the things He did in His life. Yet He chose to take upon Himself the punishment we deserved.

The other part of propitiation is also based on Christ's perfect life. Jesus did more than avoid sinning; He kept the law of God perfectly in all His actions and His thoughts. That perfect obedience is credited to us at the same time that the punishment for our sin is taken from us. We tend to think of Jesus' death as the payment for our sins, and that is absolutely true. But if this payment was all His death meant, then it would only reset our debt to zero. It's this second part of propitiation that gives us right standing before God. When God the Father now looks upon a follower of Christ, He sees us through the righteousness of His Son. So even though we aren't actually righteous, when clothed (or covered) with Christ and His blood, we are declared righteous.

Pilate Speaks

"What is truth?" I asked the king of the Jews, and I thought it was a pretty good question. I had attended the best schools of the day, studied philosophy, and was well connected politically and socially. I was also the governor of the Roman province of Judea, reporting to Emperor Tiberius, so I knew a thing or two.

My main task as governor was simply to keep peace in the region, though the Jews and their leaders made this harder than I wished. They complained often about a wandering teacher from the Galilee region, saying he was stirring up the people against Caesar and against the religious establishment. The man's name was Jesus, and I was not unaware of his reputation. As far as I knew, he went about doing good and telling stories and was said to possess a remarkable talent for healing.

When the Jewish council brought this Jesus to me and accused him of setting himself up as a king, an act of treason against the emperor, I had no choice but to question him. However, I prided myself on being a man of quick and decisive action, so I got right to the point. I asked him straight up, "Are you the king of the Jews?" His answer was a little perplexing. He did not deny being a king but said his kingdom was not of this world. I knew nothing of other worlds, but I saw no evidence that he intended to incite violence against Rome.

So I tried a different strategy, partly because of a dream that had disturbed my wife. The dream bothered her to the point of interrupting my day to tell me I should have nothing to do with this righteous man. So I offered to free a Jewish prisoner in accordance with tradition. I asked the Jews if they wanted me to release Jesus or Barabbas, a notorious criminal. This seemed like an easy and obvious choice, but people often do surprising things. They chose Barabbas.

Things got worse from there. Now the crowd started shouting and demanding that I have Jesus crucified. I did not like the idea of condemning an innocent man, but I was definitely not going to let this meaningless local dispute ruin my career. So before a riot could start, I ordered that Jesus be flogged, then delivered him to be crucified.

I often think back to my conversation with Jesus. He was intelligent, articulate, and seemingly innocent. I don't know why he didn't fight harder for His freedom. He seemed to be very clear about his purpose—something about bearing witness to the truth, speaking the truth, or being the truth. I just didn't understand. Can anyone really know the truth?

Prayer

Dear Heavenly Father,

When I think about the day when Jesus suffered and died on the cross, my heart aches. I know it's important for me to remember and think about all the details, but it pains me to imagine everything my Savior did to rescue me from sin. I know there was nothing I could do to save myself, so I am eternally grateful. But I have a hard time considering how much love it took for Jesus to give Himself up for me. When I stop long enough to really take it all in, my heart can't help but explode with praise and worship and a longing to spend eternity with You in heaven, repeating the sweet name of Jesus, Jesus, Jesus!

In His holy name I pray. Amen.

Lesson 10

Ascended, Spirit & Community

Motions

24. Ascended
25. Spirit
26. Community

Passage

Acts 1–4

Take it To Heart

But you will receive power when the Holy Spirit has come upon you, and you will be my witnesses in Jerusalem and in all Judea and Samaria, and to the end of the earth."
Acts 1:8

Jesus has returned to heaven. He completed His mission on earth and sent the Holy Spirit to be with each of His followers. This Holy Spirit, promised by Jesus, empowers His disciples to witness and testify that Jesus is the Messiah, the Son of God.

Before we forge ahead in the story, let's back up a minute. Before returning to heaven, Jesus spent forty more days walking among us instead of rushing home. Why did He do this? For one thing, it was important to show His followers that He was alive. The hope of many had died with Jesus on the cross. Even His closest friends didn't understand that the Messiah had to die and be raised again to fulfill Scripture.

It makes sense then that Jesus stuck around to give His disciples what they were still lacking. They had much to learn about the Lord and His kingdom if they were going to tell all the world about Him. We know from Luke 24:25–27, when He was walking with two of His followers to the village of Emmaus, that He began with Moses and the prophets and interpreted for them all that the Scriptures had said concerning Himself.

The additional time Jesus spent with the disciples would restore their hope, strengthen their faith, and prepare them to endure the opposition and persecution that awaited them. But they would need something more in order to preach the Good News and write about the teachings of Jesus. They would need the Spirit of God Himself to remind them of Jesus' words, inspire them to speak boldly, guide their actions, empower them to heal the sick, and comfort them in times of trouble.

After forty days, Jesus gathered His disciples one last time and instructed them not to leave Jerusalem but to wait there for the Holy Spirit to come upon them. Then they watched as Jesus was lifted into the sky and taken out of their sight. The Son had returned to heaven and taken His place at the right hand of the Father.

Ten days later was the Feast of Pentecost, a harvest celebration in which Jews from all over the known world descended on Jerusalem to worship and give thanks. The Lord chose this day to send His Holy Spirit to dwell in His followers. The arrival of the Spirit that day was accompanied by a sound "like a mighty rushing wind." This must have been a huge sound heard throughout the city, because a bewildered crowd rushed to the place where the disciples were meeting and found them telling of the mighty works of God in a language that was not their own. In fact, each foreigner heard them speaking in his own native tongue! Some wondered aloud what this could mean, while others scoffed and mocked the disciples as being drunk.

But then one of the disciples stepped forward and declared that what they were witnessing was the fulfillment of Joel's prophecy of the last days. He then began to tell them about Jesus' death and resurrection and finished by declaring that Jesus is both Lord and Christ. Many of his listeners were "cut to the heart," and they asked what they should do.

Which disciple gave this eloquent sermon that moved a multitude? Just moments after receiving the Holy Spirit, who among the apostles stood up as their leader? Peter! Perhaps it's not too surprising when you consider he often acted without thinking. Remember, he was the one who volunteered to walk on the water with Jesus. That's just Peter.

But this time it's a different Peter who steps up. This isn't the Peter who was once thoughtless and prideful. This is a changed Peter, a measured Peter, a focused Peter. This is the Comeback Kid. He has mourned over his sin, languished over his mistake, and cried himself to sleep. Then he raced to the tomb and found it empty. No, this Peter isn't rushing in to speak his own mind; he's speaking the words given to him by the Spirit. This is a Peter who has matured since the courtyard and the crowing of the rooster.

Seven weeks earlier, Peter had been at the lowest point of his life. But on the Day of Pentecost, the man who had ducked and dodged and denied Jesus to the point of cursing, that Peter—a repentant, forgiven, Spirit-filled Peter—took his stand and preached his first sermon. And the church was born. Take some time and read about it in Acts 2:14-41. It's pretty rousing stuff. Not bad for a fisherman. When Peter quotes the prophet Joel and King David, I marvel again at how the whole of Scripture complements and supports itself, how the Bible is one unified story of God's amazing love for mankind.

The crowd was overwhelmed by Peter's sermon. Having murdered God's Son, they asked what they should do. Peter told them they should repent and be baptized for the forgiveness of their sins. Three thousand heard Peter's message and were baptized. This was the beginning of the church. God's family. A community in which there was teaching, learning, praying, fellowship, and sharing. And the Lord added to their numbers each day as

more and more people were saved.

In this new community, no one had a need that went unmet. The believers were of one heart and soul, and every person felt that what he or she owned really belonged to God, so they shared everything. Many of them sold personal property and donated the proceeds to help those in need. (Then there was the incident of Ananias and Sapphira, which you can read in Acts chapter five.)

God created community. He made us to live in fellowship with Him and with others. The church is meant to be a community in which we come together as a family to celebrate His goodness, His provision, and His faithfulness. It's a community where we help one another, encourage one another, and pray for one another. It's the group of people with whom we gather to worship God and participate as a unified body in communion (also called the Lord's Table or the Eucharist). It's a community where we fulfill the command of Christ to love one another so that the world will know we belong to Him. The early church was a shining example of a beautiful community living, working, and worshiping in sweet fellowship.

EXPLORING THE MIRACLES
Read about the disciples speaking in tongues on the day of Pentecost in Acts 2:1–11.

PENTECOST

Pentecost is a Greek word that means "fifty." In the Old Testament, Pentecost was called the Feast of the Harvest and was observed fifty days after the Feast of the First Fruits (Leviticus 23). Today, Pentecost Sunday is observed fifty days after the resurrection of Jesus.

Just before Jesus ascended into heaven, He spoke to His followers and told them to stay in Jerusalem until they received God's promise and power. Ten days later, on the Day of Pentecost, Jesus' followers were meeting together when Spirit came to them, and tongues of fire, or flames, rested upon each of them. Fire in the Bible represents God's divine presence and judgment. The disciples were then filled with the Holy Spirit, who gave them the power to do God's work. How was this possible? Because the Holy Spirit is God.

The miracle was not only the filling of the Holy Spirit but also that everyone listening understood the message in his or her own language.

This miracle allowed the message of salvation to spread very quickly. About 3,000 people were baptized after Peter preached to the crowd and told them that everyone who called on the Name of the Lord will be saved.

Jesus said, "The Counselor, the Holy Spirit, whom the Father will send in my name, will teach you all things and remind you of everything I have told you" (John 14:26, CSB). Another word for counselor is *teacher*. The Holy Spirit teaches believers how to live a life pleasing to God by helping them understand God's Word. The power that raised Jesus from the dead is available to each believer through the Holy Spirit.

God's message of salvation is for all people. How do you help others understand the message of salvation?

LET'S TALK ABOUT IT

1. What do you think it must have been like when the Holy Spirit swept into that house with a sound like a mighty rushing wind? Would you have been afraid? Excited? Both?
2. Are you loud and passionate like the apostle Peter or more reserved like the apostle John? Either way, the Holy Spirit will give you power and confidence to share the good news of Jesus Christ with others. Have you ever told someone about Jesus? What did you say?
3. Have you ever been asked to preach a sermon or teach somebody about something from the Word of God? Can you see yourself one day studying to be a preacher or teacher of the gospel of Christ and His Word?
4. Have you ever told a lie? Yeah, me too. What are some things you can do to protect yourself from the temptation to be dishonest?
5. What are the qualities of a healthy church? What do you expect to find when you walk in the door? Based on what Luke wrote in Acts about the early church, what do you think church should be like?

the Holy Spirit

The Holy Spirit is the third person of the Trinity. He is God, just as the Son and the Father are God. The Spirit testifies about the work of Christ, convicts the world of sin, regenerates and renews souls, sanctifies believers, illuminates God's Word, reveals the Lord's will, empowers the church to do His work, and provides us with peace, joy, and hope (Romans 15:13). The Holy Spirit also inspired the writing of the Bible.

Some groups who claim to be Christian deny that the Holy Spirit is a person. They teach that the Holy Spirit is nothing more than the force or energy of God. To them, the Holy Spirit is an "it," not a "He." However, the early church condemned as a heresy any teaching that denied the personhood of the Holy Spirit.

In Acts 5, when Ananias and Sapphira lied about the money they made from the sale of some property, Peter told them they had lied to the Holy Spirit. A lie cannot be told to something that is not a person. You cannot lie to a brick or a tree. Lies can only be told to persons, because the intent is to deceive. Therefore, the Holy Spirit must be a person.

On the eve of His death, Jesus said that the time was fast approaching when He would have to leave. However, He promised to not leave us alone but would send us a gift. That gift is the person of the Holy Spirit, who indwells every believer. Jesus described the Holy Spirit as a helper who would guide the apostles into all truth.

Romans 8:11 tells us that Jesus was raised from the dead by the Holy Spirit and reminds us that the same Spirit lives in everyone who believes in Jesus.

The Early Church Speaks

We were Judeans, Asians, and Egyptians. We were Romans, Cretans, and Arabians. We came from all over, from three different continents, to worship in Jerusalem in celebration of the harvest. Some of us weren't even Jews! We spoke many different languages, and yet we were drawn together as one family by our belief that Jesus was the promised Messiah who came into the world to save us from our sins.

On the Day of Pentecost, we witnessed the disciples of Jesus speaking in tongues that were not their own—yet each of us understood them as though they spoke only in our own native languages. Then Peter spoke in the power of the Holy Spirit, telling us how the Christ who had died was raised up and exalted to the place of highest honor in heaven. It is said that three thousand of us were baptized into the faith that day.

From that time forward, we remained together, even those of us from faraway lands. We attended temple together, broke bread in one another's homes, and devoted ourselves to fellowship and the apostles' teaching. We were all filled with awe at the presence of the Spirit, and the apostles did many wonders and miraculous signs of God's power.

We were now members of a new family, God's family, and we had everything in common. No need went unmet. Many of us sold our possessions and gave the proceeds to those who had need—with one remarkable exception. One husband and wife sold a piece of property but held back some of the money for themselves and then lied to the apostles about it. But what mystified us was that none of us was required to sell our property; this husband and wife volunteered to do so. Nor were they forced to give any of the money to the apostles; it was their money to do with as they pleased. And yet they told the apostles they were giving them all of the money when they weren't, perhaps so they would appear to be more generous than they were.

Peter said to them, "You have not lied to man but to God." Both husband and wife fell to the floor and died when confronted with their lie. The consequences for their actions might seem extreme as you read this now, but many learned to fear the Lord that day and hold fast to the truth in obedience to God.

Prayer

Dear Heavenly Father,

I believe that Jesus is Your only begotten Son, Your Word in the flesh. I know it was You who gave different languages to mankind when people attempted to glorify themselves by building a tower to the heavens. It was Your Holy Spirit who gave Peter the wisdom, the words, and the courage to speak powerfully on the Day of Pentecost. And You made it possible for thousands of people to hear the gospel message, each in his own language, and You saved all who called upon the name of Jesus. Give me the confidence and the words necessary to share the Good News with the people I know, the people I love, and the people I meet.

In Jesus' name. Amen.

Lesson 11

SERVANT LEADERS, STEPHEN & PERSECUTION

Motions

27. Servant Leaders
28. Stephen
29. Persecution

Passage

Acts 6–8

Take it To Heart

And the word of God continued to increase, and the number of the disciples multiplied greatly in Jerusalem, and a great many of the priests became obedient to the faith.
Acts 6:7

What is courage? Is it standing up for someone who is being wronged or bullied while other people remain seated on the sidelines out of fear? Is it speaking out against injustice when everyone else chooses to stay silent? One way to describe courage is doing the right thing even when you find yourself alone in the battle.

Fear is real. Having courage doesn't mean you're fearless. Courageous people don't lack fear; they just refuse to bow to it. Having courage means you don't allow fear to decide whether or not you will stand and speak or sit and remain silent. Having courage means you choose to do the right thing despite the possible consequences. Having courage means you choose to face head-on the storm or the bully or popular opinion.

Sometimes courage is quiet and goes unnoticed by others. For example, it takes courage to live a life devoted to God. Living for God means being faithful in the little things—the small actions and choices that no one ever sees or knows about—as well as the big things that everyone shares and talks about. It takes courage to keep doing the next right thing, to pursue holiness day after day when friends or family members aren't there to recognize our faithfulness with an "attagirl" or "attaboy." That's what it means to be faithful to God. It means we keep pursuing holiness, doing the next right thing day after day. Living courageously means trusting that everything we do matters to God, whether we are taking care of His creation or taking care of His people, whether we are taking out the trash or feeding the hungry, whether we are changing a diaper or helping a friend, whether we are

stopping to talk with a needy stranger or calling a loved one on the phone.

Courage is a character trait of those who love God. In our study of the Old Testament, we saw many examples of courage in action: Noah as he built the ark; Abraham when he offered his son Isaac; Ruth as she stood by her mother-in-law, Naomi; Hannah when she gave her son, Samuel, to Eli to raise in the service of the Lord; Shadrach, Meshach, and Abednego, who stood in defiance of King Nebuchadnezzar's edict to bow to his idol; Daniel, who continued praying to God in direct violation of an unjust law; and many others. Know this: Courage never goes unnoticed by God.

Courage would be needed to spread the gospel and build the New Testament church in the face of great persecution. In the video for this lesson, we discussed how the church was being established and it became necessary to appoint leaders. Among those who were chosen to display courage in leading the church was a man named Stephen. In Acts 6, he is described as having wisdom and a good reputation, a man who was full of faith and the Holy Spirit. The disciples selected Stephen to be a servant leader, and he proved to be an excellent choice. He was "full of grace and power" and did "great wonders and signs among the people."

And then he faced opposition. Let's pause here for a moment. We've seen this play out time and again in the Scriptures. Can you think of other biblical people who were doing the right thing—the thing that God asked them to do—and faced opposition as a result? Maybe David comes to mind. Or Nehemiah. Or any number of the prophets. That's right, doing the right thing over and over, living faithfully and trusting God, often draws the attention of enemies both physical and spiritual, those who resent all things good, true, or beautiful.

And so it was in Stephen's case. He was doing good, and some people decided to try and argue with him. But when they couldn't cope with his wisdom and the Spirit with which he was speaking, they chose to lie about him. They accused him of speaking "blasphemous words against Moses and

God" and of teaching that Jesus would destroy both the temple and the law of Moses. As a result, Stephen was dragged before the Sanhedrin to answer these charges.

Have you ever been lied about? Has anyone ever claimed that you said something you didn't say? It's an awful feeling. You know you didn't do or say what you're being accused of, but how can you defend yourself? Your first impulse might be to panic or run away, but courage doesn't quit. Courage doesn't shrink from opposition. Courage stands and speaks the truth despite the presence of fear or danger.

Confronted by the authorities with his opponents' lies, Stephen stood. In fact, he was at such peace before the council that "his face was like the face of an angel." When asked if the accusations were true, he began a well-organized and thorough rebuttal of the charges. Take a few minutes to read what he said in Acts 7:1–53. Make notes in your notebooking journal as you read.

Notice that Stephen did not directly respond to the false accusations. Instead, he did something wholly unexpected: He told the story of the Jewish people, from the calling of Abraham to the building of Solomon's temple, with an emphasis on the days of Moses. This approach probably seemed odd, especially when you consider that the council was made up of so-called experts in the law of Moses and the history of the Jewish nation.

Near the end of his message, Stephen summarized his story with this devastating counter-accusation: History proved that the Jewish people themselves were guilty of the very charges that had been brought against him. They had continually stiffened their necks against God, resisting His Holy Spirit and chasing after idols. They had persecuted His prophets and killed His only Son, Jesus the Messiah. And the men on the council were just as guilty of these crimes as their forefathers!

Ouch. Talk about courageous! Stephen must have known his words would enrage the council, but he also knew that only the truth would set this people free.

The sermon Peter preached on the Day of Pentecost was similar to Stephen's testimony, including the accusation that his listeners were responsible for Christ's crucifixion. But in Peter's case, the audience was "cut to the heart." Three thousand believed and were baptized.

But the response to Stephen's message was quite the opposite. Council members fumed in anger and gnashed their teeth at him. And when Stephen gazed up at heaven and announced that he saw God's glory and Jesus standing at the right hand of the Father, the men covered their ears and cried out in a loud voice so as not to hear him. Then they dragged Stephen to a place outside the city limits, took up rocks, and stoned him until he was dead.

Yet through it all, he remained at peace and full of grace. As he lay dying, Stephen followed the Lord's example by asking God to forgive those who murdered him. That's courage. Courage stands up and speaks out. Courage stays focused and forgives.

There's one other item of note you should remember about this event. Acts 7:58 mentions that before stoning Stephen, the men of the council took off their cloaks and laid them at the feet of a young man named Saul of Tarsus. That same day, Saul embarked on a savage persecution of the church, going from house to house and city to city, dragging to prison men and women who believed in the risen Christ. As we will see in the next lesson, Jesus had mighty, world-changing plans for Saul.

EXPLORING THE PARABLES
Read the parable of the talents in Matthew 25:14–30.

DEACONS

A pastor's primary responsibilities are to preach the Good News, being prepared to do so even when inconvenient, and to correct, rebuke, and encourage the flock with great patience and careful teaching (2 Timothy 4:2). What other responsibilities do you think your pastor has? Who helps your pastor with those responsibilities?

The leaders in the early church needed help with everyday tasks so they could focus on preaching and teaching. And so they appointed deacons to be servant leaders whose job is to meet the physical needs of the church. The first deacons were selected by the twelve apostles in Acts 6:3 so they could focus on teaching the Word and not spend their time waiting tables.

The biblical guidelines for selecting deacons are found in 1 Timothy 3:8-10. Deacons must be honest, worthy of respect, faithful, trustworthy, husband of one wife, not greedy, not addicted to alcohol, and good managers of their homes. Holding the office of deacon is an honor and a blessing.

In the church today, deacons may assist the pastor or elders by serving communion, ushering, accounting, helping with repairs, organizing committees, or meeting any other need that enables the pastor and elders to focus on the spiritual needs of the church body. The pastor and elders oversee the deacons.

If you are not yet an adult, then you cannot officially serve as a deacon in the church. But you can still be helpful. What are some ways you can demonstrate honesty, faithfulness, trustworthiness, respect, and servanthood in serving the body of Christ?

LET'S TALK ABOUT IT

1. How would you define courage?
2. Has anyone ever told lies about you or bullied you? How did that make you feel? How did you respond?
3. Have you ever stood up for a friend or family member who was being picked on? Were you scared? What happened next?
4. Why do you think it's hard for people to stand up for others?
5. How was Stephen able to be so courageous and stand up to his accusers?

the gospel is good News

The message of Jesus Christ—His life and death and what it means for us—is called the gospel. The word *gospel* means good news.

These days, however, we often hear the gospel spoken in a way that makes the news far less good than it actually is. Why? Because many Christians are afraid of offending people. But the truth is that for the good news to be good, we have to understand the bad news first. The bad news is this: Every single person ever born (except Jesus) was a sinner who deserves the full wrath of God in eternal punishment. That is very bad news indeed. And it's hard to share that with people who do not yet know Christ. Yet this news tells them exactly why they need the gospel. In fact, this news is so bad that it *is* offensive (2 Corinthians 2:15–16; 1 Peter 2:7–8). That is why we must speak the truth in love and avoid being judgmental.

Our goal is to help people understand that Jesus is the only solution to a very real problem they have. It's like being told they have terminal cancer, only worse. They have a sin problem that is *eternally* fatal. And they cannot do anything to help themselves; they need someone to do it for them. Not only does Jesus provide the solution, but He makes this offer freely through grace. That is astonishingly good news that should inspire us to share it every chance we get!

Stephen Speaks

It's pretty incredible when I think back to those early days of the church. It was so exciting to be a part of what the Lord was doing, working wonders among the believers and ushering in His eternal kingdom. I couldn't get enough.

The fellowship with other believers was so sweet, and God was adding to our numbers daily. Even priests from the temple were joining us! We rejoiced with each new profession of faith in Christ, but such increase brought with it significant growing pains. For example, we were overwhelmed with the number of widows needing care. We had the generosity and means to provide for them, but we needed to get organized. Also, demands on the apostles' time were many, and it made no sense for them to give up preaching the Word to serve tables. So it was decided to select seven men to serve those in need. I accepted the call and became one of the first deacons of the church.

Things went smoothly at first, and I thanked God every day for my new responsibilities. We were helping so many people, and the work was deeply satisfying. And the Holy Spirit was working through me to do many signs and wonders among the people.

Then I was arrested and accused of speaking blasphemies against Moses and Yahweh. Nothing could have been further from the truth! But people had been paid to bear false witness against me, so I was brought before the Sanhedrin to defend myself.

But instead of trying to disprove the lies against me, I let the Holy Spirit speak through me, and I just went with the flow. After telling them the whole story of God's people, I quoted His Word where He declared that the nation of Israel was a stiff-necked people, resisting His Spirit and persecuting His prophets. Then I spoke the words that really got the council boiling. I said they were just like their forefathers, and now they had killed His Righteous One, the Christ.

That did it! I knew my fate was sealed, and yet I had within me a peace that passed all understanding. As I looked up to heaven, I saw the glory of God and Jesus standing at His right hand. My accusers picked up stones. I knew what was coming, but I was ready to meet my maker. Are you?

Prayer

God of All Grace,

I want to help Your church thrive and do the work and ministry You have called it to do. I want to serve in ways that build up the church, our Lord's body. Help me to be faithful in small things, diligent when I am given greater responsibilities, and humble in everything I do. Remind me that I am a member of Your body and that anything I do to help is a good use of my time, talents, and resources. Keep Your church healthy, strong, united, and committed to worshiping You in spirit and in truth, now and forever.

In Jesus' name. Amen!

Lesson 12

PHILIP, PAUL & PETER

Motions

30. Philip's Preaching
31. Paul's Conversion
32. Peter's Vision

Passage

Acts 8–10

Take it To Heart

So the church throughout all Judea and Galilee and Samaria had peace and was being built up. And walking in the fear of the Lord and in the comfort of the Holy Spirit, it multiplied.
Acts 9:31

We are currently studying the early church leaders: Philip, Paul, and Peter. We discussed Philip in the video. The Gospels don't say much about him, but we did learn that he was faithful with his witness and testimony, ready to go where God would send him.

Believe it or not, we meet the next church leader at the stoning of Stephen. When we first meet Saul, he is described only as a "young man." But there is so much more to this picture. I hope you enjoy a good puzzle, because getting to know Saul requires some detective work to collect the information we need to understand this man whose writing would come to change the world.

Before he became widely known by his Greek name, Paul, Saul was born a Roman citizen in the city of Tarsus. One of the largest centers of trade on the Mediterranean coast, Tarsus was located in a region we know today as southern Turkey. Saul came from a family of Pharisees, and as a young man he was sent to Jerusalem to study the Torah under Gamaliel, a high-ranking member of the Sanhedrin. Eventually, Saul himself became a Pharisee.

We pick up his story in Acts chapter nine. Saul isn't just standing by and watching coats anymore. Here we find him preparing for a road trip north to the city of Damascus, where he expects to find more Jews who believe that Jesus is the resurrected Messiah. Saul has been officially sanctioned by the high priest to bring them bound to Jerusalem for prosecution and imprisonment. In later speeches and letters, Saul would confess that he had been zealous in his hatred of Christ and His followers and believed that he was faithfully serving God by persecuting them.

As Saul nears Damascus, he is suddenly engulfed in a bright light shining down from heaven. Probably stunned or terrified or both, he falls to the ground. Then he hears a voice saying, "Saul, Saul, why are you persecuting Me?" Saul asks, "Who are you, Lord?" The voice responds, "I am Jesus, whom you are persecuting." Imagine the terror that fills Saul's heart when he realizes that he has declared himself to be the sworn enemy of the true Son of God! He probably expects to be struck dead in this moment, but instead Jesus tells him to continue his journey and enter the city. There he will receive further instructions.

As quick as it came, the bright light is gone and the voice silent. The men who are traveling with

Saul are speechless, for they heard the sound of a voice speaking but saw no one. They help Saul to his feet, and he realizes he is completely blind. He can't see a thing. This man, who had been so focused and driven to destroy Jesus' followers, has just been confronted personally by Jesus Himself.

His companions lead him into town. For three days the blindness persists, and Saul goes without food or drink. I wonder if he spent this time remembering the things he had done to the Lord and His followers. I wonder if he pondered the stoning of Stephen and how Stephen asked God to forgive those who were stoning him. We don't know for sure what Saul was thinking about during this time, but according to Acts 9:11, he was definitely praying. Have you ever spent time just waiting on God? Do you remember a prophet from our Old Testament study who had three days to rethink his disobedience? (Look up the story of Jonah.)

As Saul is praying, a believer in the city named Ananias has a vision in which the Lord directs him to go to Saul and lay hands upon him so that Saul may regain his sight. But Ananias hesitates, for Saul's reputation has preceded him. He is known to be an enemy of the faith who has done great evil to the saints. The Lord assures Ananias that Saul has been chosen to be an instrument of God and will preach the gospel to the Gentiles, people who are not Jewish.

Ananias obeys and finds Saul just where the Lord said he would be, at a house on Straight Street in Damascus. (We don't find too many addresses in the Bible, so it's surprising when we find this street name in Acts 9:11.) Upon meeting him, Ananias says, "Brother Saul, the Lord Jesus who appeared to you on the road by which you came has sent me so that you may regain your sight and be filled with the Holy Spirit." Notice that Ananias addresses

Saul as a brother. I imagine that both men had tears in their eyes in that moment. They were once enemies, but Jesus has brought them together for God's glory. Only God can do that.

The moment Ananias speaks to Saul, "something like scales" fall from Saul's eyes and he regains his sight. The last thing he had seen was the bright light on the road, and the first thing he sees now is a messenger of mercy and grace. Only God can create such wonderful moments. Now Saul could really see—better and clearer than ever before. Everything has changed. So what does he do next? The first thing Saul does is to be baptized. Only then does he eat.

Saul's conversion was dramatic and extraordinary. He wasn't just a nonbeliever; he was a persecutor of believers. He didn't just think Christians foolish for believing; he was intent on destroying those who chose to follow Christ. But God had other plans for him. He had plans to use Saul and his radical conversion story to take the gospel message beyond the Jewish nation to the Gentiles. You see, nothing is wasted with God. He is the great Redeemer, and He will use *all* of your story when you give your life to Him.

EXPLORING THE MIRACLES
Read about Jesus healing blind Bartimaeus in Mark 10:46–52.

CLEAN vs. UNCLEAN

Although God did not create anything that was bad, the Bible does make a distinction between what is "clean" and "unclean." According to the law of Moses, some animals were considered clean, while others were unclean. The same was true of food. The law also specified some situations that would make a person unclean for a while, such as having a skin disease, giving birth, or touching a dead body.

In the Old Testament, when people were made unclean, they were not allowed to be a part of worship services. In fact, they had to remain outside the camp or temple until they had been purified. Purification happened in different ways but often included a waiting period followed by a blood sacrifice or cleansing with water.

When Jesus came, He taught that the difference between clean and unclean was not something we eat or touch but is found in the attitudes of our hearts before God. It took Peter some time to fully understand this teaching. At first, he continued avoiding food that was considered unclean under the law. Then, in a vision, God revealed to Peter that the food laws of the Old Testament no longer have to be followed. Keeping one's heart pure is what matters.

The reason God called some things clean and others unclean was to teach His people about sin and the need for atonement. Some things separate us from God, and those things need to be atoned for. After the sacrifice of Jesus and the gift of the Spirit, the symbolism of clean vs. unclean food, animals, and circumstances was no longer necessary.

LET'S TALK ABOUT IT

1. Saul was a highly educated, very religious man. How then was it possible for him to stand against Christ and His disciples?
2. Saul experienced a dramatic conversion with the light of heaven and an appearance by Christ on the road to Damascus. Why do you think he needed such a big wake-up call?
3. When Saul was blind and waiting for Ananias, what do you think was on his mind? How do you think this time of reflection might have influenced his mission going forward?
4. Ananias probably had serious doubts and fears about meeting Saul. What do you think helped him obey God and trust that this was a good thing to do?
5. How do you think other Christians reacted to Saul soon after his conversion? Were they fast or slow to trust that he was sincere in his newfound allegiance to Christ? What would you have thought about the situation?

Mission Work

Although the word "mission" is not found in the Scriptures, the concept is made clear. A mission is when God sends someone to preach the gospel to a specific group of people. Jesus modeled this as He traveled around Israel, sent by the Father to redeem His people. In fact, mission work is so important to Jesus, it was His final command on earth.

Just before Jesus ascended to heaven, He told His disciples, "Go therefore and make disciples of all nations, baptizing them in the name of the Father and of the Son and of the Holy Spirit, teaching them to observe all that I have commanded you."

The lives of the apostles show just how seriously they took missions. According to tradition, they gave their lives to spread the gospel as far away as modern-day Ethiopia, Ukraine, India, and Britain. The early church also took mission work seriously, and by the beginning of the fourth century, Christianity had become the dominant world religion.

It is very important to remember that as powerful as missionary work has been, it doesn't work because of our own passion, intelligence, or charisma. In fact, God does not need missionaries at all; He can call people to Himself any way He wants. But one of the primary ways He chooses to grow His family is through the work of missions.

All Christians must commit to praying and asking how God is calling them to support missions, whether it is by devoting themselves to full-time missionary work, participating in short-term missions projects, or supporting missionary work with their finances and resources.

Saul Speaks

I was born in Tarsus, an important city in the Roman province of Cilicia. Like my father before me, I was a Jew and a Pharisee of the tribe of Benjamin. I was trained in tentmaking, which provided me a reasonably good living. But my claim to fame was the impeccable theological education I received. I studied in Jerusalem at the school of Gamaliel, where I hobnobbed with the chief priests and religious leaders of the day in hopes of one day making my mark in the world.

When the Christian martyr Stephen was stoned for blasphemy, I stood nearby, approving of his death. This event was a turning point in my career, galvanizing me to take things to another level. I truly believed the best solution to the problem of Jesus was to rid Israel of these fanatics by means of arrest and imprisonment—or death, if necessary.

Jesus had a reputation as an impressive teacher, but He was dead. Why, I thought, were these people worshiping a would-be king who was no more? Their simple-minded zeal was creating chaos in Jerusalem. Even temple priests were walking away from their duties to join this cult who called themselves "followers of the Way."

I received approval from the high priest himself to lead the charge against these blasphemers. I began by going from door to door and arresting as many of their number as I could find, both men and women. My single-minded approach to this work struck terror in the hearts of their little community, and it didn't hurt my reputation in the Sanhedrin either.

I was on my way to Damascus to ferret out more followers of the Nazarene when my whole world was turned upside down. Like many before me and many after, my life and mission were changed in an instant when I met Jesus. As I collapsed to the ground in His presence, the career I had so carefully constructed collapsed with me. In that moment, my eyes were blinded by a light from heaven, but suddenly I began to see everything more clearly than ever before.

Prayer

God of Light,

You are the God of amazing grace. Although every person is sinful in Your sight, You can save anyone who calls upon the name of Your Son, Jesus Christ. Thank You for saving Stephen and Saul and using each of them in mighty ways. Thank You for Ananias and his example of obedience. Use me to share the good news of Jesus with the people I meet, whether they are next door or on the other side of the world. Show me how You want me to help spread the gospel message to the ends of the earth.

In Jesus' name. Amen.

Lesson 13

LAW, GRACE & THE CALL

Motions

33. First Journey–Law?
34. Council–Grace
35. Second Journey–Call

Passage

Acts 13–18

Take it To Heart

But we believe that we will be saved through the grace of the Lord Jesus, just as they will.
Acts 15:11

Wasn't it exciting to learn about Paul's first missionary journey in the video? What do you remember about Saul when we first met him? He was the number one enemy of the church. He was on a mission to put Christ-followers in prison. But God had other plans for Saul's life—plans to spread the gospel message instead of stopping it.

In the early days of the church, most believers were Jewish by birth. Jesus was a Jew, and He chose Jewish disciples. He often taught in Jewish synagogues and in the temple in Jerusalem. And so it was not unusual for the first believers to preach primarily among the Jewish population. Even those who fled to other regions to escape Saul's persecution shared the gospel only with Jews in those areas. Even the apostle Peter was hesitant to take the gospel to the Gentiles at first.

Did this mean that only Jews could be saved? Not at all! Despite acknowledging that He had been sent to the Jews only, Jesus praised the faith of a Gentile woman and healed her daughter in Matthew 15:24. In Luke 7:2–10, He marveled at the faith of a Roman centurion and healed his servant. In John 4, many Samaritans came to faith through His interaction with the woman at the well. In John 10:16, Jesus said to the Jews, "I have other sheep that are not of this fold. I must bring them also, and they will listen to my voice. So there will be one flock, one shepherd." You see, Jesus came to save all people who believe in Him, both Jews and Gentiles.

In Acts 10, Peter became convinced that "God shows no partiality" and that the Good News is for all people. As he preached the gospel to the Gentile household of Cornelius, a Roman centurion, the Holy Spirit came upon all who heard the message and they began to speak in tongues, praising God. And so Peter commanded that they be baptized with water also.

In Acts 13, when news arrived that Greeks in the Syrian city of Antioch had heard the gospel and believed, the church sent a disciple named Barnabas to confirm the report and to teach them the word properly. Barnabas and Saul would teach together in Antioch for a whole year, and it was there that the followers of Christ were first called "Christians." From there, the Holy Spirit sent Barnabas and Saul to preach on the island of Cyprus, and Saul became better known by his Greek name, Paul.

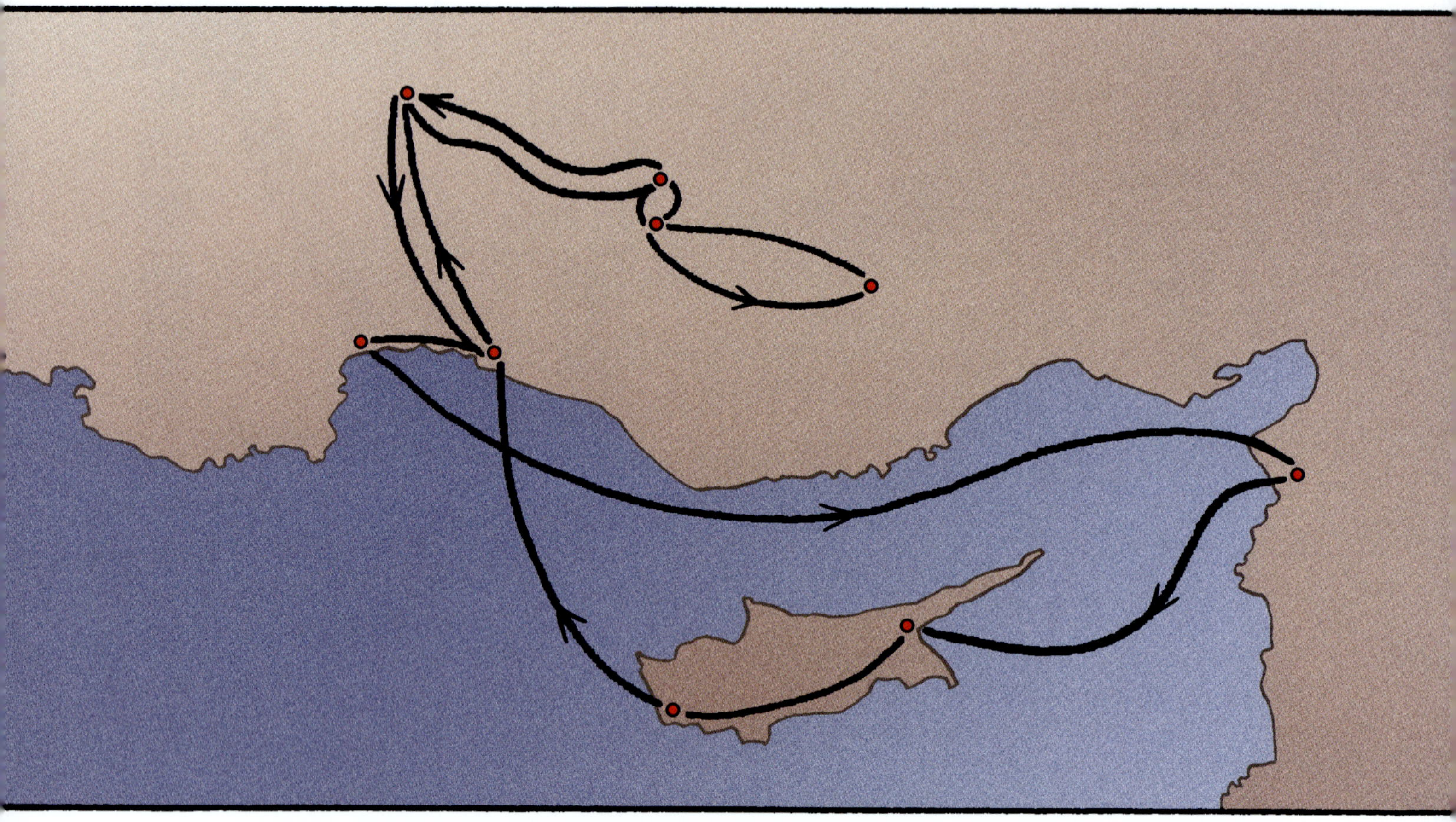

Thus began the first of Paul's missionary journeys. From Cyprus, the two men traveled to Asia Minor and the region of Galatia. The Gentiles there received the gospel with great joy, but when Jews saw the crowds gathering to hear Paul preach, they were filled with jealousy and began to stir up trouble. So Paul said to these Jews, "It was necessary that the word of God be spoken first to you. Since you thrust it aside and judge yourselves unworthy of eternal life, behold, we are turning to the Gentiles."

All this preaching to Gentiles raised some interesting questions for the young church. Although the gospel message was no longer considered to be exclusively for the Jews, the question was raised: Did the Gentile believers need to keep the law of Moses in addition to following Christ? Specifically, did they need to be circumcised as the Jews were? And so the apostles and church elders came together

in Jerusalem to consider the question.

A church meeting about circumcision may sound boring and kind of gross, but hang with me. The real question was one of holiness—that is, being set apart from the world's way of doing things and devoting ourselves instead to God's purposes. In Leviticus 19:2, God called His people to "be holy, for I the LORD your God am holy." Holiness was the issue in Moses' time, and it was the issue in the early days of the church. The question was this: Was holiness more about what a person did—what he ate, where he worshiped, how he marked his body—or was it about the condition of his heart? What was true then is true today: God wants your heart, your whole heart.

The council would eventually conclude that both Jews and Gentiles are saved through the grace of the Lord Jesus, not by the law. In other words, salvation is the free gift of God offered to all mankind.

Yes, there was much debate. But Peter reminded everyone that Cornelius's household received the Holy Spirit from God just as the Jewish disciples had on the Day of Pentecost. Paul and Barnabas then told of the many miracles and wonders that God had worked through them among the Gentiles. Finally, James, the leader of the church in Jerusalem and the half-brother of Jesus, spoke of the Old Testament prophecies considering the salvation of the Gentiles and judged that the church should not make it difficult for anyone to follow Christ. He suggested instead that they write to all the churches and tell them that Gentile believers were not required to keep the Jewish laws.

This first church council is a picture of a healthy meeting of God's people coming together to address a difficult question. They discussed the issue, arrived at a decision, and then made a statement to the whole church. Take some time to read the whole discussion in Acts 15. Write in your notebooking journal about the statement they issued, where they sent it, and who was selected to carry it to the churches.

With renewed excitement and unity of purpose, Paul was prepared to set out on his second missionary journey. He knew where he wanted to go and with whom. However, God had other plans.

He sent Paul elsewhere and gave him two new partners in ministry, Silas and Timothy. Then Paul had a vision in the night, in which a man from Macedonia urged him, "Come and help us." Paul believed this to be a sign from God, and so they made immediate arrangements to preach in the Macedonian cities of Philippi, Thessalonica, Berea, and others before going on to Athens and Corinth.

It is difficult to describe what it's like to know when God is calling you to do something as an individual. God has never spoken aloud to me, but I have experienced a prompting that I knew was from Him. The key to hearing from God is to always be seeking Him. Make it a habit during prayer to listen quietly and wait on Him. Also, pay close attention when the Holy Spirit nudges you to speak to someone. Know and believe that God loves you and will guide you. You probably will never hear from Jesus in a blinding flash of light as Paul did, but if you seek and obey and trust Him, you may begin to recognize when He is directing your steps.

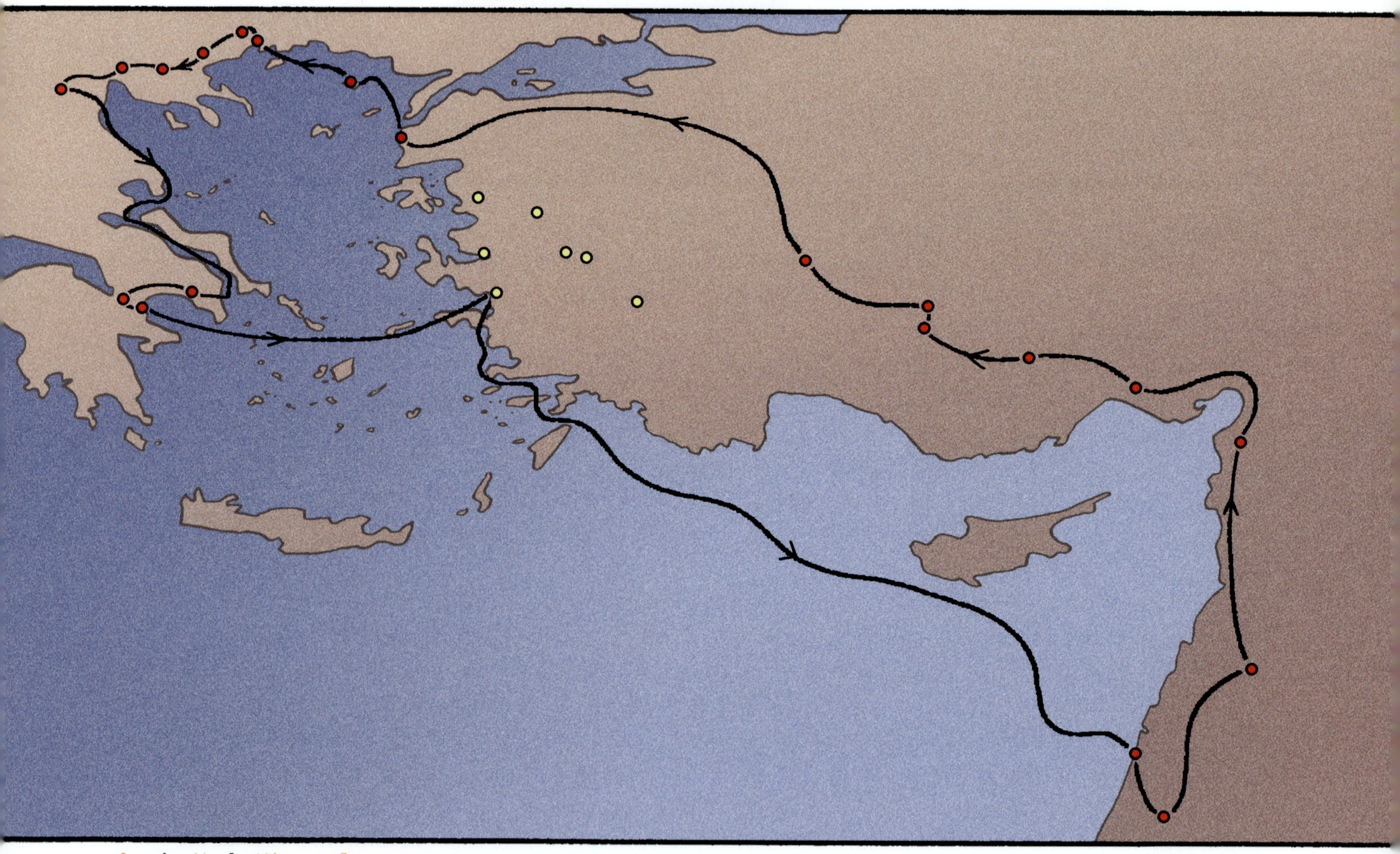

EXPLORING THE PARABLES
Read the parable of the wise and foolish builders in Matthew 7:24–27.

TENTMAKING

How do you earn money? Do you receive an allowance for doing household chores such as cleaning your room, vacuuming, or mowing the lawn? Do you get paid to babysit or do chores for your neighbors? What kind of work do you want to do when you're old enough to have a job?

The apostle Paul made tents, a trade he most likely learned from his father. It's likely that he took small, portable tentmaking tools with him on his missionary journeys and partly funded his travels by making and repairing tents part-time.

Traveling is never free, and some of Paul's missionary trips lasted for years. Even if local Christians provided him a place to stay, how did he pay for his meals and other necessities such as writing materials? In ancient times, philosophers often made a living by traveling from town to town and charging their listeners for the wisdom they shared, but Paul refused to do this (1 Corinthians 9:12–18). However, when taking the gospel to other cities such as Thessalonica, he did accept material support from the Philippian church, which he had founded. But we know that Paul also earned money by plying his trade as a tentmaker. In Corinth, he worked and stayed with Aquila and Priscilla, who were also tentmakers (Acts 18:1–5).

A tentmaker in biblical times commonly made tents using leather and cilicium, a cloth made from the long hair of a goat native to Paul's home province of Cilicia. He would have used knives and awls as tools to sew the tents together. Paul used his earnings from tentmaking not only to support himself but also to help the community and give to the poor.

As you grow older, you will probably earn money in many ways to support yourself or a family, as well as help people in the community, but your primary job will always remain the same. Like Paul, it's your job to share the gospel with others. How are you doing so far?

LET'S TALK ABOUT IT

1. Have you ever been to a church or denominational convention? Have you read about any of the historic church councils, such as the First Council of Nicaea in AD 325? What is so important about these kinds of meetings?
2. Have you ever heard of the Apostles' Creed or the Nicene Creed? If so, have you memorized one or both? If not, look them up and read them.
3. Thinking back on your study of the Old Testament, how was circumcision once a symbol of being part of God's family? What do you think Paul meant when he wrote in Romans 2:29 that "circumcision is a matter of the heart"?
4. God called the people of Israel His chosen nation. Have you ever stopped to think about how wonderful it is that Gentiles can also be part of God's kingdom?
5. How sensitive are you to the leading of the Holy Spirit? Has God ever given you a message that you just had to share with someone?

grace & truth

When God gave the law to Moses, He was not providing a way for His people to be saved from their sins. Instead, He gave the Jews a law that no one could ever fully keep. The Lord used this law to reveal the deep sinfulness and guilt that all people have before an unimaginably holy and righteous God. In other words, the law reveals our need for a savior, someone who can do for us what we could never do for ourselves.

It's important to remember that God doesn't have to save a single person. We certainly don't deserve a savior, for we all have sinned and fallen short of God's perfection (Romans 3:23). Yet He chose to send His only Son on a rescue mission to save us from our sins. John's Gospel describes Jesus as coming from the Father "full of grace and truth" (John 1:14). Grace means receiving favor that we do not deserve, and we certainly do not deserve salvation. Truth means the way the world really is, and the foundation of all truth is the God who made all things.

Grace and truth also tell us about God's steadfast love. In giving Moses the law—which itself was gracious because it revealed God's will when He did not have to tell us anything about Himself—the Lord gave the children of Israel a system of sacrifice through which they could rightly worship Him. Those sacrifices of animals were temporary fixes, but they pointed to a time when the Messiah would come and, as the Lamb of God, provide a sacrifice that would cover people's sins once and for all.

Barnabas Speaks

How are you doing today? I sure hope you enjoy your time reading this lesson. And in case I haven't already said this, I think you are doing a great job! Keep up the good work.

What's your name? When I was a boy on Cyprus, I was called Joses. But when I became a follower of Jesus, the apostles called me Barnabas, which means "Son of Encouragement," probably because I loved to serve others.

I'd like to welcome you to this study of the missionary journeys of the apostle Paul. Although Paul was the main preacher during our trips together, I did quite a bit of work, including encouraging Paul when he got tired or hungry. He was doing a great work for God's kingdom, but he was still a human and prone to discouragement when people didn't respond to the gospel. He wanted every man, woman, and child to be saved. I did too. But God was bringing in such a large harvest of new souls that I didn't complain.

Paul and I were good teammates. A dynamic duo, if you will. I asked Mark to join us on the first of our mission trips. He left early and returned to Jerusalem, which wasn't a big deal to me. Like I said, it's hard to get me down about hardly anything. But Paul was upset. So much so that when I suggested Mark join us on our next journey, Paul said, "No way." We argued, and Paul and I went our separate ways, but we remained friends and brothers in Christ. I had to wish him well, first, because it's just who I am, and second, because he was sharing the Good News of Jesus Christ.

Keep reading. Keep working in your notebooking journal. You're almost to the end of the forty motions in the New Testament outline. In just a few more lessons, you'll begin looking at each of the twenty-seven books in the New Testament. It's going to be awesome!

Prayer

God of all Creation,

You established Your church to stand firm against the gates of hell. And You invited Gentiles to join the nation of Israel in Your family, Your body, Your church. May Your kingdom come and Your will be done on earth as it is in heaven. Help me to be ready to hear Your direction, submit to Your Spirit, and go where You send me to share the Good News of Jesus Christ, the Savior of every person who calls upon His name.

It's in His holy name I pray. Amen.

Lesson 14

BUILDING, TRIALS & ROME

Motions

36. Third Journey–Build
37. Trials
38. Fourth Journey– Rome

Passage

Acts 16–28

Take it To Heart

The following night the Lord stood by him and said, "Take courage, for as you have testified to the facts about me in Jerusalem, so you must testify also in Rome."
Acts 23:11

Someone once said that all the best stories are true. Indeed, the best stories are often incredible, sometimes almost unbelievable. This is certainly true of the life of Paul. During three missionary journeys—that we know of—he boldly proclaimed the gospel. On some occasions he was welcomed with open arms, and other times he was stoned, beaten, conspired against, imprisoned, and run out of town.

Paul's third missionary journey was longer than the previous two. First, he returned to Ephesus, where he remained for at least two years. Then he returned to Macedonia and Achaia, where he spent time building up the churches he had planted on his first two journeys. Finally, Paul made his way back to Jerusalem despite several warnings from friends that he would be arrested and delivered to the Roman authorities if he entered the city. His reply: "I am ready not only to be imprisoned but even to die for the name of the Lord Jesus."

At first Paul was welcomed in Jerusalem, and he reported everything that had happened on his journey. But troublemakers showed up at the temple and falsely accused Paul with lies and half-truths. I'm old enough to know better, but it still stuns me when people are willing to lie against someone. I just don't understand why some people want to hurt others. In this case, they wanted Paul arrested, or worse. They succeeded in starting a riot, and Paul was seized and beaten by the mob. Roman soldiers bound Paul and were taking him away when he asked to be allowed to speak to the crowd. Given permission, he began to speak to the people in Hebrew. Why do you suppose it's significant that Paul chose to speak in this language?

Acts 22:1–21 records Paul's statement to the crowd. Take a moment to read it. Basically, he shared his personal testimony, including his persecution of Christians, meeting Jesus on the road to Damascus, his blindness and baptism, and how God called him to preach to the Gentiles. Up to this point, the crowd listened quietly. But when Paul mentioned the Gentiles, they started rioting again. In the chaos caused by their convicted hearts, Paul was escorted away.

In recent years, there has been a considerable amount of talk about inclusiveness, the idea that businesses, schools, governments, and other groups should be allowing and accommodating people who have historically been excluded because of their race, gender, sexuality, or beliefs. But what about the church? It's important to understand that yes, the gospel is exclusive, meaning that the forgiveness God offers is only available through the one person of Jesus Christ. But His sacrifice and death as the perfect Lamb of God is inclusive, allowing for all people to be saved when they believe in Jesus.

Here's the beauty of God's plan. Salvation is freely offered to all who will receive it. The gate is narrow, but it is wide open. The free gift of eternal life is offered with no distinction made between people groups. In the Old Testament, of course, God chose a specific group, the nation of Israel, to receive His favor. But even then there were times when God grafted foreigners into His family—people such as Ruth and Rahab. In the New Testament, the way to eternal life is opened to everybody who believes that Jesus is the Son of God, their Savior.

That is really good news! However, some people don't like to include others. They want to be selfish and keep good things to themselves. Excluding others is especially selfish when it comes to God's forgiveness and salvation. People who want to keep these gifts all to themselves clearly don't know God. Do you remember John 3:16? "For God so loved the world, that he gave his only Son, that whoever believes in him should not perish but have eternal life." God loves people so much that He sent His Son to live among us and to die for us. And He welcomes into His family every person who chooses to trust and obey His Son.

Let's get back to Paul's story. The tribune who arrested him decided that Paul should be "examined by flogging." This is the same brutal punishment given to Jesus before He was crucified. But as the soldiers stretched him out and prepared their whips, Paul identified himself as a Roman citizen by birth. This may seem like no big deal, but it was huge. By law, Roman citizens could not be scourged without a trial and conviction. Paul had received neither, so the soldiers were ordered to put away their whips.

Paul remained in Roman custody for quite some time, but the Lord came to him with words of

assurance and a foreshadowing of what was to come: "Take courage, for as you have testified to the facts about me in Jerusalem, so you must testify also in Rome." This would prove to be a comfort to Paul in the coming years. But he didn't leave immediately. He would face three trials first—one each with Felix, Festus, and Agrippa.

After a hearing with Felix, the governor of Judea, Paul remained in custody for two years, although his friends were allowed to visit and attend to his needs. When Festus replaced Felix as governor, he too questioned Paul. But Paul appealed to Caesar, as was his right as a Roman citizen. After a conversation with Agrippa, the king over Judea, Paul was sent to Rome.

Although he was treated well on the journey, it wasn't a straight shot, and getting there was a trial in itself. The voyage took several months because of various difficulties, including being shipwrecked on the island of Malta. Yet during this time, Paul could rest on God's assurance that he would arrive in Rome safely to testify about the gospel. How did Paul encourage the sailors? And what happened to Paul that caused the natives of the island to be

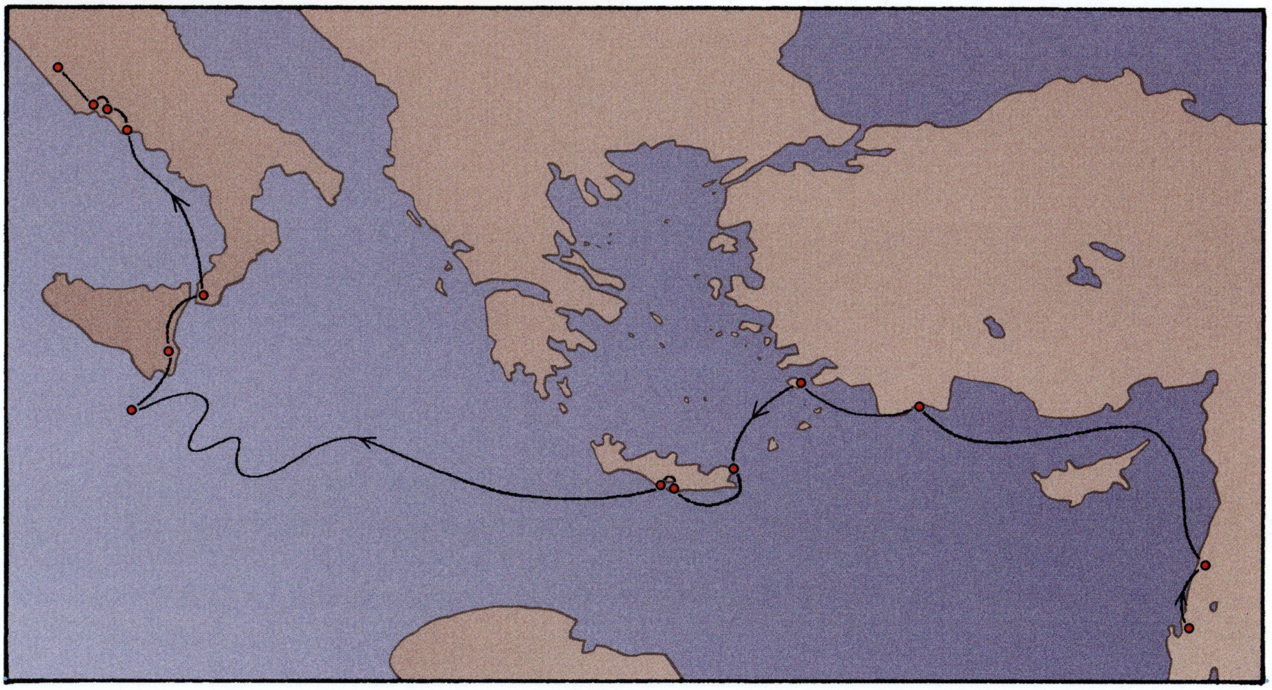

concerned? You can read the whole account in Acts 27 and 28:1–16.

When he finally arrived in Rome, Paul wasted no time in calling together the Jews in the city in order to state his case to them. Some believed his teaching about Jesus, but others didn't. Although he was under house arrest for two more years while awaiting trial, Paul welcomed all who came to him, "proclaiming the kingdom of God and teaching about the Lord Jesus Christ with all boldness and without hindrance."

What happened to Paul after that? We don't know, because this is where the book of Acts ends. We know he was tried once in Rome, although some believe he was arrested and tried a second time after making a fourth missionary journey, possibly to Spain. According to the early church historian Eusebius, in the end Paul was martyred in Rome by the Emperor Nero.

EXPLORING THE MIRACLES
Read about Jesus calming the storm in Mark 4:35–41.

ROMAN CITIZENSHIP

Why is citizenship important? When you are recognized as a citizen of a country, you have the rights, privileges, and protection given to that country's people. In the United States, for example, those rights include freedom of speech, the right to a jury trial, the right to vote, and the freedom to worship as you choose.

The apostle Paul was a Jew, but he was also a Roman citizen because he was born in the free city of Tarsus. As a Roman citizen, Paul had the right to vote, hold public office, and own property. He also could not be tortured unless he was condemned to die. This fact saved Paul from flogging by Roman soldiers.

Although Roman citizenship had its privileges, Paul taught about another, more important citizenship. In Philippians 3:20, he wrote that every Christian is a citizen of heaven. That's right, you became a citizen of heaven when you accepted Jesus Christ as your Lord and Savior. What are the rights and responsibilities of heavenly citizenship? Your right is to live with Jesus in heaven for all eternity. You have also been given the Holy Spirit, who is transforming you to become more like Jesus (2 Corinthians 3:18) while empowering you to be an effective ambassador of heaven. Your responsibility is to help grow the kingdom of God by sharing the gospel with people who don't yet know Jesus (2 Corinthians 5:17–21).

LET'S TALK ABOUT IT

1. The apostle Paul lived an adventurous life, including many hardships. How do you think he was able to endure through it all?
2. Have you ever had someone lie about you or try to get people to gang up against you? If so, how did that make you feel?
3. Paul was determined to share the gospel of Jesus Christ with as many people as possible. Are you prepared to tell other people about Jesus? Is there something you still don't understand about the gospel? If so, what?
4. Paul wrote several letters during his time in prison. What kind of letters do you write? Can you picture yourself writing a letter, article, or book explaining some aspect of the gospel of Christ? If so, what would you like to write?
5. If you were with Paul in the Roman prison, what would you have said to encourage him?

trials & testing

We all have difficult times in life when we must endure some kind of physical or emotional pain. In Acts 14:22, Paul says that we must suffer many hardships to enter the kingdom of God. A hardship might consist of an illness or injury, an unwanted change, a broken relationship, money problems, a deep personal loss, unfair accusations, or even persecution for believing in Jesus. When we find ourselves in situations like these, we might wonder why God allows bad things to happen to us if He is truly all-powerful.

But instead of questioning whether God is really in control when bad things happen, we should be comforted knowing that because He is in control, our suffering is not meaningless. Remember, there is no such thing as good luck or bad luck; life is not governed by random chance. Testing and trials all happen for a reason.

Sometimes "bad" things that happen are the natural consequences of living in a fallen world corrupted by sin. Other times, a hardship might be the result of an attack by our spiritual enemy, Satan. There are also times when God is using a difficulty to discipline us and teach us as any loving father would. In any case, we need to understand that the Lord makes all things work together for the good of those who love God and are called according to His purpose (Romans 8:28). It's not just the things we like and make us happy that work for our good, but all things work for our good.

The problem is, we often have a hard time seeing the good that comes from the trials we face, especially while we're going through them. So when trials come, it's important we remember that our sovereign God is good, He is trustworthy, and He loves us extravagantly. Rejoice, therefore, knowing that trials will strengthen your faith as you rely on God to see you through them (Romans 5:3–5; James 1:2–4). As painful as suffering can be, God uses it to grow us, strengthen us, and shape us into the image of His Son (1 Peter 4:12–14).

The Sanhedrin Speaks

We were the Great Sanhedrin, the supreme court and ruling council of the Jews. Although Judea was under Roman occupation, our authority in matters of Jewish law was unquestioned. We numbered seventy—Sadducees, Pharisees, and scribes—in addition to the high priest, and we convened in the Temple every day, except during feasts and Sabbath days.

We believed we had solved our "Jesus problem." During one memorable Passover week, we delivered the Nazarene to the Roman governor of Judea, Pontius Pilate, complete with witnesses ready to testify of the carpenter's blasphemy and treason. Even when Pilate attempted to release Jesus on a technicality, we managed to force the governor's hand, ensuring the crucifixion of the one who claimed to be the king of the Jews and threatened to undermine our authority among the people.

Unfortunately, the council's disdain of the carpenter was not unanimous. Nicodemus and others sympathized with and defended his actions before the council. Another council member, Joseph of Arimathea, went so far as to claim the body and provided him a burial in Joseph's own tomb! This disloyalty did not help matters when, just days later, wild rumors began spreading throughout the city that the Nazarene had risen from the dead.

Before long, a cult grew up around this legend. They called themselves Christians and were led by the ragtag crew of fishermen who had followed Jesus in the final years of his life. Everywhere they went now, they turned the world upside down, upsetting the established order of things. Repeatedly, they were arrested, beaten, and ordered not to preach in the name of Jesus. We even stoned one of their leaders to death. Yet this persecution seemed only to encourage them, and their numbers increased daily.

Even priests and Pharisees were joining their cause! One of them, Saul of Tarsus, also called Paul, became a particularly painful thorn in our sides. The council's many efforts to silence him mostly came to nothing. On one occasion, his arrest and appearance before the Sanhedrin resulted in a violent brawl between the Sadducees and Pharisees in the council chambers, resulting in Paul escaping our clutches once more.

What is it about this Jesus and his followers that has eluded our grasp and frustrated our attempts to squash this movement once and for all?

Prayer

Dear Heavenly Father,

You used the apostle Paul mightily to spread the gospel of Christ around the world. Paul was courageous, bold, and faithful. You also created me with a plan for me to do good work and to bring glory to You. Shape me, train me, and call me. Send me to shout out the Good News that the world may know You, love You, and worship You!

In Jesus' name. Amen!

We spend considerable time waiting. Waiting and often anticipating. We wait for our toast to pop up. We wait for dinner to be ready. We wait in line to pay for our groceries. We wait for church to begin. Traffic and commuting also require that we practice patience. We wait for Christmas. We wait for vacations, birthdays, and springtime. Incredibly, the average American spends thirteen hours each year just waiting on hold for customer service! All over the world, for all kinds of reasons, humans wait. It's just part of life.

Can you think of some Bible characters who had to wait for what God promised? What is something you're waiting on? How long have you been waiting? What are some things you do while you're waiting?

Time spent waiting is valuable time that we can either waste or use wisely. Yes, there are times when we all grow tired and restless while waiting, but some of us are especially quick to give in to impatience and frustration. And while sometimes it's fair to say that the wait is longer than it should be, that doesn't mean the situation gives us permission to be rude or unkind to others. Let's face it: Learning to wait well isn't easy.

Several times in the Bible we see God's people waiting on Him. Abraham, Joseph, and David are just some of the Old Testament heroes who waited many years for God to fulfill His promises to them. Does that seem strange to you? If they were faithful, why did they have to wait? After all, God has infinite power and resources to bring to bear on any situation.

But waiting is not without its benefits. Can you think of some?

One important benefit of waiting on God is that it teaches us to trust Him. When God makes a promise, He always fulfills it. However, only God knows the perfect time to fulfill that promise, and He won't allow it to come to fruition one minute before—or after—the designated time. Waiting requires that we rest in God's perfect timing, trusting not only that He knows best what we need and when we need it but also that He will be faithful to make it happen.

We are flawed humans with a sinful nature and a limited ability to understand. We often want things that are either not good for us or not as good as what God has planned. And when we want something, we usually want it now. But waiting on God's perfect timing gives us time to reconsider what it is we think we want. There have been many times in my life when I thought I wanted or needed something now, only to discover through waiting that I really didn't want or need it after all, because God had something far more wonderful planned for me.

Another benefit of waiting is that it develops character, at least when we do it right. Waiting well is the goal, and that means waiting without complaining, grumbling, or arguing. While waiting, we can practice valuable character qualities, although that's something we tend to avoid doing whenever possible. For example, we generally don't want to practice patience. Many of us think we just don't have time for it. The problem is, when we're impatient, many of us are so anxious to get going that we start going in the wrong direction! King Saul did just that, and the Holy Spirit departed from him, according to 1 Samuel 16:14. In the New Testament, we learn that patience is a fruit of the Spirit and is well worth cultivating in our lives. Is it any wonder then that having and exercising patience makes life so much less stressful? You will also find that waiting on God helps you to practice contentment, thankfulness, and joyfulness.

The Bible repeatedly encourages us to wait on the Lord, to put our hope and faith in Him. Isaiah 40:31, a favorite passage for many, tells us, "They who wait for the Lord shall renew their strength; they shall mount up with wings like eagles; they shall run and not be weary; they shall walk and not faint." No matter how bad things get, no matter how many trials we endure or how much we suffer for our beliefs, we must never lose heart. For God will provide us strength and courage and joy

forever if we are patient and wait on Him.

One thing every Christian eagerly awaits is the return of Jesus. In fact, Romans 8:22 tells us that all of creation is "groaning" in anticipation of this glorious event! At the end of the book of Revelation, we read the climactic statement in which Jesus says, "Behold, I am coming soon." We are now living in the last days—the time between when Jesus ascended to heaven and the time when He returns. And it is during this time that we need to practice waiting well.

The apostle Peter was speaking about the return of Jesus when he wrote, "The Lord is not slow to fulfill his promise as some count slowness, but is patient toward you, not wishing that any should perish, but that all should reach repentance" (2 Peter 3:9). In other words, God doesn't want anybody to spend eternity in hell, and so He has given us this time to tell others about Jesus and His love.

Remember the directive that Jesus gave His disciples just before He went up into heaven? He told them, "Go into all the world and preach the gospel to all creatures." This command is not just for missionaries who take the gospel to foreign lands. Preaching the gospel is a job for each and every one of us! We are meant to share the Good News of Jesus Christ with the people whose lives intersect with ours. These are the last days, and we are running out of time to share the gospel with people who need to hear about Jesus.

EXPLORING THE PARABLES
Read the parable of the watchful servants in Matthew 25:1–13.

THE SECOND COMING

Throughout the history of Christianity, believers have taken great hope and comfort in the promise that Jesus will return one day. In fact, almost every generation of believers has thought Christ's return would happen in their lifetime.

Many signs are mentioned in Scripture of things that must happen before Jesus comes again. But the Bible also says that no one can know the day or the hour of His return. Instead, believers must remain strong in their faith and live as if Christ could return at any time.

The return of Christ will be the final event in the history of the world as we know it. This is when the final judgment will happen—believers will be rewarded and given eternal life, and unbelievers will receive eternal punishment.

There are several different views in the church about when Christ will return. Some believe the "rapture of the saints" is an event that will happen before Christ's return and begin a time of great tribulation on the earth. Some believe Jesus returns at the Last Judgment.Some believe that His coming will usher in a thousand-year reign of Christ, during which Satan will be bound and cast into a pit. After a thousand years, Satan will be loosed for a time and lead many people into a final rebellion against the Lord, but this rebellion will end with the devil and his followers being defeated and thrown into the lake of fire for eternity.

Even within these views there are different interpretations of the timing of the events. But most agree that Jesus will create a new heaven and new earth where evil will no longer be able to affect creation and we will dwell with God and worship Him forever.

LET'S TALK ABOUT IT

1. What is something you've been waiting for? Do you find it hard to wait? Why?
2. What can you do to practice waiting better?
3. Do you ever stop and think about what it will be like on that glorious day when Jesus returns? What do you need to do to prepare to meet God face-to-face?
4. What are some good ways to start a conversation about Jesus with a friend? What about with a stranger?
5. How much time do you spend thinking about heaven? Are these peaceful thoughts? How much do you long to enjoy eternity in the presence of Jesus Christ?

denominations

Throughout the history of Christianity, there have always been disagreements about how to interpret some teachings of Christ and the apostles, how to practice the faith, and how to organize the church. Unfortunately, many of these disagreements have led to arguments, which have caused division in the church. These divisions have created different groups of believers with different beliefs and practices.

There are three main branches of Christianity: the Roman Catholic church, the Eastern Orthodox church, and Protestant churches. The three branches have such deep differences that they have little to do with one another beyond their shared belief that Jesus Christ is the Son of God. Within each branch there are also various groups who disagree on beliefs and practices within their specific tradition. The divisions within the Protestant branch are called denominations.

Most denominations have been formed around certain beliefs that are so important to the group, they feel they cannot worship in a congregation that does not hold the same beliefs. Different denominations have been formed out of disagreements over how baptism should be done and what it means, understanding the gifts of the Holy Spirit, how church government should work, and many other things, some more important to the Christian faith than others. America has been the birthplace of hundreds of denominations 1) because the country has never had a state-sponsored church, 2) because the U.S. Constitution encourages religious freedom, and 3) because of a general spirit of independence that is uniquely American.

What unites all believers at all times in all places is a belief in a few certain doctrines so important that you're not a Christian if you reject any one of them. These include the Trinity, the divinity of Jesus, that He died for our sins and rose again bodily on the third day, that Christ is our only hope of salvation, and that He will return to judge the world and establish His kingdom for eternity.

John Speaks from Patmos

"In the beginning." Just writing those words again brings back so many memories. Moses used these powerful words in his account of Creation, and I was inspired to use them again in my telling of the story of Jesus, the Christ and the one and only Son of God.

When I met Jesus, I was a young buck, full of energy and enthusiasm. As I walked at His side, I would marvel that not only was I alive for the appearing of the Messiah, but I was also privileged to be one of His inner circle. He called me His beloved disciple. Anyone who spent time with Him felt loved, but I can only try to tell you how special He made me feel.

Then things seemed to unravel. Jesus was arrested and tortured, and I could only stand and watch with His weeping mother as Jesus was nailed to a cross. My soul was crushed at His death, and I no longer knew what to think.

But everything changed when He arose from the dead. Suddenly, I was filled with renewed hope for the future. Then Jesus sent His Holy Spirit to fill His disciples, giving us a clearer understanding of His teaching and the deeper meaning of His death and resurrection. The Spirit emboldened us to preach His words with power and authority, accompanied by many signs and wonders.

People were believing and being baptized in droves. Of course, the chief priests and government officials didn't like this one bit, and they set out to silence those who publicly professed faith in Jesus. At first, this meant imprisonment and beatings, but when Stephen was stoned for preaching the name of Jesus, all bets were off.

Now I am the last of the original twelve apostles. All the others have lost their lives in the name of the Lord. One by one, my friends were martyred for their faith. I was prepared to do the same, but instead I was exiled to the tiny island of Patmos to live out my days. Most who were sent there ultimately died of starvation or exposure to the elements or were killed by other prisoners.

One morning, as I was enjoying my morning walk along the shore, the Spirit told me to write down a vision that God was about to show me. And what a glorious vision it was! I saw heaven open and reveal to me signs, letters, bowls, horses, and the Lord Jesus Himself. I was witnessing things to come, a prophetic glimpse of the end of the age. You know it as the book of Revelation.

I wrote about Jesus in the beginning, and I wrote about Jesus at the end. And my testimony is true.

Prayer

Most Sovereign God,

Thank You for the Bible! I believe that it is a real and accurate history of events that You ordained and allowed for Your purposes, our salvation, and Your glory. This is Your story, and I rejoice knowing that You are a loving, merciful, and gracious God. Thank You for making Yourself known to me and for adopting me into Your family.
I love You and look forward to the day when Jesus will return and claim all believers as His own. Until that time, help me to wait well. Help me to be faithful to walk in the footsteps of my Savior and to spread the Good News wherever You send me.

All glory to You, Your Son, and the Holy Spirit! Amen.

NEW TESTAMENT Outline

Quick Reference to the 40-Point Outline

Story Line:
Jesus Comes

1. Greece–Language

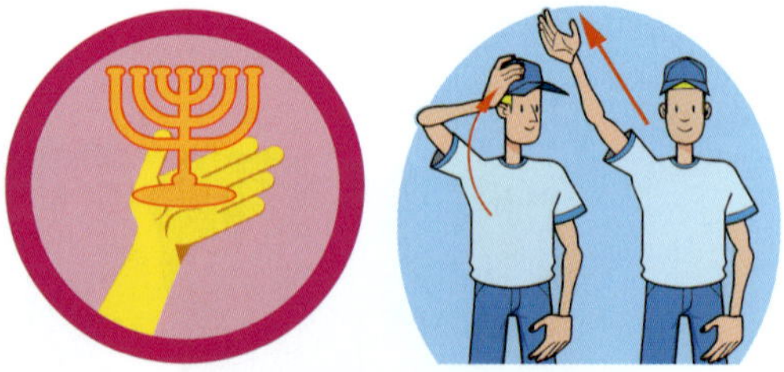

2. Israel–Hopes

3. Rome–Roads

4. Birth

5. Baptized by John

6. Tempted by Satan

7. Second Birth

8. Woman at the Well

Story Line: Jesus Ministers

9. Rejection–Selection

10. Parables–Miracles

11. Testimony of Peter

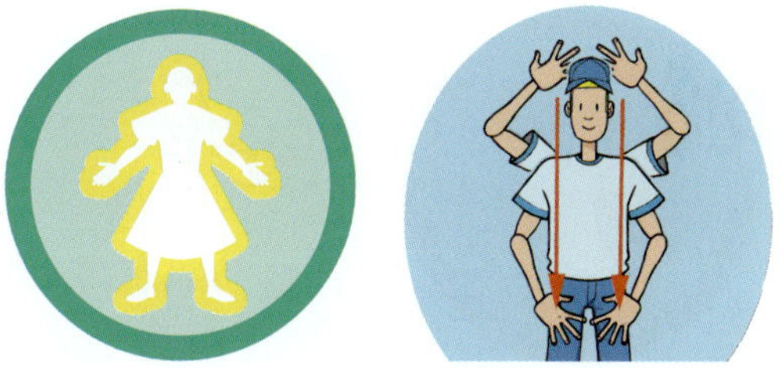

12. Transfiguration

13. Counting the Cost

14. Seeking the Lost

15. Lazarus Raised

16. Zacchaeus Praised

Story Line: Jesus Dies and Lives

17. Triumphal Entry

18. Temple Cleansing

19. Last Supper

20. Prayed–Betrayed

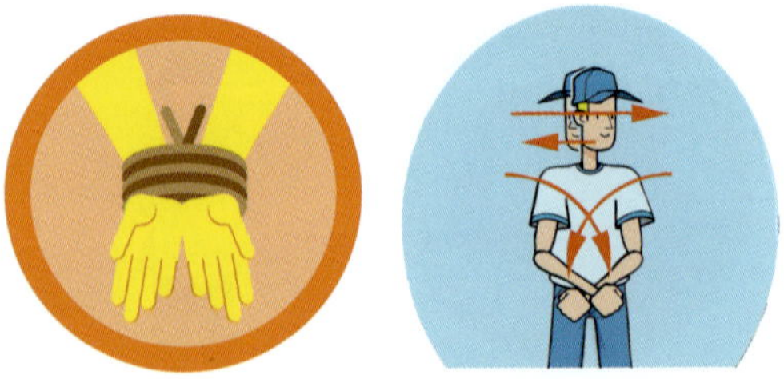

21. Tried–Denied

22. Crucified

23. Resurrected

24. Ascended

Story Line:
The Church Begins

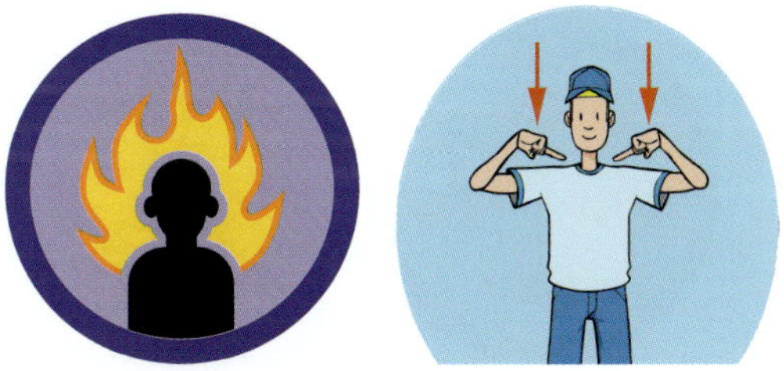

25. Spirit

26. Community

27. Servant Leaders

28. Stephen

29. Persecution

30. Philip's Preaching

31. Paul's Conversion

32. Peter's Vision

Story Line:
Letters and Revelation

33. First Journey–Law?

34. Council–Grace

35. Second Journey–Call

36. Third Journey–Build

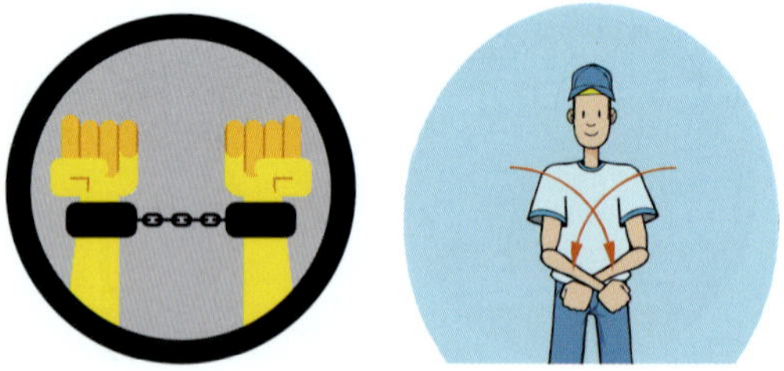

37. Trials

38. Fourth Journey–
Rome

39. Apostles Speak

40. Wait–Christ

PART 2

NEW TESTAMENT

27 Books

Lesson 16
MATTHEW

King

Matthew • AD 60–65 • Jews • Synoptic

Mary • Joseph • Jesus • John the Baptist

Disciples • Pharisees & Sadducees

Genealogy traced back to Abraham

Sermon on the Mount • Miracles • Teaching

MATTHEW

So all the generations from Abraham to David were fourteen generations, and from David to the deportation to Babylon fourteen generations, and from the deportation to Babylon to the Christ fourteen generations.

Matthew 1:17

Jesus is the King of the Jews.

Bible Reading

Matthew 5–7

Key Word

King

Take it To Heart

So all the generations from Abraham to David were fourteen generations, and from David to the deportation to Babylon fourteen generations, and from the deportation to Babylon to the Christ fourteen generations.

Matthew 1:17

Matthew Speaks

"Your taxes are due today!" I must have shouted this thousands of times in my job as a tax collector. I have to admit, my position came with a good amount of power and authority. People tried to avoid me, but I always caught up with them eventually. And they knew it was time to pay up.

It's true that tax collectors were not popular with the people, but I made a good living working for the Romans. I didn't like my employers any more than my fellow Jews, but I understood their position. There were roads to build, armies to equip, and a bureaucracy to maintain. These things cost money.

Meanwhile, I had a nice home, fancy robes, and plenty of food. But I was especially proud of the fact that I always wore new sandals. Most people wore the same pair for most of their adult life, long after the sandals had worn thin, so that their feet were always dusty and uncomfortable. Every year I would buy myself a new pair just to remind myself how much better I was doing than the commoners in town. I may not have had many friends, but I had my things.

Then I met someone who changed my life. He talked about riches that couldn't be stolen and possessions that would never rust or wear out. I was intrigued, even after I learned He was talking about things that were not of this world. I was eager to learn more from this man called Jesus.

One day He was speaking on a hillside where a crowd had gathered. He started teaching about things that sounded familiar. I knew the Old Testament law, and I knew it well. But this man made me see everything I thought I understood from a new perspective. For example, the law said I must not kill, but Jesus went further and said I should not hate in my heart. The law said I must not commit adultery, but Jesus said I should not even lust in my heart. He taught that it wasn't enough to follow the letter of the law; my heart must be right before God.

Then He invited me to join His group of disciples. I knew I needed to learn more from Him. I soon forgot all about my tax collection duties, my savings, and even my sandals. All of that paled in comparison to the riches that were mine by following the King of the Jews.

EXPLORING THE MIRACLES
Read about Jesus feeding the five thousand in John 6:1–15.

The Fulfillment of Prophecy in Matthew

God did not merely promise His people that He would send a Messiah. He also revealed through His prophets dozens of details about the Messiah so that the Jews might recognize Him when He appeared. Also, some wicked men falsely claimed to be the Messiah, but the prophecies concerning Him were so specific that it gave the people a way to judge who was lying.

Some of the details that were foretold included that He would be a descendant of David, born in Bethlehem to a virgin, be called from Egypt, minister in Galilee, and appear at a specific time after Jerusalem was restored. Although not all theologians agree as to the exact number of Old Testament prophecies made about the Messiah, there are at least sixty. That's more than enough to paint a very specific picture of the Messiah hundreds of years before He was born.

Matthew wrote his Gospel mainly to his fellow Jews. He knew they would be familiar with these prophecies, and he went out of his way to show how Jesus fulfilled all of them. He often used the word "fulfill" to make sure his meaning was not misunderstood.

GENEALOGIES

A genealogy is a chronological list of a person's ancestors. And though it's embarrassing to admit it, when we run across them in the Bible, we often skim or even skip these passages. Although they might seem like unimportant details that interrupt the flow of the story, the Holy Spirit included them for important reasons.

For example, a genealogy connects episodes in biblical history that are separated by gaps in time. They can provide a rough guide to making a timeline of that history. The Hebrews used them to determine if someone qualified for the priesthood. The genealogy of Jesus of Nazareth, as provided in the Gospel of Matthew, shows that He was a descendant of King David, thus fulfilling Old Testament promises and prophecies. Matthew provides Jesus' genealogy through His earthly father, Joseph, whereas the Gospel of Luke provides His genealogy through His mother, Mary.

For modern-day readers, genealogies help tell the story that runs throughout all of Scripture, which is that God is making a people for Himself. For example, God's promise was to Abraham and his descendants. Who are Abraham's descendants? The genealogies tell us. And yet, not everyone in the genealogy was faithful to God. In such cases, the genealogies reveal God's covenant faithfulness even when His people were unfaithful. And that should be an encouragement to us when we stumble ourselves.

Prayer

Dear Father in Heaven,

I know Jesus is the Son of God. I also know that Matthew recorded His genealogy to remind us that Jesus is also the Son of Man—the descendant of human beings who lived upon the earth. Each of these people has a story to tell, and each one played a part in the eventual birth of Jesus. I thank You that Your prophets foretold that Jesus would be a descendent of King David and born to a young virgin in the city of Bethlehem. All these prophecies came true, and they remind me that this was all part of Your master plan to save me from my sins. Thank You, Father!

In Your Son's precious name I pray. Amen.

Lesson 17
MARK

Servant

John Mark • AD 60–68 • to Romans • Synoptic
Jesus • John the Baptist
Disciples • Pharisees & Sadducees
Miracles • Calling of the 12 • Teachings

MARK

"But whoever would be great among you must be your servant, and whoever would be first among you must be slave of all. For even the Son of Man came not to be served but to serve, and to give his life as a ransom for many."
Mark 10:43–45

Jesus is the action-oriented Servant of God.

Bible Reading

Mark 8–9

Take it To Heart

"But whoever would be great among you must be your servant, and whoever would be first among you must be slave of all. For even the Son of Man came not to be served but to serve, and to give his life as a ransom for many."
Mark 10:43–45

Key Word

Servant

Mark Speaks

I was born in northern Africa, but soon after, my parents migrated to Galilee due to unrest in our homeland, eventually settling in Cana. When my father died suddenly, the big fisherman Simon Peter took me under his wing. He was a pretty rough character then, but he was married to a relative of my father, and in many ways, he became like a father to me. He made sure I got a good education, including training in the classics and the law of Moses. My mother felt indebted to Simon Peter, and I looked up to him and admired him.

When I was still a young man, Peter walked away from his life as a fisherman to follow Jesus of Nazareth, a man he believed to be the Messiah and Son of God. Peter changed after Jesus was unjustly crucified, and he became the leader of Jesus' followers. By this time, we had moved to Jerusalem, and the church there often met in our home. So I couldn't help but learn about Jesus myself.

After being baptized with water and the Holy Spirit, I followed Peter around, learning all I could about the Messiah's life and teachings. After accompanying the apostle Paul and my cousin Barnabas on one of their mission trips, I grew passionate about one day returning to Africa to spread the Word of God there.

But first, I was moved to write down as much as I could of the miracles and words of Jesus as told to me by Peter, who had witnessed these events firsthand as His close companion and disciple. Peter spoke of Jesus as a King and the divine Son of God, but he also described the Lord as a humble servant. I thought it was important for people to know both sides of our Savior in order to follow His example until He returns.

EXPLORING THE PARABLES
Read the parable of the sower in Matthew 13:1–9.

Fasting

Fasting is a spiritual discipline in which we choose not to eat for a time as an offering to God. Prayer and fasting are often done together in times of seeking the Lord. The Bible gives many examples of God's people fasting when there is great suffering, a need for guidance, or a time of repentance.

Fasting helps us spiritually in a number of ways. Fasting reminds us that we are to rely on God for all we need and that every good thing we have comes from Him. When we fast, we can spend our mealtimes in prayer so that the absence of food is filled with time spent in God's presence. Fasting is also a way to discipline our bodies by not letting our desires control us. In other words, by not responding to hunger for a time, we strengthen our ability to resist gluttony and other sinful desires.

In the Old Testament, fasting was so important in the law of Moses that it was a required part of observing Yom Kippur, the Day of Atonement. Other fasts were kept at different times in Israel's history to commemorate important events and God's deliverance from them. In the New Testament, we see Jesus, Anna, Paul, and others fasting, but specific times are not designated when all believers must fast.

SCRIBES

Scribes were legal experts. They had knowledge of the law and wrote commentaries about different points of law. Scribes also had the authority to draft legal documents such as marriage contracts and mortgages. Every village had at least one scribe.

Scribes were highly educated and well respected in the community. In fact, many of the rules they created in their commentaries were taught as if they were more important than the law itself. Sadly, the scribes were experts in the letter of the law but often missed the spirit behind the law. This led to many a conflict between the scribes and Jesus.

One of the jobs of a scribe was to copy important documents, including the Scriptures themselves. They copied everything by hand using a pen made from a reed and ink made by mixing soot and water. This work was meticulous and exacting and preserved the Old Testament part of our Bibles.

The scribes had many rules for copying the Scriptures. Here are just a few of them:

- They had to repeat each word aloud as they wrote it.
- They were required to wipe their pen and wash their entire bodies before writing YHWH, or Yahweh, the most holy name of God.
- All letters, words, and paragraphs had to be counted, and the entire document they were working on became invalid if two letters touched each other.

You may think you have to follow a bunch of grammar rules when you write, but can you imagine having to follow the rules of a scribe? The next time you're given a writing assignment, remember the scribes and your work might not seem so difficult.

Prayer

Dear Heavenly Father,

I believe that Jesus is Your Son. I believe that although equal to You in every way, He humbled Himself, took on human flesh, and served mankind. How is it that the Creator waited upon His lowly creation? I may not be able to fully understand the height and width and depth of His love, but I believe He died for me and rose again. Help me each day to resist the temptations of this world and follow in Christ's footsteps by showing compassion and mercy to everyone around me.

In the wonderful name of Jesus, amen.

Lesson 10
LUKE

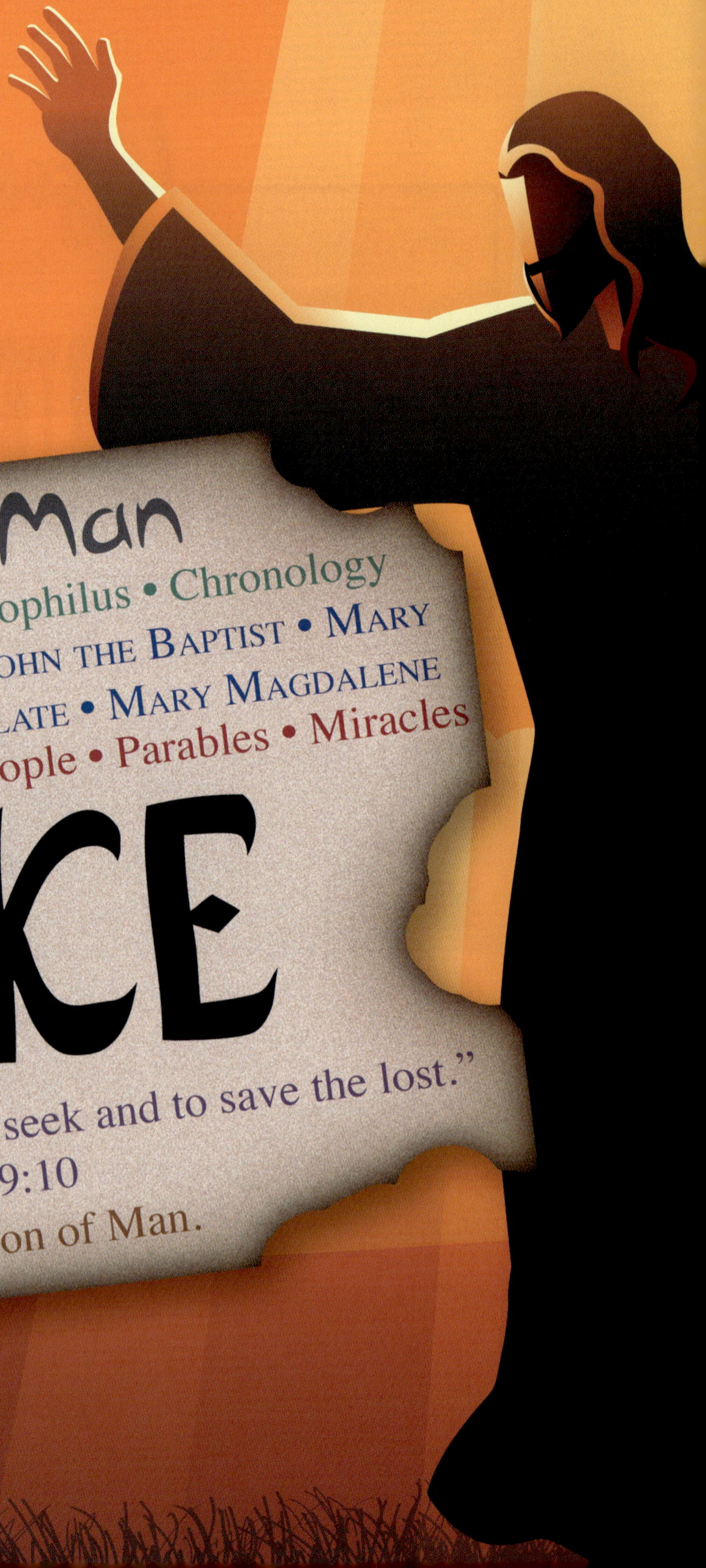

Son of Man

Luke • AD 60–65 • Greeks • Theophilus • Chronology
Jesus • Elizabeth • Zechariah • John the Baptist • Mary
Disciples • Herod the Great • Pilate • Mary Magdalene
Genealogy • Relationship with People • Parables • Miracles

LUKE

"For the Son of Man came to seek and to save the lost."
Luke 19:10

Jesus is the Son of Man.

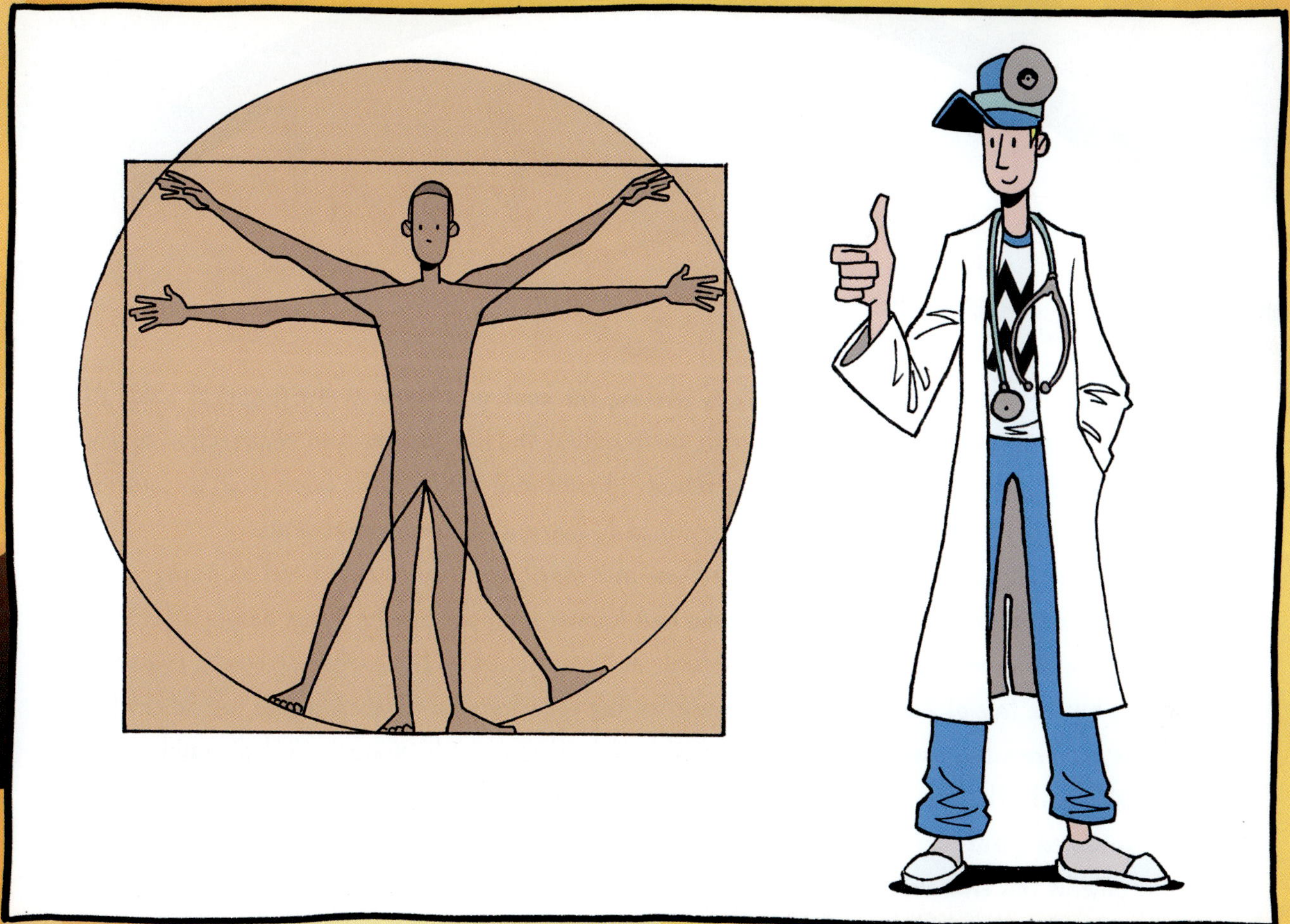

Take it To Heart

"For the Son of Man came to seek and to save the lost."
Luke 19:10

Bible Reading

Luke 1–3

Key Word

Perfect Man

Luke Speaks

You might wonder why I undertook the task of writing the book you know as the Gospel of Luke. After all, others had already written about the events surrounding the life, death, and resurrection of Jesus Christ, and I myself was not a witness to these things. I heard and believed the Good News as told to me by Paul, and from that moment on, I was determined to learn all I could about Jesus.

I not only read the accounts written by Matthew and Mark, but I also sought out as many eyewitnesses as I could find, men and women who had known Jesus personally. I was deeply affected by stories of His love and compassion toward individuals not mentioned in the earlier accounts. I was struck, for example, by the tale of Zacchaeus, the diminutive tax collector who climbed a tree just to catch a glimpse of Jesus. Then there was the thief who confessed faith even as he was crucified alongside our Lord. I was also taken with the two men who were taught by a stranger on the road to Emmaus, unaware this was the resurrected Christ.

My purpose in this endeavor was to write down for the benefit of others everything I learned in my investigation of Christ's mighty works and His teachings in the order they happened. As a physician, I was particularly interested in the many who were healed at His word. I made no assumptions but recorded only the facts as I was able to confirm them. I trust that I was guided and inspired by the Holy Spirit in this task.

I then set out to write an accurate history of the early years of the church and the courageous acts of the apostles in spreading Christianity to other cultures. I traveled with Paul on his second and third missionary journeys, working at his side. It wasn't always easy being Paul's companion. He lived a hard, uncompromising, and sometimes dangerous life. He made enemies easily, especially among those in authority who called him a troublemaker who dishonored God's temple and flouted the authority of Rome. This made Paul the subject of much slander and persecution.

In the end, I remained by his side in Rome as he awaited execution by the murderous Emperor Nero. During this time and throughout our travels, I took every opportunity to record the remembrances of Paul and the other apostles that I might set them down for all time in the book you know as Acts.

EXPLORING THE PARABLES
Read the parable of the prodigal son in Luke 15:11–32.

temptation

God's moral law has been written on the hearts of all people. Part of what it means to be a person made in God's image is that we know the difference between right and wrong. When we fail to do what is right, we sin. But before we sin, we think about the choice we are faced with. When we are attracted to a choice that goes against God's moral law, that is called "temptation."

Living in this fallen world, we all have temptations we struggle with, often for our whole lives. But being tempted is not a sin; Jesus was tempted but did not sin. We sin when we act on the temptation. There are times, however, when we enjoy just the thought of disobeying God. That is also a sin because it's a way of acting on the temptation, even if we don't actually do the thing we are fantasizing about.

And then there are sins of the heart. Pride, unrighteous anger, hatred, lust, envy, greed, selfishness, and covetousness are just some of the sins that can live in the human heart. You can try to hide these attitudes from others, but they are still sin. And if you hold on to them and think about them, they will often lead you into sinful actions.

Where does temptation come from? Either from Satan or our own sinful flesh, never from God. God does not tempt us, but He does allow us to be tempted. Temptation is not necessarily a bad thing, because God will use it to build our character and strengthen us spiritually. It's a kind of testing or trial. God promises that when we are tempted, He will never let us be tempted more than we can bear (1 Corinthians 10:13). No matter how powerful a temptation might be, we always have the strength to resist. God always gives us a way out.

CRUCIFIXION

Crucifixion is one of the most painful and brutal forms of execution ever invented. Although people were crucified before the rise of Rome, it was the Roman Empire that made it so well-known. This type of execution was so humiliating and agonizing that it was used only for the worst criminal offenders and rebels against Rome. In fact, crucifixion was always carried out publicly to discourage criminal behavior and uprisings.

When a person was crucified, the large nails or spikes were driven through his wrists—not the palms as often depicted in art—and into the crossbeam. The feet or ankles were also nailed to the cross in a way that made the legs bend at the knees.

When the cross was raised, the jolt of the upright beam dropping into the hole would dislocate the shoulders of the victim. This put so much weight on the chest that the lungs were crushed. The victim would need to somehow take the weight off his chest in order to breathe. Yet he couldn't pull up with his arms because of his dislocated shoulders, so his only option was to push up with his legs using the nail in his feet for leverage. It should come as no surprise that we get the word excruciating from crucifixion.

If the person being crucified was in good physical condition, it was possible he could live up to a week while mounted on the cross. However, most victims were brutally scourged beforehand and therefore did not survive long. Death usually resulted from asphyxiation, blood loss, shock, dehydration, or some combination of these things.

If a soldier wanted the victim to die quickly, he could break the shins of the individual so he could no longer push his weight up. Sometimes a soldier would test to see if the victim was dead by running a spear through the body, as was done to our Lord and Savior.

Prayer

Most Gracious Father,

I thank You that Jesus lived a sinless life and saved me from my sins by willingly dying on the cross. I can't imagine the physical pain and suffering He endured. And worse, there was the spiritual agony He faced when You, Father, had to turn away from the sin He was carrying on the cross. I am eternally grateful that the sacrifice of Jesus, the perfect Lamb of God, was acceptable in Your sight. As hard as it is to think of everything that happened on that hill, it is the place I must go back to remember what it took to save a sinner like me.

In the glorious name of Jesus, my Savior, amen.

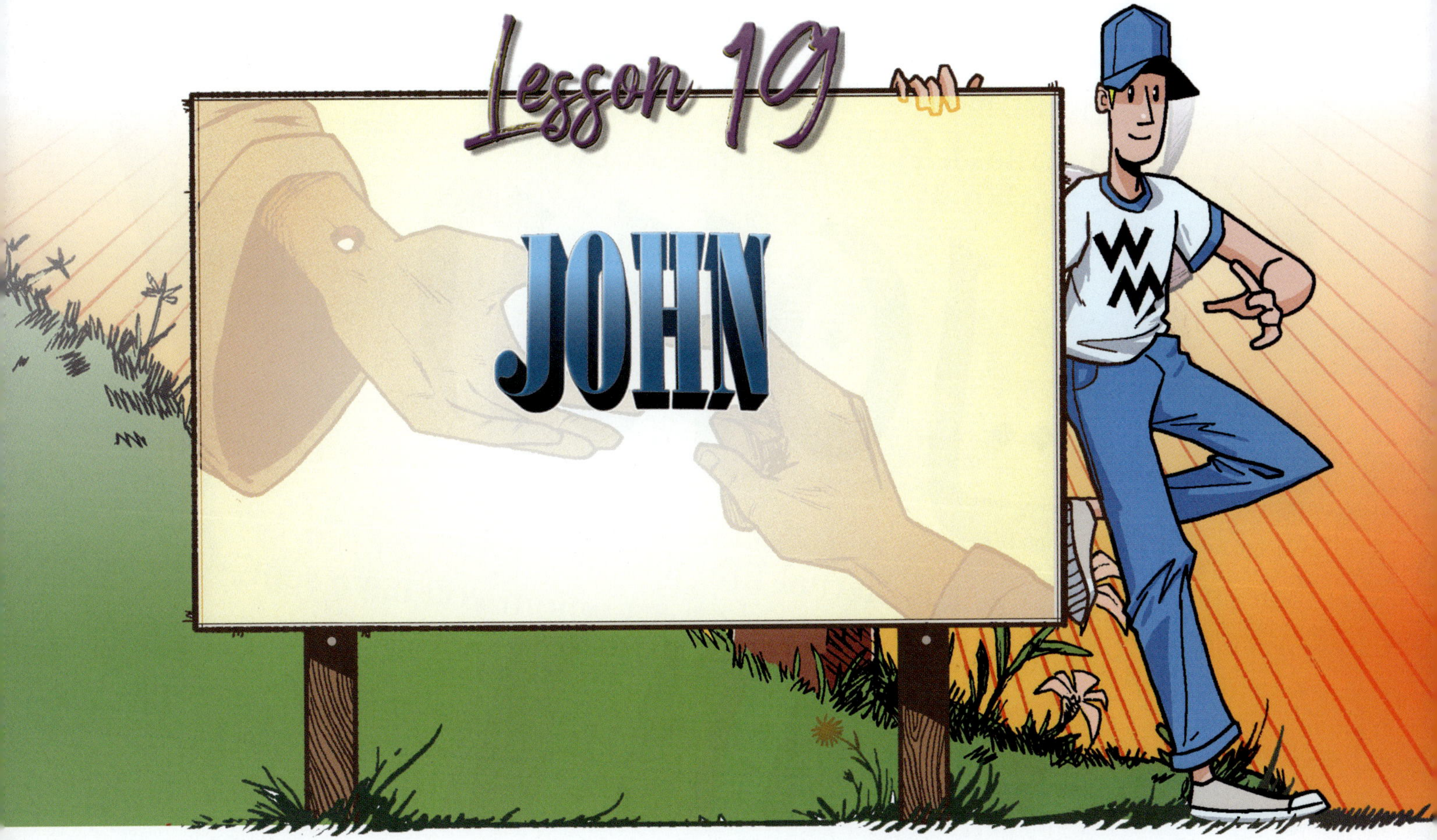
Lesson 19
JOHN

Son of God

John • AD 85–90 • Everyone • Evangelical

Jesus • John the Baptist • Disciples • Jesus' Mother

Mary, Martha, Lazarus • Pilate • Mary Magdalene

92% Unique • Upper Room Discourse

JOHN

"And this is eternal life, that they know you,
the only true God, and Jesus Christ whom you have sent."
John 17:3

Jesus is the Son of God.

Key Word

Son of God

Take it To Heart

"And this is eternal life, that they know you, the only true God, and Jesus Christ whom you have sent."
John 17:3

Bible Reading

John 1

John Speaks

When Jesus asked us to follow Him, James and I were mending our nets with my father, Zebedee. Our partners in the fishing business, Andrew and Peter, were with Him. We believed Jesus to be the Messiah, but He was calling us to walk away from our family and our livelihood. He said He would teach us to be fishers of men. James and I looked to our father, who gave us a knowing nod. So we dropped our nets and left everything to follow the Lord.

James and I had a reputation for being brash and hotheaded and quick to fight. Someone probably should have warned Jesus about us, but He didn't need their advice. He already knew what was in a man. He even called us the Sons of Thunder, perhaps because of our temperament, and named us among His twelve apostles.

After we had spent time learning from Him, Jesus gave the twelve of us authority over demons and the power to cure diseases, and He sent us out two-by-two into the villages. We cast out many demons and healed those in need, and we were feeling pretty good about ourselves. Soon after we returned to the Lord, we were seeking lodging for the night when we were turned away by a Samaritan village. I'm embarrassed to tell you that James and I asked, "Lord, do you want us to call fire down from heaven to destroy them?" Had we learned nothing of grace from our time with Him?

Then there was the time James and I foolishly asked that He promise us the places of honor on either side of His throne. I am forever grateful that Jesus was patient with us. Indeed, the more time we spent with Him, the more I grew to love Him. And I know He loved me. When I wrote of His time among us, I chose to refer to myself as "the disciple whom Jesus loved." In some ways, He was like a protective big brother, a gracious father, or a generous uncle—and yet He was so much more to me. He was my Lord, my Savior, and my best friend. And I long for the day when I will be with Him again for eternity.

EXPLORING THE MIRACLES
Read about Jesus turning water to wine in John 2:1–11.

born Again

When Nicodemus came to Jesus in John 3, Jesus told him that to see the kingdom of God he must be born again. Although this phrase is now commonplace to us, it sounded completely bizarre to Nicodemus. How could a person be born a second time? But this picture of what happens to each of us when we come to believe tells us that our very nature changes by faith in Christ. We are truly changed from one thing into another.

We were born separated from God by our sinful natures, which we inherited from Adam. We sin because we are sinners, and there is no way we cannot sin. We are alive in a physical, earthly sense, but we are dead spiritually. But when a person becomes convinced that the gospel is true and puts his or her trust in Christ, that person becomes spiritually alive. This experience is what Jesus meant by being born again.

When we are born again, it's because we have been called to faith by the Holy Spirit. Our faith is a gift from God. We can't cause ourselves to be born again any more than we could make ourselves be born physically. Regeneration—being born again—gives us new life in Christ. As a result, we reflect our rebirth by putting God at the center of our lives instead of ourselves. And that changes everything we do, think, and strive for.

"Therefore, if anyone is in Christ, he is a new creation. The old has passed away; behold, the new has come" (2 Corinthians 5:17).

7 SAYINGS FROM THE CROSS

If asked, could you explain the purpose of Christ's life? Knowing His seven last sayings from the cross can help us to understand the purpose of His coming to live among us.

Jesus prayed from the cross, "Father, forgive them, for they know not what they do" (Luke 23:34). During His final hours on earth, Christ chose to forgive those responsible for His death.

When one of the thieves crucified on either side of Jesus asked to be remembered when He came into His kingdom, Jesus replied, "Truly, I say to you, today you will be with me in paradise" (Luke 23:43). He spoke words of forgiveness and eternal life to the thief.

Jesus said to His mother, "Woman, here is your son." Then He said to John, His disciple, "Here is your mother" (John 19:26–27, NIV). Christ was concerned for the ones who loved Him and asked John to take Mary into his home and care for her.

In death, Christ was alone, and He cried out, "My God, my God, why have you forsaken me?" (Matthew 27:46). God, His Father, could not look on the sins of humankind that Christ carried as He died to secure our salvation.

Near the end, Jesus said, "I thirst" (John 19:28). The physical suffering of Christ is difficult to imagine. He was beaten, wore a crown of thorns that cut into His head, and staggered through the city as He bled from His many wounds.

A jar of wine vinegar was there at the cross, so someone soaked a sponge in it, placed the sponge on a stalk of the hyssop plant, and lifted it to Jesus' lips. When He had received the drink, Jesus said, "It is finished" (John 19:30). Bunches of hyssop were used to brush the blood of the sacrificial lamb on the doorposts of the Hebrews on the night of the first Passover, which symbolized the blood that Christ would shed for the salvation of every believer.

Then Jesus cried out in a loud voice, "Father, into your hands I commit my spirit!" (Luke 23:46). And having said this, He breathed His last. With His final words, Christ spoke to God, His Father.

Jesus used few words on this world-changing day to express His purpose of bringing love, compassion, forgiveness, and sacrifice. How many words would you need to tell the purpose of your life?

Prayer

Father in Heaven,

I long to spend eternity with You! Even now, I want to know You, to love You, and to worship You. I think the best part about eternal life is going to be hanging out with You, being in Your presence, listening to Your voice, looking into Your face, and getting a hug from You. Thank You for the hope of heaven and eternal life. Until that time, I will think about You every chance I get.

Through Jesus Christ I pray. Amen.

Lesson 20
ACTS

Holy Spirit

Luke • AD 62–65 • Greeks, Theophilus • History

Peter • James • John • The Holy Spirit • Saul/Paul

Barnabas • Cornelius • Timothy • Lydia • Silas

Government Officials

Establishment of the Church • Sermons

Persecution of the Church • Missionary Trips • Paul's Trial

ACTS

And Peter said to them,
"Repent and be baptized every one of you in the name of
Jesus Christ for the forgiveness of your sins, and you
will receive the gift of the Holy Spirit." ... And they devoted
themselves to the apostles' teaching and the fellowship,
to the breaking of bread and the prayers.
Acts 2:38, 42

Jesus is the bright light who meets
Saul on the road to Damascus.

Take it To Heart

And Peter said to them, "Repent and be baptized every one of you in the name of Jesus Christ for the forgiveness of your sins, and you will receive the gift of the Holy Spirit." . . . And they devoted themselves to the apostles' teaching and the fellowship, to the breaking of bread and the prayers.

Acts 2:38, 42

Bible Reading

Acts 1–2

Key Word

Church

Philip Speaks

The believers of Jerusalem were scattered as a result of Saul's persecution, but this did not prevent us from preaching the word. I myself went to the city of Samaria and proclaimed the Christ openly. The Spirit was with me, and the people listened. Empowered by the Spirit, I healed many who were lame or paralyzed and drove unclean spirits out of those who were possessed. And the city rejoiced.

There was also a sorcerer in the city by the name of Simon. For some time, Simon had astonished the people of Samaria with his magic while claiming to be someone of great power. But when he saw the people believing the gospel and being baptized, he chose to be baptized too and began following me about, amazed at the signs and wonders the Spirit was doing through me.

However, Simon was more enamored of power than of Christ, for when the apostles Peter and John came and began baptizing the people with the Holy Spirit by laying hands on them, Simon offered them money if they would give him the Spirit too. Peter came down hard on Simon, declaring that his heart was not right before God, for the gift of God cannot be bought and sold.

After this we took the gospel to Samaritans in other villages. Then one day, as I was praying, the Spirit said, "Rise and go toward the south, to the road that goes down from Jerusalem to Gaza." This was a desert place, but I went as instructed. Eventually, I came upon an Ethiopian man, a eunuch and the treasurer to Queen Candace. He was returning from Jerusalem where he had gone to worship. As he was riding in his chariot, he read aloud from a scroll of the prophet Isaiah. I called to him and asked him if he understood what he read. "How can I," he asked, "if no one explains it to me?" Then he stopped and invited me to sit with him, and we continued down the road.

He had been reading a prophecy of the Messiah, so I told him about Jesus Christ and shared the gospel with him. At that moment, we came upon a desert oasis with water, and he asked me to baptize him then and there. So I did. But as I brought him up out of the water, the Spirit whisked me away, and I suddenly found myself in the seaport of Azotus. I can only imagine what the Ethiopian thought when I vanished. I never saw him again, but I pray that he took the gospel to his homeland and spread the word there as a result of this mighty work of the Spirit!

EXPLORING THE MIRACLES
Read about Peter healing the lame beggar in Acts 3:1–10.

the fellowship of believers

Although your Christian faith is a deeply personal thing, God does not want you to go it alone. When you gave your life to Jesus Christ, God adopted you into His family of believers called the church. And, as in any household, God's family works better when everyone works together.

Part of being made in God's image means that we are made to live in relationship with other people. Remember that God has always lived in harmonious relationship as three persons—Father, Son, and Holy Spirit. Relationship is part of who He is, and so He always intended for people to live and work together in love.

In fact, God made His family to be dependent on one another. He gave you certain gifts, or talents, that you are meant to use to help other believers. Meanwhile, the gifts He has given to other believers will be a blessing to you. But this "gift exchange" can only happen if you are spending time with other Christians, worshiping, ministering, and doing life together.

The Greek word used in the New Testament for the gathering of believers is *ekklesia*. Although this word didn't have a religious meaning to the Greeks, it literally meant "a called-out assembly," which fit the idea of the church family perfectly. That's because the members of God's family have been called by Him to be set apart from the world for a life of holiness, both as individuals and as a whole.

CHURCH COUNCILS

Do your parents ever call a family meeting where everyone gathers to talk about something important to the whole family? That's what the historic church councils were, except that the family of God was scattered all over the ancient world, and they came together to settle disagreements about what God is like and what it means to be a Christian.

Although there are different branches of Christianity and a number of different denominations and branches within the branches, there are some things that all Christians believe. These things define what Christianity is, and these beliefs were recognized and spelled out by the church councils.

The first ecumenical council—that is, a meeting of church leaders and representatives from around the world—was called by the Emperor Constantine in AD 325. Bishops came from all over to the city of Nicaea, in what is now Turkey, to discuss whether Jesus was created by God the Father or whether He was Himself eternally God. The council produced a statement of belief called the Nicene Creed, which was then sent to churches everywhere.

The bishops met again in Constantinople in AD 381. Among other decisions, this council updated the Nicene Creed by clarifying that the Holy Spirit is a divine person and equal to God the Father and God the Son. Five later councils confirmed that human beings are born with a sinful nature inherited from Adam and that Jesus is both fully God and fully human. Mostly, the later councils reinforced the decisions of the earlier councils.

Altogether, there were seven councils that settled the core beliefs that define what it means to be a Christian. In addition to the Nicene Creed, the councils produced other statements summarizing these beliefs, including the Apostles Creed and the Athanasian Creed.

Since the church split into Eastern Orthodoxy and Roman Catholicism in the eleventh century, there have been councils within each branch but none that included the other.

Lord and Creator of All,

The world belongs to You. You created it all, and You love all people in all nations. And You desire that everyone should accept Your free gift of salvation through Jesus, Your Son. But some people have never heard about Jesus. These people need a messenger. Lord, send me! I want to share the Good News and the hope of heaven with others. Give me the words, the passion, the energy, and the courage to proclaim Your love, Your glory, and Your salvation to the ends of the earth.

In Jesus' name I pray. Amen.

Lesson 21
1 & 2 THESSALONIANS
AND GALATIANS

Returning

Paul • AD 51 • believers in Thessalonica • Letter

Paul • Silas • Timothy • The Church

Salvation & Sanctification • Affliction

Persecution of the Church • How to Live • Prayer

1 Thessalonians

And may the Lord make you increase and abound in love for one another and for all, as we do for you, so that he may establish your hearts blameless in holiness before our God and Father, at the coming of our Lord Jesus with all his saints.

1 Thessalonians 3:12–13

Jesus is the King coming back to earth.

Key Word

Stay on Target

Take it To Heart

And may the Lord make you increase and abound in love for one another and for all, as we do for you, so that he may establish your hearts blameless in holiness before our God and Father, at the coming of our Lord Jesus with all his saints.

1 Thessalonians 3:12–13

Bible Reading

1 Thessalonians 4

Peace

Paul • AD 51–52 • believers in Thessalonica • Letter

Paul • Silas • Timothy • The Church

Assurance of Christ • Signs • Persecution of Church

Prayer for Strength • Warning Against Idleness

2 THESSALONIANS

May the Lord direct your hearts to the love of God and to the steadfastness of Christ.

2 Thessalonians 3:5

Jesus is the Lord of peace.

Key Word

Work While You Wait

Take it To Heart

May the Lord direct your hearts to the love of God and to the steadfastness of Christ.
2 Thessalonians 3:5

Bible Reading

2 Thessalonians 2

Freedom

Paul • AD 48–49 • believers in Galatia • Pastoral

PAUL • PETER • BARNABAS • TITUS • FALSE TEACHERS

Law vs. Faith • Confirmation of Paul's Authority

False Teachers • Freedom in Christ • Fruit of the Spirit

GALATIANS

I have been crucified with Christ.
It is no longer I who live, but Christ who lives in me.
And the life I now live in the flesh I live by faith in the
Son of God, who loved me and gave himself for me.
Galatians 2:20

Jesus sets us free from the law.

Key Word

Unshackled

Take it To Heart

I have been crucified with Christ. It is no longer I who live, but Christ who lives in me. And the life I now live in the flesh I live by faith in the Son of God, who loved me and gave himself for me.

Galatians 2:20

Bible Reading

Galatians 5

Silas Speaks

What do you do when you experience difficulty in life? What if someone is being unfair or telling lies about you? Do you get upset? Angry? Do you whine or complain to anyone who will listen? Do you sit around dreaming up something rotten you can do to get "payback"? Or do you just close your door and cry for a while? I'd like to suggest a different approach: Try singing!

I know what I'm talking about. My name is Silvanus, though you may know me better as Silas. I was a close friend and coworker of the apostle Paul, and you can be certain the devil opposed us wherever we preached the gospel. Let me tell you about the time we were badly mistreated for doing good in the city of Philippi.

There was a slave girl in this city who was possessed by a spirit of divination, and her owners had made a great deal of money by charging people to have the girl tell their fortunes. When Paul had cast the evil spirit out of the girl, her owners were outraged that he had cut off their source of income. So they brought us before the city magistrates and falsely accused us of disturbing the peace. The magistrates ordered that we be stripped of our clothing and beaten with wooden rods and thrown into prison. There our feet were secured in chains. Did we deserve this treatment? No. In fact, because Paul and I were both Roman citizens, this punishment was quite illegal. But did we grumble and complain? No. We rejoiced, for God was more than able to redeem our suffering for His glory.

Around midnight, we were actually praying and singing hymns to the Lord—and our fellow prisoners were listening—when a great earthquake shook the prison. The doors flew open, and the chains fell off all the prisoners. When the jailer woke and saw the open doors, he thought we had all run away, so he drew his sword to kill himself for having failed in his duty. But Paul cried out, "Do not harm yourself, for we are all still here!" Then the jailer rushed in and fell at our feet, asking what he must do to be saved. I answered simply, "Believe in Jesus." So the jailer took us home, washed our wounds, and fed us. That night, he and his entire household believed and were baptized. And these few formed the beginning of the church in Philippi.

What can you learn from our experience? First, when you're walking through hard times, it's important to keep a friend close at hand. Second, the world is far more intrigued with our faith when we rejoice than when we complain about how we're treated. And finally, when you focus on the joy of knowing Jesus, your problems will look a whole lot smaller!

EXPLORING THE PARABLES
Read the parable of the workers in the vineyard in Matthew 20:1–16.

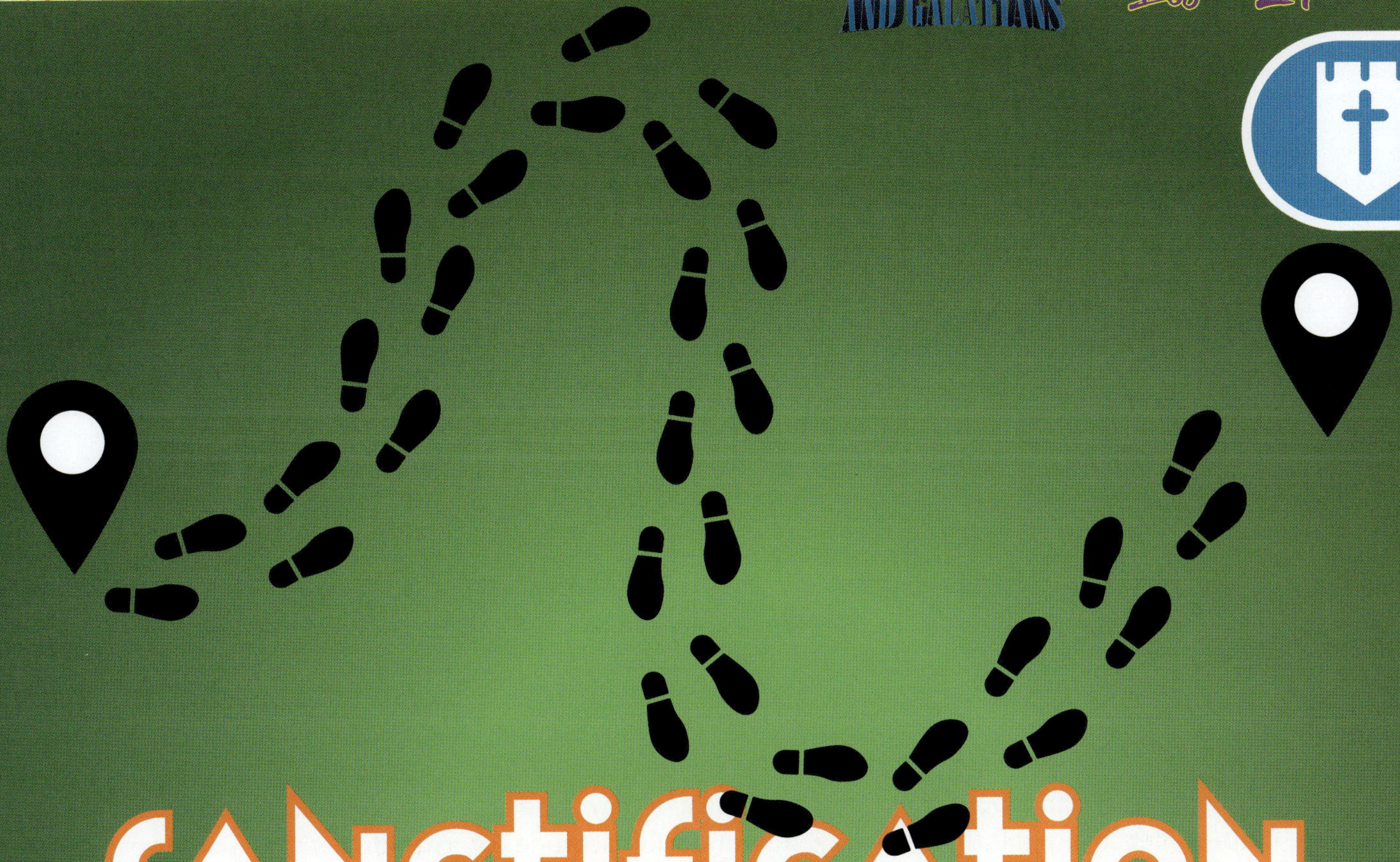

SANCTIFICATION

When you placed your faith in Jesus, you became legally sinless before God. Jesus sacrificed Himself "in order to present you holy and blameless and above reproach" to His Father (Colossians 1:22). Thus, God sees you as having the perfect obedience of Christ. This is called "justification." But just because you are justified does not mean you will now live perfectly; you will still struggle with sin. However, through the power of the Holy Spirit, you are growing and maturing spiritually and becoming more like Christ. This process of growth is called "sanctification."

Sanctification began the moment you became a believer and will last your entire lifetime. You will never reach perfection in life; only at death will your sanctification be complete. During your life, there will be periods when you grow spiritually by leaps and bounds, and there will be times when you feel like you're barely crawling in your faith. There will be times when you battle certain sins over and over and may even feel defeated by them. There may even be a particular sin that plagues you for most of your life. But that doesn't mean you're not growing. In fact, being aware of your sin and growing to hate it is a sign of your continuing sanctification.

Although sanctification greatly affects the things you do and the choices you make, it is about far more than following rules or doing the right thing. Obeying rules is not sanctification. Sanctification is the renewal of your heart and mind so that you desire the things of God more and more. When you want to please God, it affects everything you do and every choice you make.

THANKFULNESS

Galatians 5:22–23 lists nine virtues that Paul calls the fruit of the Spirit. Thankfulness is not mentioned in the list, but the Bible makes it very clear that Christians should cultivate an attitude of thankfulness in their lives:

> Rejoice always, pray without ceasing, give thanks in all circumstances; for this is the will of God in Christ Jesus for you. (1 Thessalonians 5:16–18)

> Let the word of Christ dwell in you richly, teaching and admonishing one another in all wisdom, singing psalms and hymns and spiritual songs, with thankfulness in your hearts to God. (Colossians 3:16)

It's really easy to think you deserve good things. Sometimes this can turn into selfishness where you only notice the things you don't have. The fastest way to turn around this bad attitude is to start focusing on the many blessings you surely have in your life. Here are some basic ones to get you started: life, breath, health, food, clothes, shoes, a safe place to sleep, a family who loves you.

Many people can count on only one meal a day, one pair of shoes, and one set of clothes. Yet many of them display a wonderful attitude of thankfulness. If you ever get down and start thinking you don't have a reason to be thankful, maybe you'll remember those who are less fortunate. Then you can say a prayer for them and ask God to fill your heart with thankfulness.

Of course, you have so much more than food, shoes, and toys to be thankful for. Hebrews 12:28 reminds us to "be grateful for receiving a kingdom that cannot be shaken" and to "offer to God acceptable worship, with reverence and awe." Praise God!

Prayer

Dear Heavenly Father,

Your Word tells us that Jesus will return to earth to claim His own. I definitely want to be in that number! And my hope is built on the solid rock of Your Word, which gives me the confidence and joy to look forward to that great day. I don't know if I'll be alive when the trumpet sounds and Jesus descends from the heavens, but I know that day is definitely coming. If I am dead and buried, then I will be one of the first to rise and meet Him in the air. Come quickly, Lord Jesus!

In Your holy name I pray. Amen.

Lesson 22
1 & 2 CORINTHIANS

Sanctification

Paul • AD 55 • believers in Corinth • Pastoral

PAUL • BRETHREN • TIMOTHY

The Church • Divisions • Morality • Marriage

Worship • Resurrection • Definition of Love

1 CORINTHIANS

Or do you not know that your body is a temple of the Holy Spirit within you, whom you have from God? You are not your own, for you were bought with a price. So glorify God in your body.

1 Corinthians 6:19–20

Jesus is love.

Take it To Heart

Or do you not know that your body is a temple of the Holy Spirit within you, whom you have from God? You are not your own, for you were bought with a price. So glorify God in your body.

1 Corinthians 6:19–20

Bible Reading

1 Corinthians 13

Key Word

Correcting the Saints

Authority

Paul • AD ~56 • believers in Corinth • Pastoral

PAUL • TITUS • TIMOTHY

Trials • Restoration • Giving

Warning Against False Teachers • Authority

2 CORINTHIANS

For what we proclaim is not ourselves, but Jesus Christ as Lord, with ourselves as your servants for Jesus' sake. For God, who said, "Let light shine out of darkness," has shone in our hearts to give the light of the knowledge of the glory of God in the face of Jesus Christ.

2 Corinthians 4:5–6

Jesus is our strength in weakness.

Key Word

Anatomy of an Apostle

Bible Reading

2 Corinthians 8–9

Take it To Heart

For what we proclaim is not ourselves, but Jesus Christ as Lord, with ourselves as your servants for Jesus' sake. For God, who said, "Let light shine out of darkness," has shone in our hearts to give the light of the knowledge of the glory of God in the face of Jesus Christ.

2 Corinthians 4:5–6

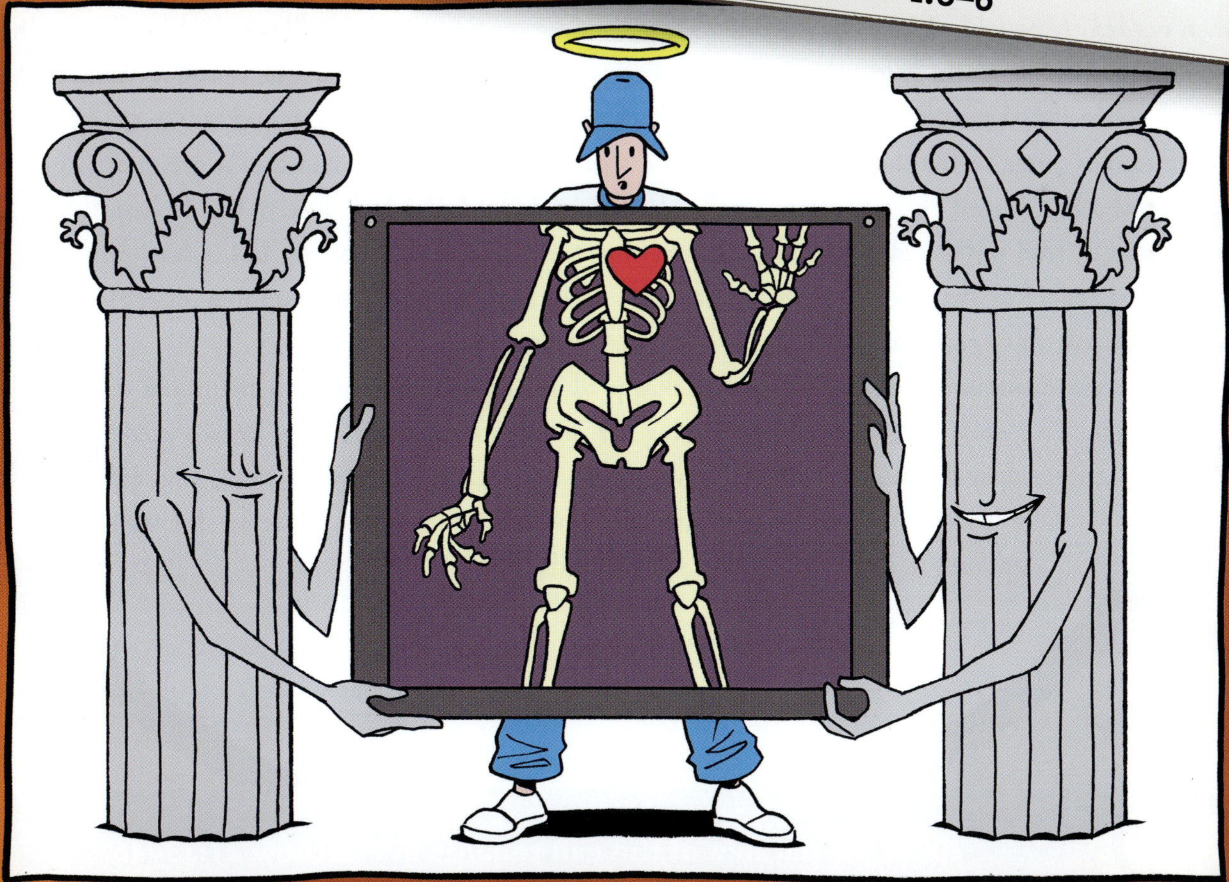

Titus Speaks

My name is Titus. Please bear with me, as I'm better known for carrying and receiving letters than I am for writing them. My friend Paul, on the other hand, is quite famous for sending letters. In fact, Paul's letters make up nearly half the books in the New Testament!

Paul taught me about Jesus during his first missionary journey. Although I was a Greek and a Gentile, I quickly came to love the Lord with all my heart! I wanted more than anything to serve God, and so Paul took me with him as a kind of assistant. I occasionally took down notes and letters as he dictated them, and sometimes I acted as an interpreter. I was also quick to offer an encouraging word when needed. I thought of Paul as a second father, and he considered me his "true child" in the faith.

As I grew in the faith, Paul came to count on me as a trusted coworker in the ministry. Sometimes, he sent me to churches as his representative to act as a troubleshooter and peacemaker. Once, when a deep conflict arose in the church at Corinth, Paul wrote a severe letter denouncing a group of false teachers who had caused the dissension. I not only delivered this letter but then stayed to help the church heal as Paul instructed me. Sadly, his letter has since been lost to history, but after I brought him a good report of the church's progress, he wrote them another, more encouraging letter, which I also delivered. You know this letter as the Bible book Second Corinthians.

Several years later, Paul placed me in charge of the church he started on the island of Crete. This work kept me very busy caring for all the new believers. Paul knew I would need encouragement and a reminder of what was important to teach Christians who did not yet fully understand how to do what is good in God's eyes. So he wrote me the letter that appears in your Bible as the book of Titus!

EXPLORING THE PARABLES
Read the parable of the evil tenants in Matthew 21:33–46.

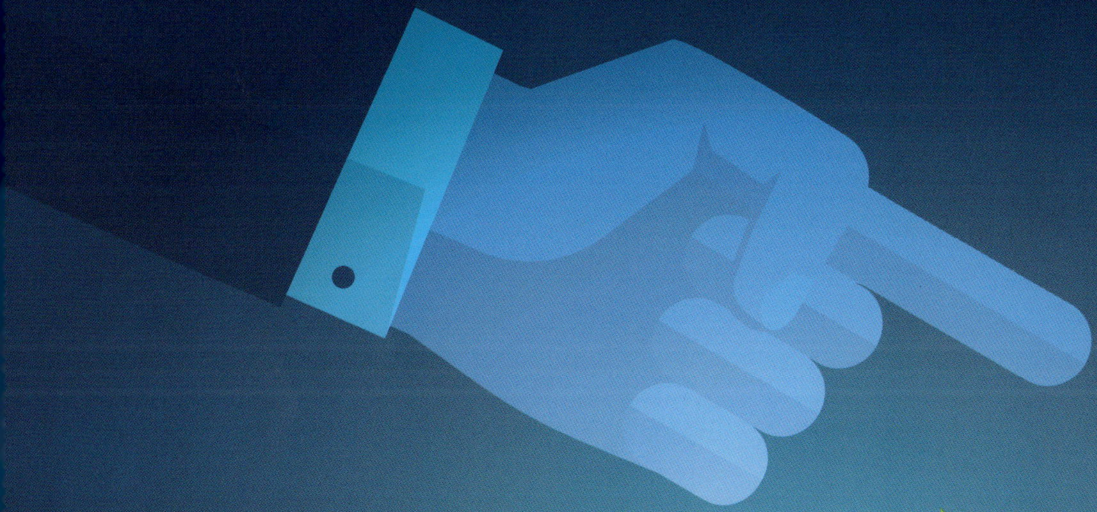

discipline

The word *discipline* comes from the Latin word for "student," which also gives us the word *disciple*. When a believer is learning more about the faith and being mentored in the ways of God, he or she is being discipled. That's why the followers of Jesus are called "disciples." In this sense, discipline isn't a kind of punishment. Discipline is instruction, training, or a practice that helps the student to continue to grow in understanding, self-control, and spiritual maturity.

But the word *discipline* also means "to correct." When referring to the process used to correct wrong behavior, discipline can feel like a negative thing because it can be painful for the person receiving correction. But biblical correction is, in truth, a positive thing because it helps us to recognize and repent of our sin and consistently live out God's moral law. Discipline in this sense steers us away from harmful choices and encourages us toward healthy, life-giving things. Hebrews 12:11 reminds us, "For the moment all discipline seems painful rather than pleasant, but later it yields the peaceful fruit of righteousness to those who have been trained by it."

Our Father in heaven loves us, and He corrects us for our own good. But He also corrects us for the good of God's family. Sin is dangerous and a harmful influence, and when one of us publicly strays from God's moral law, it can quickly sow disunity and impurity among the church.

When a believer sins against another, Scripture provides a process the person must go through to be restored to fellowship in the church. If the person who has sinned refuses to change or accept discipline, that person may ultimately be cut off from the church. Although no one wants this, sometimes it is necessary to protect the church and to convince the sinner of his or her sin so that he or she can repent.

Church discipline at any level is never to be undertaken lightly or in a judgmental spirit. Different traditions have different processes for administering discipline and restoring the individual, but part of the goal must always be to develop and maintain the spiritual health of the congregation as a whole.

Agape Love

What are some of the things you love? Do you love ice cream? Pizza? Your church? Your mom and dad? God? You might love all these, but is all love the same? The Bible speaks about a few different types of love. Two of these are *phileo* love and *agape* love.

Phileo love is the love between true friends, someone with whom you can share your deepest thoughts and feelings. When Jesus arrived to find Mary and Martha mourning, their brother Lazarus was already dead. Jesus knew He was about to raise Lazarus from the dead, yet He openly wept because of His *phileo* love for Lazarus.

In I Corinthians 13, the apostle Paul writes about another kind of love: *agape* love (pronounced Ah-GAHP-ay). This is an unconditional love, the most important kind of love, and Paul vividly describes it for us:

> Love is patient, love is kind. It does not envy, it does not boast, it is not proud. It does not dishonor others, it is not self-seeking, it is not easily angered, it keeps no record of wrongs. Love does not delight in evil but rejoices with the truth. It always protects, always trusts, always hopes, always perseveres. Love never fails. (I Corinthians 13:4–8, NIV)

Agape love is known by what it does. It's not just a feeling. God loves with an *agape* love. He so loved the world that He gave His only Son to die in our place. Jesus did not want to die, but He loved us so deeply that He did what God the Father asked Him to do.

Having and showing *agape* love requires that we make a choice. Jesus said that whoever has received His commands and obeys them, that person is the one who loves Him (John 14:21). Christ commands us to love one another. As He has loved us, so we must love one another, and by this everyone will know that we are His disciples (John 13:34–35).

Now get this: God also asks us to love our enemies with *agape* love. *Agape* love is sometimes referred to as unconditional love. This means we love people regardless of how lovable they are and whether or not they love us. Jesus died for us when we were still God's enemies (Romans 5:10). So even if we don't have a good feeling toward our enemies, we can choose to act toward them in a loving way.

God of All Love,

You love us perfectly. You are love. And Jesus gave us many examples of how to show love toward You and toward our fellow man. Love is so important to You that Jesus said Your greatest commandments are to love You and love our neighbors. Help me to get a handle on agape love and live by it in a way that pleases You. Father, let Your Spirit so fill my heart with Your love that I overflow with love that is sincere and pure!

I ask this through Christ for Your glory. Amen.

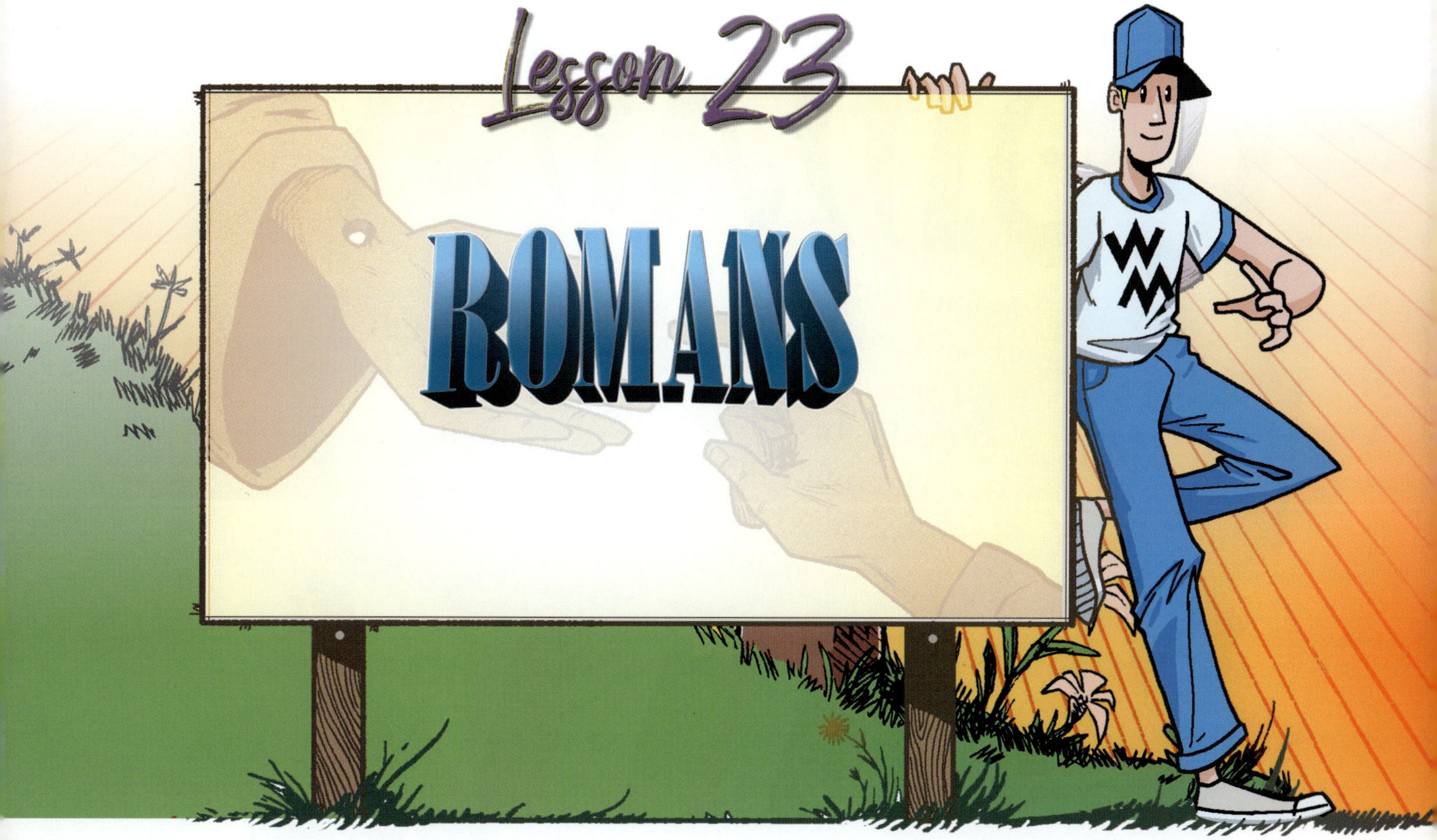
Lesson 23
ROMANS

Righteousness

Paul • AD 56 • believers in Rome • Doctrine

Paul • Tertius • Brethren • Timothy • Gaius

Foundations of the Faith • Sin • Salvation

Sanctification • Sovereignty • Service • Roman Road

Argument of Faith vs. Works

ROMANS

For I am not ashamed of the gospel,
for it is the power of God for salvation to everyone who
believes, to the Jew first and also to the Greek. For in it the
righteousness of God is revealed from faith for faith,
as it is written, "The righteous shall live by faith."

Romans 1:16–17

Jesus is the source of our righteousness and salvation.

Bible Reading

Romans 6–8

Take it To Heart

For I am not ashamed of the gospel, for it is the power of God for salvation to everyone who believes, to the Jew first and also to the Greek. For in it the righteousness of God is revealed from faith for faith, as it is written, "The righteous shall live by faith."

Romans 1:16–17

Key Word

Paid in Full

Paul Speaks

I had envisioned telling you something more along the lines of "What I Did on My Roman Holiday." For despite being a Roman citizen, I had never actually visited Rome, and I was eager to visit my brothers and sisters in Christ who lived in that great city.

But now I was headed to Rome under very different circumstances. As you know, I was falsely accused in the temple and arrested some time ago. I have now been imprisoned for more than two years despite there being no evidence against me. I stood trial a second time before the Roman governor, Festus, who knew I was innocent yet hesitated to release me, as he did not wish to provoke the Jews who accused me.

Therefore, I appealed to Caesar, as was my right as a citizen of Rome. This meant I would be taken to Rome and tried in the imperial court, where local politics held no sway. Some have asked why I appealed to Caesar when my innocence was clear and my release inevitable. I did so because the Lord had come to me in the night and said, "Take courage, for as you have testified to the facts about me in Jerusalem, so you must testify also in Rome."

And so I was taken aboard a sailing ship, accompanied by my beloved friend Luke, the believer Aristarchus of Thessalonica, and a centurion of the Augustan Cohort named Julius. Julius treated me kindly and allowed me to go to my friends and be cared for. However, the journey was a difficult one for all aboard. The winds were against us, food and supplies ran out, and storms battered the ship. But an angel of God appeared to me and promised that all on the ship would survive. So when some of the sailors wanted to escape in a rowboat, I said that they must remain onboard, under the protective hand of God.

Although we would be shipwrecked on the island of Malta, everyone who sailed with us survived, and we gave thanks to God. Three months later, we were able to continue our journey to Rome. And there I spoke the Good News of Jesus Christ before Caesar—just as God had said I would.

EXPLORING THE MIRACLES
Read about Jesus healing the man with a withered hand in Luke 6:6–11.

righteousness

Proverbs 15:9 tells us that God detests the ways of the wicked, but He loves a person who "pursues righteousness." When the Bible speaks of pursuing righteousness, it isn't talking about doing whatever "feels" right to you. God's own character is the only standard for what is right and just, and all of our thoughts and actions are judged by this standard. When a person's thoughts and actions are in keeping with God's moral law, that person is considered righteous.

Yet according to Romans 3:10, none of us is righteous. "No, not one." All of us have sinned and fallen short of God's glory (Romans 3:23).

So what does this mean for us? Because God is perfectly holy and His standard of righteousness is perfect, He cannot let sin go unpunished. And we can never repay the debt we owe for failing to keep His law. We deserve punishment. But God loves us so much that He sent His Son to live a perfect life and be righteousness for us. By believing in Jesus, we stand before God in the righteousness of Christ. His perfect obedience is credited to us because of His sacrifice on the cross.

Because you have received so great a gift, the only reasonable response is to turn away from sin and instead walk in righteousness. Or as Paul puts it, "Cast off the works of darkness" and "put on the Lord Jesus Christ" (Romans 13:12–14). To pursue righteousness means to respond to God's gift by doing acts of love, honesty, generosity, courage, mercy, and other traits that reflect God's character.

"Righteous are you, O Lord, and right are your rules" (Psalm 119:137).

JUSTIFICATION

No one has to teach a child to sin. Adam's disobedience brought sin into the world, and so every person since has been born with a sinful nature. We choose to sin because of this sinful nature. In fact, people are so sinful that we cannot even do a little bit of work to help earn our salvation. This is what makes the sacrifice of Jesus Christ so essential: He does for us what we cannot do for ourselves.

Christ's death on the cross paid the debt we owe for sinning against the holy God who created us. But Jesus did far more than that since taking on our punishment really only pays our debt back to zero. His work on the cross also credits us with His perfect obedience to God's law.

If you have chosen to believe in Jesus, it is because in God's wondrous grace and mercy, He has given you the gift of faith (Ephesians 2:8). This faith has given you the ability to believe and receive the work that Jesus did on your behalf.

When you responded to His call, God then responded by forgiving your sins and began seeing you as righteous before Him. This is called justification. To be justified means that you have been declared legally innocent and free from the guilt of your sins.

Of course, justification does not mean you will never sin again or don't need to confess when you do sin. In fact, keeping God's moral law is not something you can do on your own. Only the Holy Spirit can transform your heart so that you want to keep God's commandments, so ask for His help every day to choose obedience.

Prayer

Most Holy and Righteous God,

I am not ashamed to live by faith through the power of Your Son, Jesus Christ. My heart is open to You. You know all my secrets and desires. Cleanse the thoughts of my heart, Holy Spirit, and help me to want to do what is right. Help me to perfectly love You, Lord, so that I may glorify You and worthily magnify Your holy name!

Through Christ my Lord, amen.

Lesson 24
EPHESIANS & PHILIPPIANS

Fullness

Paul • AD 60–62 • believers in Ephesus • Letter

PAUL • TYCHICUS

Encouragement • Unity • Illustrations of the Church

2 Prayers • 6 Mysteries • Family Relationships

Armor of God

EPHESIANS

For by grace you have been saved through faith.
And this is not your own doing; it is the gift of God,
not a result of works, so that no one may boast.
Ephesians 2:8–9

Jesus is He in whom we stand firm.

Key Word

Body Building

Bible Reading

Ephesians 6

Take it To Heart

For by grace you have been saved through faith. And this is not your own doing; it is the gift of God, not a result of works, so that no one may boast.

Ephesians 2:8–9

Joy

Paul • AD 60–62 • believers in Philippi • Letter

Paul • Timothy • Epaphroditus

Joy in All Circumstances • Service

Christ's Humble Example • How to 'Shine'

Confidence in Christ • Pressing On • 8 Things to Think On

PHILIPPIANS

For to me to live is Christ, and to die is gain.
Philippians 1:21

Jesus is our confidence and joy.

Bible Reading

Philippians 2

Key Word

Happily Humble

Take it To Heart

For to me to live is Christ, and to die is gain.
Philippians 1:21

Epaphroditus Speaks

It's important that you put forth your best effort in all things, whether doing chores, serving in ministry, or working a job. As Paul might say, whatever you do, work at it with all your heart, for it is the Lord Jesus you are serving.

However, it is possible to overdo it, however good our intentions. Some of us have a habit of taking on too much, volunteering for every service opportunity or work assignment when our schedules are already full. If we don't take time to rest, eat, and sleep as needed, we can push our bodies to the breaking point. I learned this the hard way.

When our church in Philippi learned the apostle Paul was under house arrest in Rome, it was quickly decided that we should take up a collection and send him money for food and clothing. We would also send him a helper, someone to attend to his needs. When the call was raised for a volunteer, I leapt to my feet and practically begged for the privilege of serving the man who had brought the gospel to Macedonia.

And so it was that I was chosen to make the long journey to Rome. Upon my arrival, I devoted myself to the work of Christ, assisting Paul in matters both personal and missionary, for despite his captivity, he continued to preach the Good News to any and all who would come to him. I was Paul's hands and feet in the city, and I was determined not to limit the reach of his ministry. However, I became so consumed by the work that I neglected to attend to the needs of my own body.

I fell seriously ill, almost to the point of death. But God had mercy on me and restored my health over time. When I was better, Paul thought it best that I return to Philippi to alleviate the worries of my family and friends, who had received word of my sickness. He sent me home with the most beautiful letter to the Philippian church. In it he called me his brother, fellow worker, and fellow soldier and asked the brothers and sisters to receive me with joy and honor.

EXPLORING THE MIRACLES
Read about Jesus healing Jairus's daughter and about the woman who touched His robe in Luke 8:40–56.

THE ARMOR OF GOD

Turn on just about any televised sport, and you will see athletes wearing specialized equipment to protect them from injury. A professional hockey goalie puts on a helmet, mask, glove, pads, blockers, chest protector, and skates and carries a large stick onto the ice each game. That's fifty pounds of equipment designed to protect the goalie as the opposition shoots hard rubber projectiles at him or her, often at speeds of a hundred miles per hour!

Did you know that God has given you special equipment to wear? The difference is that you are a participant in a battle much bigger than any sporting contest, and your opponent isn't trying to score a goal or win a game. Satan "comes only to steal and kill and destroy" (John 10:10). Your enemy is dangerous and determined, but God provides everything you need to fight this spiritual battle. Ephesians 6:11 calls your equipment "the whole armor of God."

Satan is the father of lies; the belt of truth surrounds you so that you don't fall victim to his schemes. A warrior's breastplate protects his vital organs from blows that would otherwise be fatal; the breastplate of righteousness protects your spiritual heart. A warrior wears protective footwear to run bravely into battle; the gospel of peace is your spiritual footwear as you witness to others.

A warrior's shield stops arrows from piercing his body; the shield of faith protects you from the wicked one's fiery darts of deception. A helmet protects the warrior's head from serious injury; the helmet of salvation protects your mind from believing anything that contradicts the truth of Scripture. A sword is used to attack and destroy the enemy; the sword of the Spirit is the Word of God. This is the weapon that Jesus used to defeat Satan in the wilderness, and this same Word is available to you, but you must know it and practice it and carry it into battle.

Finally, draw strength from God by praying and talking with Him throughout the day, every day. Have you put on the armor of God today?

grace

One of the most profound ways in which we experience God's goodness is when we realize that the only thing we deserve from God is punishment for our sins and yet He gives us salvation. This is called grace. Grace is often defined as "unmerited favor." In other words, God gives us something good that we did not earn and do not deserve.

In Ephesians 2, Paul writes at length of just how amazing God's grace is. He starts by describing you and me as being dead in our sins. What can dead people do for themselves? Nothing. Not one thing. And yet when we were dead, God chose to make us alive in Christ by giving us the gift of faith. Think about that for a moment. We didn't even have the ability to believe the gospel without first receiving faith through God's grace. That means we can't even boast about the smart thing we did in choosing to believe in Christ!

What is the worst thing anyone has ever done to you? Would you offer that person grace before they asked for forgiveness? Would you go so far that you would sacrifice your most precious possession in order for that person to receive your grace? That is what God did. Except your sin was far worse than any wrong someone did to you, and the sacrifice God made was far more costly. That's how much He loves you. That's how amazing God's grace is.

Prayer

God of All Creation,

I rejoice in Your love and all the spiritual blessings that come with being Your child. I know I have a terrible enemy who wants to take me from You and destroy my witness. Yet I am confident to stand firm in Christ, praying in the Spirit at all times. Help me to put on Your whole armor every day and to set my mind on things that are true, honorable, pure, and worthy of praise. No matter what I face, I know that Christ will give me everything I need, including the strength to press on.

For Your glory, amen.

Lesson 25
COLOSSIANS & PHILEMON

Hope

Paul • AD 60 • believers in Colossae • Letter

PAUL • TIMOTHY • TYCHICUS • ONESIMUS • EPAPHRAS

Supremecy of Christ • Freedom in Christ

Warning About False Teaching • How to Live

4 Mysteries • 4 Therefores

COLOSSIANS

For in him the whole fullness of deity dwells bodily, and you have been filled in him, who is the head of all rule and authority.

Colossians 2:9–10

"Christ in you, the hope of glory."

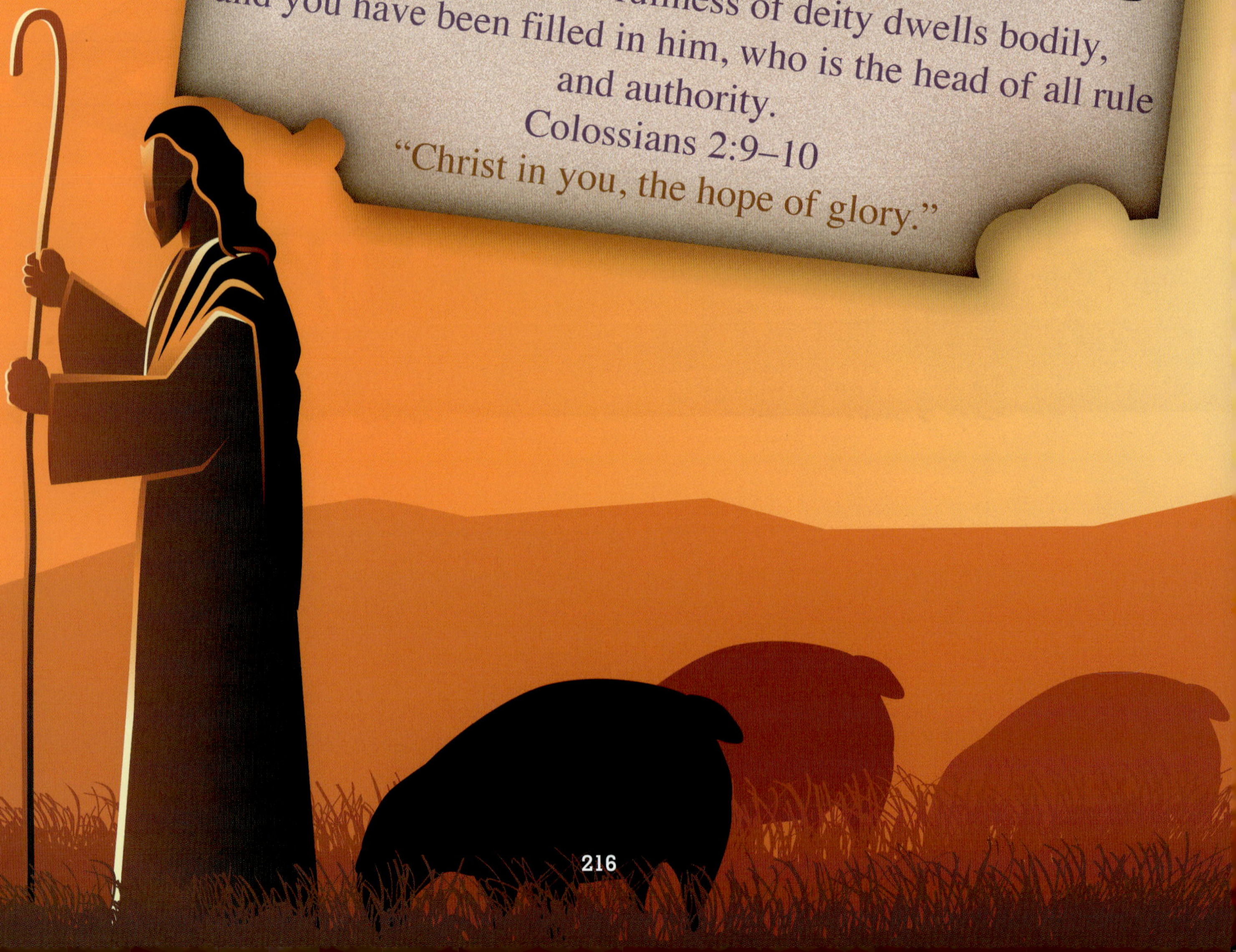

Bible Reading

Colossians 1:1–3:17

Take it To Heart

For in him [Christ] the whole fullness of deity dwells bodily, and you have been filled in him, who is the head of all rule and authority.
Colossians 2:9–10

Key Word

Commander in Chief

Redeemer

Paul • AD 60–62 • Philemon • Letter

Paul • Philemon • Onesimus

Forgiveness • Debts Paid • Submission and Respect

Christian Brotherhood

PHILEMON

For this perhaps is why he was parted from you for a while, that you might have him back forever, no longer as a bondservant but more than a bondservant, as a beloved brother.

Philemon 1:15–16

Jesus is the One who paid our debt.

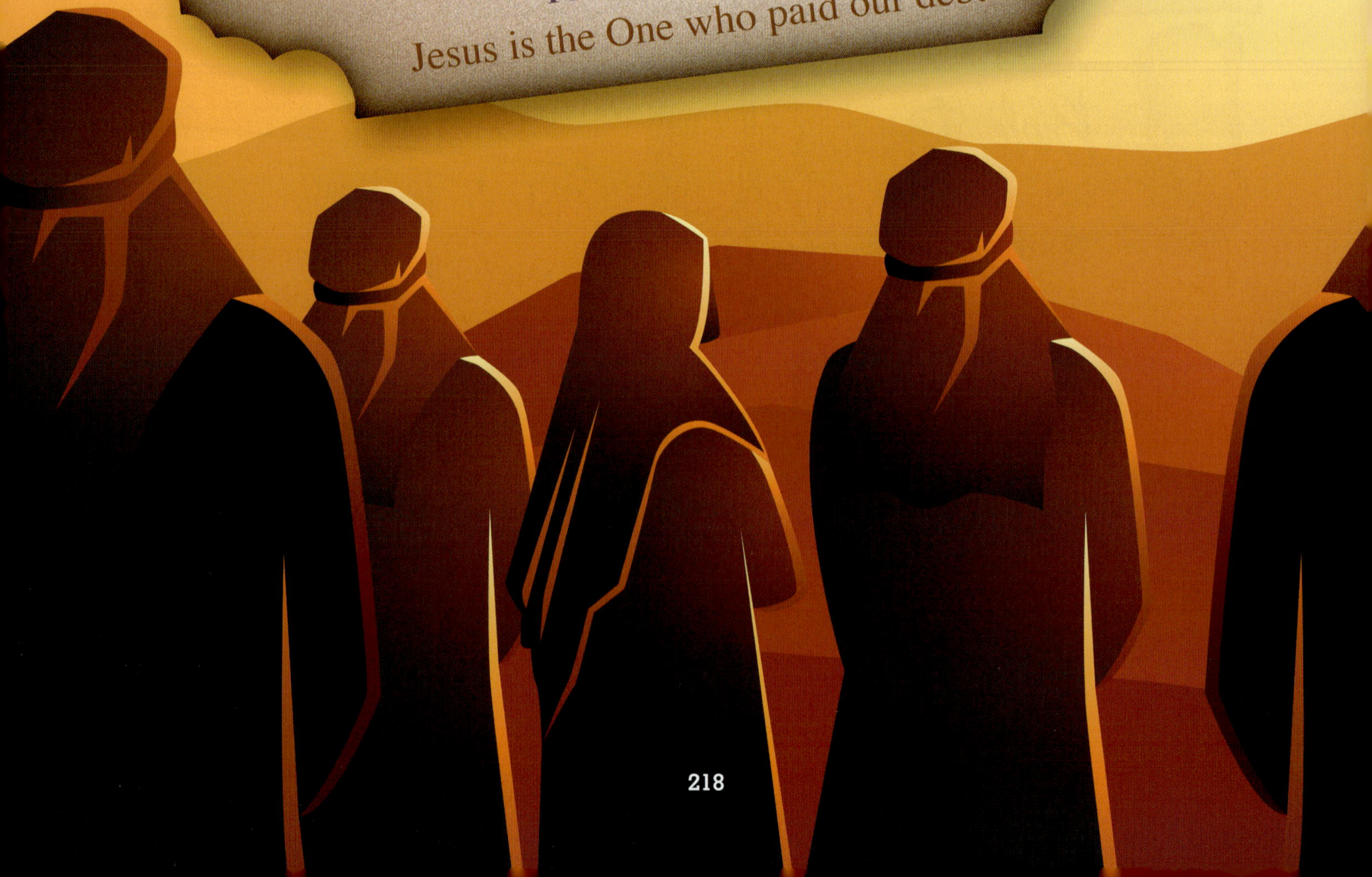

Bible Reading

Philemon 1

Key Word

Bondage to Brotherhood

Take it To Heart

For this perhaps is why he was parted from you for a while, that you might have him back forever, no longer as a bondservant, but more than a bondservant, as a beloved brother.

Philemon 1:15–16

Philemon Speaks

You probably know my friend Paul, who is also called Saul. I became a follower of Jesus after listening to Paul preach several sermons. He was passionate, but more importantly, he spoke the truth. I believed, repented of my sins, and turned my life over to Christ. Later, I shared the gospel with my wife, Apphia, and we were baptized.

Afterward, I remained close with Paul, and he even wrote me a letter when he was imprisoned in Rome. But what's interesting is that he gave the letter to a man named Onesimus and asked him to deliver it to me. Paul knew full well that Onesimus was my slave who had run away. I could have easily had him thrown into prison! But since I saw him last, Onesimus had accepted Jesus as his Lord and Savior. Now Paul urged me to received him as a brother in Christ. I admit, that option had not occurred to me, but when Paul spoke, I listened.

Paul's letter is a short message. In fact, it is one of the shortest books in the Bible—only twenty-five verses. He wrote to me of forgiveness and reconciliation and started by calling himself a prisoner of Christ Jesus. Ouch! That stung a little, but you know what? That's exactly what I needed to hear to heal my relationship with Onesimus.

By the grace of God, the encouragement of Paul, and the prompting of the Holy Spirit, I accepted Onesimus as my friend and brother in Christ. He may have been my slave once upon a time, but I was the one feeling set free that day.

EXPLORING THE PARABLES
Read the parable of the unforgiving servant in Matthew 18:21–35.

the sufficiency of jesus

One of the hardest things to understand about Christianity is that we don't need anything else but Jesus to be with God. Yes, the Bible is clear that salvation is a free gift from God, but it's hard to wrap your mind around the idea that something so important and life-changing (and life-giving) could be so simple and easy. It seems like there must be something more to it. No doubt that's why many heresies and false religions are based on the idea that Jesus is not enough. They often teach that we must do something to earn our salvation, like possess special knowledge that was hidden or even follow someone who claimed to be a prophet long after Jesus died.

But the truth is that everything you need for salvation and the Christian life can be found in Christ. There are no additives or artificial ingredients necessary. According to Paul, the fullness of God's nature dwells bodily in Jesus (Colossians 2:9). There is nothing lacking in God, so there can be nothing lacking in Jesus. Jesus is enough. Enough for what? Everything!

His perfect life and humanity made Him a sufficient substitute for us on the cross. His divinity made Him sufficient to pay the infinite debt we owed for our sins. And He is sufficient to give us strength and perseverance for our daily lives and our battle against sin. Because Jesus was a perfect and acceptable sacrifice to God, we are made perfect and acceptable as God's children.

BROTHERHOOD

When your grandparents were growing up, people at church would often greet each other as "Brother Wilson" or "Sister Jones." This was meant to express affection and the family-like bond we have with our fellow believers. When a person is saved, he or she is adopted into the family of God. So even though we aren't biologically related to most other Christians, we are part of the same family. As children of God, it makes sense that we would think of each other as brothers and sisters.

Two people may enjoy a very close relationship because they are related biologically and come from a family where love is freely expressed and everyone feels safe to share in the ups and downs of life. Sometimes two people have a close relationship because they have undergone a life-altering experience together. Think of the players on a sports team. Working closely together through a long season and winning a championship creates a lasting memory that can bind people together for many years. Often military buddies develop a close brotherhood by fighting side-by-side against a common enemy and then making it home safely.

As a Christian, you are part of a brotherhood of believers. These are your teammates, your fellow soldiers, your family. Worshiping God together, celebrating life together, and serving together in ministry are all ties that bind. All of you are blessed to be part of God's family and the brotherhood (and sisterhood) of believers.

Prayer

Dear Heavenly Father,

Thank You for my brothers and sisters in Christ. I'm so glad that You have given us this family to bear one another's burdens and encourage one another in faith and good works. Help me to clothe myself in compassion, kindness, humility, gentleness, and patience for the family of God, and help me to always be ready to forgive just as You have forgiven me. Knit our hearts together in love so that we will live in perfect harmony as Your children.

In Jesus' name I pray. Amen.

Lesson 26
HEBREWS

High Priest

Unknown • AD 64–68 • Believers • Letter

Paul • Titus

Warnings • Pay Attention • Unbelief
Danger of Falling Away • Hall of Faith • Let Us
References to Old Testament

HEBREWS

Since then we have a great high priest who has passed through the heavens, Jesus, the Son of God, let us hold fast our confession.
Hebrews 4:14

Jesus is the last word from God and our great High Priest.

Bible Reading

Hebrews 11:1–12:3

Take it To Heart

Since then we have a great high priest who has passed through the heavens, Jesus, the Son of God, let us hold fast our confession.

Hebrews 4:14

Key Word

Milk to Meat

Apollos Speaks

Leaders are learners—that's my motto. I learned to treasure knowledge and wisdom as a young Jewish man in Alexandria, Egypt, a city founded by the Greeks and home to the world's greatest library. There I studied mathematics, languages, music, philosophy, art, science, and rhetoric, in which I learned to express ideas and persuade others. But my first love was the Word of God. Moses, David, Solomon, Ezra, the mighty prophets of the Lord—these were my mentors and my inspiration.

When word reached me in Alexandria of John the Baptist and the miraculous events surrounding the life and death of Jesus of Nazareth, something sparked in my soul. I could not ignore or dismiss the fact that many of these happenings echoed the scriptural prophecies about the Messiah. So I set out immediately for Jerusalem, determined to learn all I could of Jesus and John.

When I confirmed for myself that Jesus was indeed the Messiah, I began moving from place to place, telling anyone who would listen of His miracles and teaching the baptism of John. Then everything changed in Ephesus, where I stood in the synagogue and taught about the repentance of sins and faith in the Messiah. Afterward, I was approached by a kindly couple who told me that although my facts were correct, my understanding was incomplete.

Husband and wife, Priscilla and Aquila were friends and associates to the one called Paul, a learned man whose name and reputation I had encountered in my journeys. They explained to me the deeper significance of the Messiah's death and resurrection and revealed the gift of the indwelling Holy Spirit. They told me how Jesus had charged His followers to take the message of salvation to the ends of the earth, making disciples of both Jews and Gentiles. I was overjoyed at this Good News and grateful for the instruction of Priscilla and Aquila.

From that time forward, I preached the gospel wherever I was sent, watering where Paul had planted, bolstering the faith of those who believed, and using the Scriptures to publicly refute those Jews who denied that Jesus is the Messiah.

EXPLORING THE PARABLES
Read the parable of the mustard seed in Matthew 13:31–32.

Christ's Perfection

The perfection of Christ means that Jesus lived a sinless life. He kept God's law without violating it even once. You might think it must have been easier for Jesus since He is God, but even though Jesus was fully God, He was also fully human. Hebrews 4:15 assures us that He was tempted to break God's law in every way that we are. Yet through it all, Jesus never failed to do God's will.

In the Old Testament, a lamb was sacrificed at every Passover. This was a symbol that pointed to the coming Messiah, the Lamb of God. By perfectly doing God's will, Jesus was made an acceptable sacrifice for our sins. We deserved eternal punishment, but Jesus suffered on our behalf. His perfection was able to overcome all our imperfections.

Christ's perfection is how a righteous and holy God is able to punish sin and also welcome us into His presence. Without Christ's perfection we could never be forgiven by God or reconciled to Him.

THE HALL OF FAITH

Hebrews 11 is sometimes called "The Hall of Faith." This chapter recognizes and remembers many heroes of the faith from the Old Testament. It starts by defining faith as the assurance of things hoped for and the evidence of things not seen. Then begins a roll call of great heroes of the past who believed God in big ways.

The first person listed is Abel, who is commended for offering acceptable sacrifices to God. How did he know what to offer God when there was no law yet written to tell him how to make a sacrifice? By faith.

Then we hear how Enoch was taken up into heaven and did not see death because he had pleased God. Why is that important? Because as the next verse tells us, without faith it is impossible to please God.

Next, we find Noah. Then Abraham and Sarah. Abraham is known as "the father of faith," which is probably why a large portion of Hebrews 11 is devoted to the story of how Abraham was willing to sacrifice his only son because he trusted that God would be able to bring him back from the dead. Isaac is followed by Jacob, who is followed by Joseph.

By faith Moses chose to endure the hardship of slavery rather than to enjoy the pleasures of sin for a season. By faith Moses was not afraid of Pharaoh, and by faith he kept the Passover. By faith he led the Israelites across the Red Sea on dry ground.

Following mentions of Rahab, Gideon, Barak, Samson, Jephthah, David, Samuel, and the prophets, the chapter concludes with a reminder that many martyrs lived by faith and died having not yet received what was promised.

Hebrews 12 then begins with this challenge to all believers: "Therefore, since we are surrounded by so great a cloud of witnesses, let us also lay aside every weight, and sin which clings so closely, and let us run with endurance the race that is set before us, looking to Jesus, the founder and perfecter of our faith."

Prayer

God of Heaven,

I can't thank You enough for all that Jesus was and is. He is God the Son, yet He stepped down from His throne to live among us. He is human, yet He never sinned. He is Your perfect Passover Lamb, and He gave Himself as a sacrifice for us. He completed the work You gave Him to do on earth, and now He sits at Your right hand, interceding on our behalf. Your Word also records how faithful You have been and how many men and women walked by faith and believed You before they saw Your promises come to pass. I can see I would be a fool to reject You. So I stand by faith in Your Son, my Savior, Jesus Christ.

In His name I pray. Amen.

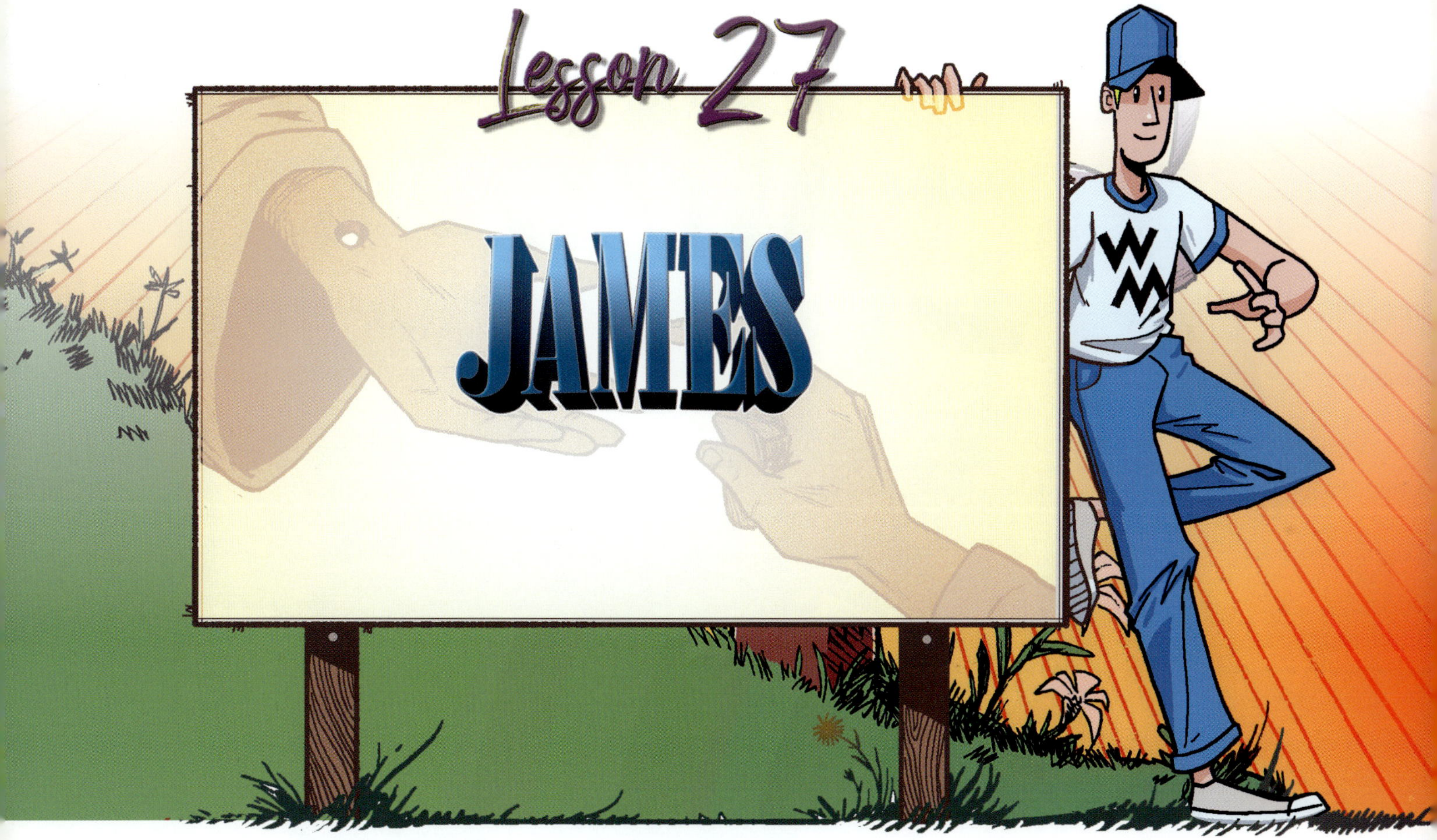
Lesson 27
JAMES

Lawgiver

James • AD 44–49 • Jewish Christians • Letter

JAMES • CHRISTIANS

Warnings • Partiality • Faith & Works
Taming the Tongue • Need for Wisdom
Enduring Suffering • Power of Prayer

JAMES

But be doers of the word, and not hearers only,
deceiving yourselves.
James 1:22

Jesus is the Lawgiver.

Bible Reading

James 1–5

Take it To Heart

But be doers of the word, and not hearers only, deceiving yourselves.

James 1:22

Key Word

Faith Gauge

James Speaks

My name is James, son of Joseph of Nazareth. My mother, Mary, was chosen by God to give birth to the Messiah while she was still a virgin. Jesus Christ, our Lord and Savior, was my half-brother.

I am ashamed to remember that I did not always believe Him to be the Messiah. I knew that Jesus had power I did not understand, but instead of listening to His words or believing His works, I taunted Him like a petulant brother. I dared Him to go to Jerusalem and show what He could do, even though I knew His life was in danger. "Go to where your followers can see your miracles," I said. "No one will ever hear of you if you hide yourself in Galilee. If you can do such wonderful things, show yourself to the world!"

I grieved deeply in the hours after His execution. But in the days after His tomb was found empty, Jesus appeared to me, alive and well, and I knew. I believed. So when He ascended to heaven, I joined our mother and His disciples in Jerusalem to pray and await the coming of the Holy Spirit.

In the months to follow, I learned from Peter, John, and the others, and I served the believers in any way I could. I did not boast that I was a blood relative of our Savior, and I refused any special treatment as such. Later, I was humbled to be chosen as an elder in the young church. Some came to call me James the Just.

Please help others to learn from the foolishness of my younger days. If you know a skeptic, someone who stubbornly refuses to believe, tell them the story of how I missed what was right in front of me—in my father's house even! Then tell them how my life was forever changed when I met the resurrected Christ.

EXPLORING THE PARABLES
Read the parable of the good Samaritan in Luke 10:25–37.

Faith & Works

The New Testament is very clear that we are saved by faith alone. There is nothing we can do to earn or add to our salvation. Our works are not part of the equation, according to Ephesians 2:8–9. And yet the book of James says that faith without works is dead. In fact, James offers the examples of Abraham and Rahab to say, "A person is justified by works and not by faith alone" (James 2:24).

Many Christians have been confused by what looks like a contradiction in Scripture. But we need only look a little deeper to see what James is getting at.

Have you ever heard the phrase, "Where there's smoke, there's fire"? Smoke doesn't exist on its own but is the product of fire. And fire always makes smoke, or at least it did in the time of James. What James is saying is that there's an important relationship between faith and works. Just as fire produces smoke, true faith produces works. The two go hand-in-hand. However, the smoke itself cannot produce heat and light any more than works can justify you before God.

In other words, James is saying that if you have genuine faith, then you will also do good works. And if your faith is not leading you to do good works, then it's not really faith.

TAMING THE TONGUE

"Abracadabra!" Ever wonder why stage magicians say that? It is thought to come from a Hebrew phrase meaning "I create as I speak." That's what God did when He brought creation into existence merely by speaking. Words are so powerful that they were the tools God used to make everything that exists! And the Gospel of John begins by saying that Jesus existed eternally as God and in the beginning was called the Word.

These facts tell us that the way we use words is very important, especially when speaking to others. In the third chapter of his book, James warns us about the power our words have to both bless and curse. He says the tongue is like a tiny flame that starts a raging forest fire or a small rudder that steers a great ship. Little things can have huge consequences, "setting on fire the entire course of life"!

Proverbs 18:21 says that life and death are in the power of the tongue. We can use our tongues to worship God, speak blessings, and be an encouragement to others. On the other hand, our tongues can speak words that deeply hurt people, are bitter toward God, tell lies, or even deliver curses.

Jesus reminds us that the words we speak reflect the content of our hearts and that, when He returns, we will answer for every careless word we have spoken (Matthew 12:34–37). Controlling what you say and how you say it is a sign of your spiritual maturity.

Prayer

God Almighty,

Give me the courage and desire to step out of my comfort zone and do the good works that You have created me to do. Let the words of my mouth and the meditation of my heart be acceptable to You, my rock and my redeemer! Help me to choose carefully what my ears hear, what my eyes see, where my feet go, and what my mouth says. Give me wisdom and understanding so that I can bring You glory in everything I think, say, and do.

In Jesus' name. Amen!

Lesson 20
1 & 2 TIMOTHY AND TITUS

Eternal

Paul • AD 63–66 • Timothy • Letter

PAUL • TIMOTHY

Organization of the Local Church • Sound Doctrine
Church Life • Personal Discipline

I TIMOTHY

But as for you, O man of God, flee these things. Pursue righteousness, godliness, faith, love, steadfastness, gentleness. Fight the good fight of the faith. Take hold of the eternal life to which you were called and about which you made the good confession in the presence of many witnesses.
1 Timothy 6:11–12

Jesus is the King eternal, immortal, invisible, the only God.

Take it To Heart

But as for you, O man of God, flee these things. Pursue righteousness, godliness, faith, love, steadfastness, gentleness. Fight the good fight of the faith. Take hold of the eternal life to which you were called and about which you made the good confession in the presence of many witnesses.

1 Timothy 6:11–12

Bible Reading

1 Timothy 3

Key Word

Leadership Manual

Guard

Paul • AD 65–67 • Timothy • Letter

PAUL • TIMOTHY

Personal Letter • Encouragement • Warning: False Teachers

Spiritual Battle • Importance of Preaching

2 TIMOTHY

Do your best to present yourself to God as one approved,
a worker who has no need to be ashamed,
rightly handling the word of truth.
2 Timothy 2:15

Jesus is able to guard what I have entrusted.

Key Word

Combat Manual

Take it To Heart

Do your best to present yourself to God as one approved, a worker who has no need to be ashamed, rightly handling the word of truth.

2 Timothy 2:15

Bible Reading

2 Timothy 2, 4:18

Able

Paul • AD 64 • Titus • Letter

PAUL • TITUS

Church Organization • Godly Living
Missionary Trips • Paul's Trial

TITUS

The saying is trustworthy, and I want you to insist on these things, so that those who have believed in God may be careful to devote themselves to good works. These things are excellent and profitable for people.
Titus 3:8

Jesus is the One through whom we have become heirs having the hope of eternal life.

Key Word

Conduct Manual

Take it To Heart

The saying is trustworthy, and I want you to insist on these things, so that those who have believed in God may be careful to devote themselves to good works. These things are excellent and profitable for people.

Titus 3:8

Bible Reading

Titus 2

Timothy Speaks

When I was a child in Lystra, my mother and grandmother taught me God's Word. They read it to me every morning at breakfast, and I would try to recite it back to them. When I learned to write, I was soon able to pen long passages of Scripture, mostly from memory. This was just life at my home. My mother and grandmother loved God's Word, the bread of heaven, and I learned to fill my heart and mind with truth—a full and satisfying meal indeed.

Paul the apostle always spoke kindly of my mother and grandmother and commended their genuine faith. He said that my upbringing had prepared me to recognize the Messiah, and so it was that I heartily responded to the call of Christ when Paul came to preach in our town.

I was still a young man when Paul asked me to accompany him on his second missionary journey. He became my mentor, and I became his co-worker and travel companion. Together with Silas, we visited the churches at Philippi, Thessalonica, and Berea. Later, we ministered in Athens and Corinth. Sometimes, Paul would leave Silas and me to continue working with the local church while he traveled on alone. Several years later, when Paul knew I was ready, he sent me on my own to shepherd the believers in Ephesus.

I want to encourage you with something that Paul wrote in a letter to me. He said that I should not let anyone despise me because of my young age. He said I should let my words and actions always be an example of love, faith, and purity. He knew how much I loved God's Word, so he also urged me to devote myself to the public reading and preaching of Scripture. I now encourage you to do the same.

EXPLORING THE MIRACLES
Read about Jesus healing the woman with a disabling spirit in Luke 13:10–17.

Suffering

No matter where in the world or when in history people were born, no matter how rich or poor, they all experienced suffering. Jesus said that we too would suffer in this life (John 16:33). For some, suffering afflicts us by way of injury or disease. Others suffer difficulty as a result of an earthquake, fire, flood, or storm. Others suffer violence that someone does to them. Suffering is part of living in a fallen world.

But God is sovereign over every person and everything, and that means nothing that happens is ever meaningless. That doesn't mean we will always know what the meaning is, for sometimes God does not choose to reveal it to us. But we do know that God is infinitely good and loving and that He uses our suffering and trials for our good.

Sometimes the greatest good can come only from suffering. The best example of this is the crucifixion of Jesus, which was the most evil act ever committed and the greatest amount of suffering anyone ever experienced. Yet our eternal salvation—an astounding good—would be impossible without the extraordinary suffering Jesus endured.

Although we can't always know exactly why God allows us to suffer, we can know and take comfort in the truth that suffering shapes our character to be more Christlike. And it makes us rely on the Lord in a way that we could never do except through suffering. Therefore, suffering is ultimately a way in which we are refined and shaped for God's purposes. We are made richer by it, not poorer.

WIDOWHOOD

When a woman's husband dies, she becomes a widow. Do you know a widow? Does your church reach out to help widows and others who are going through a difficult time in life? Perhaps your church helps feed those who do not have enough food or pays the electric bill for a widow who is poor. Maybe you know someone who has painted a house or done yardwork for a widow.

In Bible times, women mostly depended on their husbands for their livelihood. A few were businesswomen, but most women stayed home to care for the family and house. And often when her husband died, a widow had no way to make money for herself or her children. In the Old Testament, Hebrew widows often gleaned—gathered grain from the corners of a landowner's field—for food. Tithes were shared with her, and her cloak could not be taken from her as a promise to repay a loan.

The apostle Paul instructed the church to take care of the older widows, and he was specific about some of the details. For example, a widow had to be over the age of sixty, lead a godly life, and have no family members to take care of her. In Paul's time, a younger widow usually remarried and her new husband provided for her.

James the Just said that taking care of the needs of orphans and widows is part of a religion that is pure and faultless (James 1:27). It is the responsibility of Christ's followers to take care of people who have great difficulties in life. How can you and your family help widows and others in your community who are in need?

Prayer

Father God,

You care about me and the people of Your pasture. When difficult times come my way, You provide me comfort, healing, strength, and hope. You even put people in my life to lift me up, be a friend, and walk beside me. You call some to pray on my behalf and send others to provide me with advice and counsel. Help me likewise to have compassion on people who are suffering or enduring trials—the widow, the orphan, the prisoner, the lonely. Let me respond with kindness and mercy and help in practical ways. Help me to give food to the hungry and a cup of cold water to the thirsty in Your name and for Your glory.

In Jesus' name. Amen.

Lesson 29
1 & 2 PETER AND JUDE

Chief Shepherd

Peter • AD 64–65 • Believers • Letter

PETER

Holiness • Submission to Authority
Suffering • Being Watchful

1 PETER

But in your hearts honor Christ the Lord as holy, always being prepared to make a defense to anyone who asks you for a reason for the hope that is in you; yet do it with gentleness and respect.
1 Peter 3:15

Jesus is our Chief Shepherd.

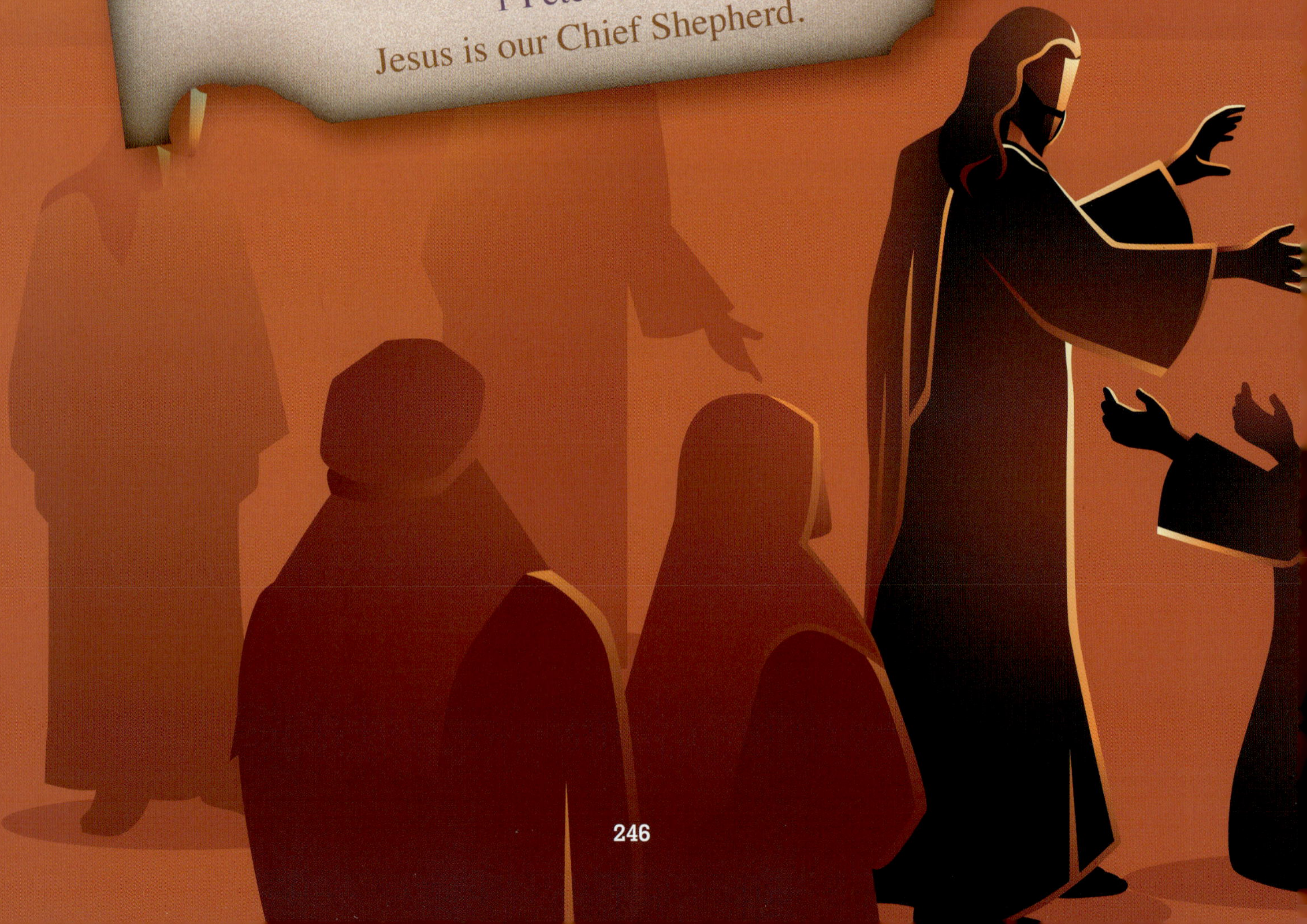

Bible Reading

1 Peter 4

Key Word

Pain with a Purpose

Take it To Heart

But in your hearts honor Christ the Lord as holy, always being prepared to make a defense to anyone who asks you for a reason for the hope that is in you; yet do it with gentleness and respect.

1 Peter 3:15

Morning Star

Peter • AD 65–67 • Believers • Letter

PETER

Eyewitnesses • False Prophets and Teachers

The Day of the Lord Is Coming

2 PETER

His divine power has granted to us all things that pertain to life and godliness, through the knowledge of him who called us to his own glory and excellence.

2 Peter 1:3

Jesus is not wanting that any should perish, but that all would come to repentence.

Key Word

Poison in the Pew

Bible Reading

2 Peter 1

Take it To Heart

His divine power has granted to us all things that pertain to life and godliness, through the knowledge of him who called us to his own glory and excellence.

2 Peter 1:3

Keeper

Jude • AD 67–80 • Believers • Letter

JUDE

Destiny of the Ungodly • Persevere

JUDE

Beloved, although I was very
eager to write to you about our common salvation,
I found it necessary to write appealing to you to contend
for the faith that was once for all delivered to the saints.
Jude 1:3

Jesus is the One who is able to keep us from falling.

Key Word

Fight for the Faith

Bible Reading

Jude 1

Take it To Heart

Beloved, although I was very eager to write to you about our common salvation, I found it necessary to write appealing to you to contend for the faith that was once for all delivered to the saints.

Jude 1:3

The Women of the New Testament Speak

My name is Phoebe. I served at the church in Corinth at the seaside village of Cenchrea. The Lord used me as a helper and benefactor to many, including our brother Paul, who tasked me with delivering his now-famous letter to the Roman church. Perhaps you're surprised to hear of a woman ministering in such big ways, but many women played important roles in the early days of the Christian faith.

Of course you know of Mary, mother of our Savior, Jesus Christ. But do you know of Anna the prophetess, who dedicated her life to worshiping God in the temple? She recognized the Messiah immediately, though He was but an infant, and was among the first to spread the news of His coming (Luke 2:36–38).

Mary Magdalene was among the most devoted followers of our Lord Jesus during His ministry. She did not abandon Him in His time of suffering but was present at His trial, His sentencing, His beating, and His crucifixion. Mary Magdalene was the first person to encounter Jesus after His resurrection (John 20:11–18).

Priscilla and her husband, Aquila, were tentmakers who opened their home to Paul and brought him into their business while he founded the church in Corinth. Priscilla and Aquila are commended in Scripture for their hospitality, service, and ability to build up others in the faith (Acts 18). Later, they established a home church in Ephesus.

Dorcas, also known as Tabitha, was known in the city of Joppa for her many good works, such as making clothes for the poor and needy. When she fell ill and died, grieving believers sent word to the apostle Peter in a nearby town. After Peter came and raised her from the dead, word spread throughout the city and many came to believe in Jesus Christ.

So many other women in church history, most unnamed, have set profound examples for us with their commitment to the faith, their devotion to God's Word, their powerful prayers, their insightful teaching and writing, their service to the church, and their love for humanity.

EXPLORING THE PARABLES
Read the parable of the good shepherd in John 10:1–18.

eternal security

As we have seen, when you were born, you were born with a sin nature. Therefore, you did not have the ability to choose God. The faith you now have is a gift given to you by God in His grace and mercy. Without this gift, you could not have believed in Jesus. Once you received the gift, you responded by believing in Him and His work on the cross. And because you believed, the righteousness of Christ is credited to you. God accepts you as His adopted child because when He looks at you, He sees the perfect obedience of Jesus, not your sins.

Notice that in all the things that went into your salvation, you didn't do any of them except believe, and even the faith you have is a gift from God. Salvation is absolutely and completely God's work and His alone. None of us can earn it, deserve it, or contribute to it in any way. And this is cause for great comfort for all believers because it means we have eternal security. In other words, Jesus has given us eternal life, and no one can take it away from us (John 10:28–29).

Christ's work of paying for your sins on the cross is finished (John 19:28–30). Jesus is now seated at the right hand of the Father, meaning His work is completed (Mark 16:19). It is not "possibly" finished or "potentially" finished, waiting for you to complete it. The work of Christ is actually finished. And because God does not change and no one and nothing can thwart the will of God, you cannot lose your salvation. It's a done deal. Although there may be times when you feel like you're not holding onto God's hand closely or well, you can be certain that He has you firmly in His grip. "For I am convinced that neither death nor life, neither angels nor demons, neither the present nor the future, nor any powers, neither height nor depth, nor anything else in all creation, will be able to separate us from the love of God that is in Christ Jesus our Lord" (Romans 8:38–39, NIV).

HOSPITALITY

Most of the time, it's easy to be welcoming and gracious to people we know and love, such as friends and family. But when we show that same kindness to strangers, it's called hospitality. In fact, the Greek word translated as *hospitality* in the New Testament means "love of strangers." This trait is so important to Christlike character that the apostle Paul twice listed it among traits that church leaders "must" have (Titus 1:8; 1 Timothy 3:2).

No matter how many friends you have on social media or how many people you know, there are far more people who are strangers to you. These are the people to whom you should be hospitable when you have the opportunity.

When your family travels to a place where you don't know anyone, your parents simply make reservations to stay at a hotel. Hotels are part of what we call the "hospitality industry" because of the fact that it serves strangers. But there were no hotels and few inns when the Bible was written, so hospitality was a very important part of that culture. Where did Paul stay when he was on one of his missionary journeys? Travelers often stayed with total strangers. Not only that, but their hosts fed them too, often for two or three days or more.

In today's culture, it's easy to live isolated from others and never have to deal with strangers face-to-face. But you are called to be different from the rest of the world. Being hospitable and showing kindness to a stranger is a way to demonstrate the gospel. Start by sharing a smile or saying "Hi" at the grocery. Big things often have small beginnings. You never know how God will use a simple act of kindness.

Prayer

God of all Creation,

You are all-knowing and all-powerful. And yet You are so great that I'm amazed I can know anything about You. When people doubt Your existence or question that Jesus is equal to You in every way, I want to be able to defend these truths. Help me to be ready to give reasons for the hope I have in You and to do so with gentleness and respect. Thank You for giving me everything I need to witness effectively.

In Jesus' name. Amen.

Lesson 30
1, 2 & 3 JOHN
& REVELATION

Light / Love

John • AD 80–95 • Believers • Letter

JOHN

Fellowship • Walking in the Light • Antichrists
Children of God • Love • Overcoming

1 JOHN

That which we have seen and heard we proclaim also to you, so that you too may have fellowship with us; and indeed our fellowship is with the Father and with his Son Jesus Christ. And we are writing these things so that our joy may be complete.
1 John 1:3–4

Jesus is pure light.

Key Word

Fellowship Barometer

Bible Reading

1 John 1

Take it To Heart

That which we have seen and heard we proclaim also to you, so that you too may have fellowship with us; and indeed our fellowship is with the Father and with his Son Jesus Christ. And we are writing these things so that our joy may be complete.

1 John 1:3–4

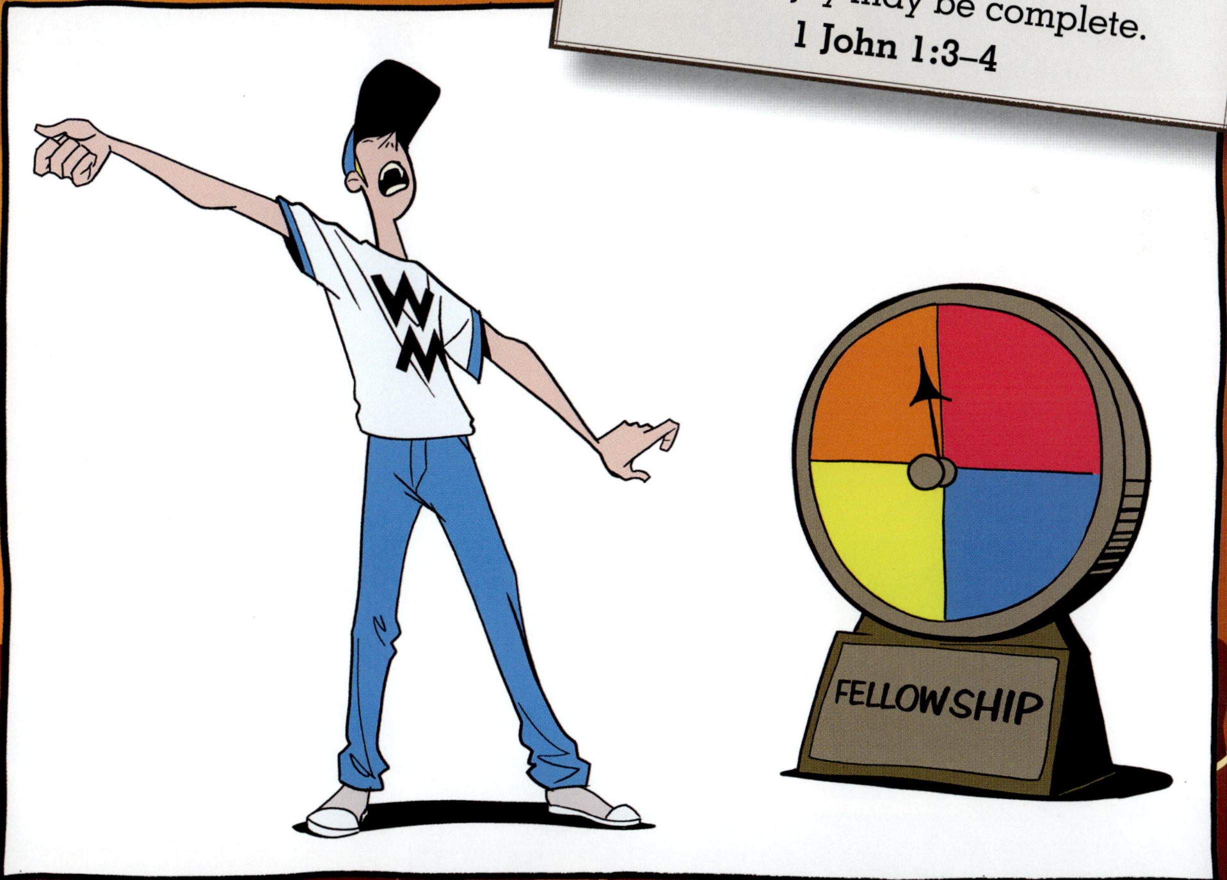

Eternal Truth

John • AD 80–95 • Believers • Letter

JOHN

Walking in Truth • Love One Another

Abide in Christ's Teaching • Watch Out for Deceivers

2 JOHN

Everyone who goes on ahead and does not abide in the teaching of Christ, does not have God. Whoever abides in the teaching has both the Father and the Son. If anyone comes to you and does not bring this teaching, do not receive him into your house or give him any greeting.

2 John 1:9–10

Jesus is God in human flesh.

Take it To Heart

Everyone who goes on ahead and does not abide in the teaching of Christ, does not have God. Whoever abides in the teaching has both the Father and the Son. If anyone comes to you and does not bring this teaching, do not receive him into your house or give him any greeting.

2 John 1:9–10

Key Word

Bolt the Door

Bible Reading

2 John 1

The Name

John • AD 80–95 • Believers • Letter

JOHN

Hospitality • Imitating Good

3 JOHN

Beloved, do not imitate evil but imitate good. Whoever does good is from God; whoever does evil has not seen God.
3 John 1:11

Jesus is the who.

Key Word
Open the Door

Bible Reading
3 John 1

Take it To Heart
Beloved, do not imitate evil but imitate good. Whoever does good is from God; whoever does evil has not seen God.
3 John 1:11

Alpha & Omega

John • AD 95–96 • Believers • Prophecy

John

Vision • Messages to the Churches • Lamb Who Was Slain
Seven Seals • Great Tribulation • Two Witnesses
Wrath of God • The Beast & the False Prophet
Second Coming • Judgment • New Heaven & Earth

REVELATION

Blessed is the one who reads aloud the words of this prophecy, and blessed are those who hear, and who keep what is written in it, for the time is near.
Revelation 1:3

Jesus is the King of kings, the Lord of lords, our bright and morning star.

Bible Reading

Revelation 19–22

Key Word

Coming Events

Take it To Heart

Blessed is the one who reads aloud the words of this prophecy, and blessed are those who hear, and who keep what is written in it, for the time is near.

Revelation 1:3

Gaius Speaks

My friends, I have received a letter from my dear friend John, the beloved disciple, who was present at the crucifixion of our precious Lord. I was pleased to open my home to John when he brought the gospel of Jesus Christ to our city and established the church here. He instructed me in the faith and has since allowed me to serve God by showing hospitality to those who carry the Good News to Asia.

The letter was delivered by a missionary called Demetrius, who has come with a group of Christians to preach the gospel in our region. Of course, I offered them my home. John knows that he does not impose on me by sending messengers of God to sleep in my rooms and eat at my table, for I take great joy in providing such as I have to our brothers in the faith.

I do not say this to puff myself up or sing my own praises. The Lord has given me the means to provide aid and assistance to those who are called to proclaim the gospel far from the comforts of home. That's not to say that it is always convenient or comfortable for me to take in total strangers. But every instance is an opportunity for me to place my trust in God and demonstrate the love of Christ.

Each of us has a responsibility to care for and support the missionaries of God. Remember, our Lord Jesus was on a mission far from home, having no place to lay His head, yet He was surrounded by people of faith who cared for Him and met His needs as they were able. We should do the same for those who proclaim His message in our day.

EXPLORING THE MIRACLES
Read about Jesus cleansing the ten lepers in Luke 17:11–19.

Antichrist

One of the most mysterious people in Scripture is a world ruler who will bring great persecution to the church in the end times. He will become so powerful and oppressive that he will be stopped only by the return of Christ. The Bible calls this person "the man of lawlessness" and "the antichrist." He is thought to be "the beast" spoken of in Revelation 13.

The word *antichrist* simply means "against Christ." Anyone who teaches that Jesus is not the Christ is an antichrist because the person is teaching a false gospel (1 John 2:22). But since the beginning of Christianity there have been many men who believers thought were the Antichrist prophesied to appear in the end times. Nero, Napoleon, Hitler, Stalin, and even several popes have been called the Antichrist by some. Although many have been a kind of antichrist, they were not *the* Antichrist.

When the Antichrist is revealed, he will be someone "who opposes and exalts himself against every so-called god or object of worship, so that he takes his seat in the temple of God, proclaiming himself to be God" (2 Thessalonians 2:4). In other words, he will not only reject all religions, but he himself will claim to be God and demand to be worshiped.

By the power of Satan, the Antichrist will perform false miracles that deceive many. He will likely achieve world domination and rule with absolute authority. Given the enormous evil done by those who were thought to be the Antichrist in the past, we can be sure that the actual Antichrist's rule will bring pain and suffering to people in a way the world has never seen.

He will also oppress the Jews (Daniel 9) and wage war against the followers of Christ (Revelation 13:7). But the Antichrist is a man doomed to destruction, for Jesus Christ will defeat the beast upon His return, and he will be thrown into the lake of fire (Revelation 19:19–20).

HEAVEN

Although God is everywhere all at once and not limited to a particular place, He does reveal Himself fully in one particular place. That place is what we call heaven. Although invisible to us while we are on earth, heaven is a very real place. It's not just a happy, peaceful feeling or a state of mind. In heaven, God's glory is a blessing to all who reside there. Hell, on the other hand, is where God reveals His glory in wrath.

All beings in heaven worship God. This includes angels and believers who have died. The souls of believers who have died are with God in heaven, awaiting the day of judgment when they will receive glorified bodies like Christ took on when He was resurrected from the grave.

Because of how it is depicted in art and popular culture, many people have a cartoony image of heaven that pictures it as a place where dead people are given wings and a harp and sit around on a cloud all day. Heaven could not be more different from that! There are no limits to God's perfection, which means that we can never know all His love, all His goodness, or all about anything else He is. Even though we will live forever with Him, we will never stop learning new things about God and new reasons to worship Him.

Dear Lord of Heaven,

When I think about finding myself in Your glorious presence, seeing You face-to-face for the first time, I wonder if I'll be able to even speak. At times I think I might just fall down face-first before Your throne as Your angels cry, "Holy, holy, holy!" At other times, I imagine myself singing and dancing for joy in Your presence, or running into Your arms for a reassuring hug. All I know is that I long to be with You, to see Your glory and magnify Your holy name.

Come quickly, Lord Jesus!
Amen.

NEW TESTAMENT Books

Quick Reference to the 27 Books

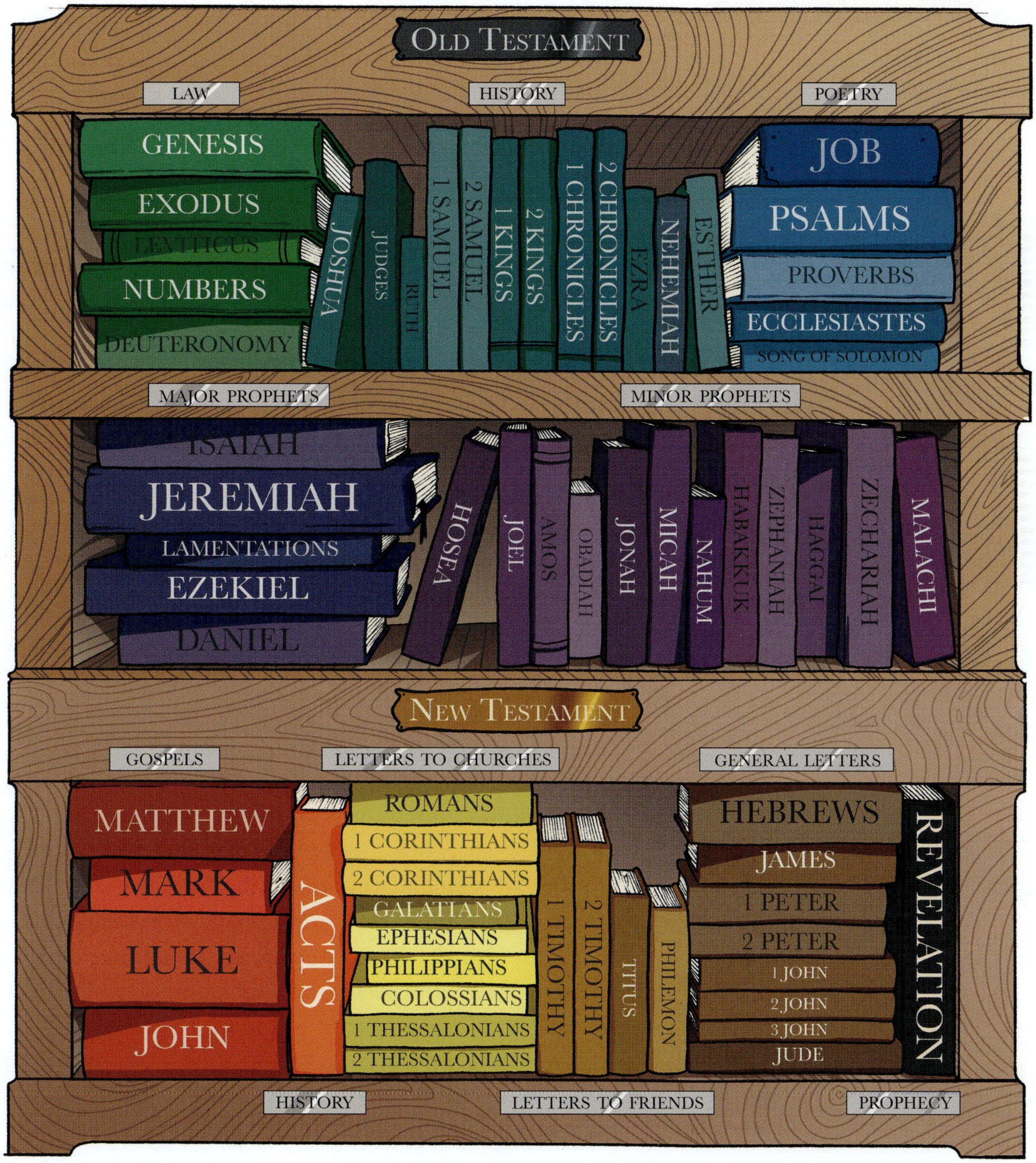

Matthew

King

When you combine a "mat" and a "U," you get something that sounds like "Matthew." This welcome mat leads you directly to a **king**, the key word for the book of Matthew. Matthew, a Jewish tax collector, became a disciple of Jesus, the Jewish Messiah, and wrote a book to his fellow Jews to establish the identity and authenticity of Jesus' claims. In the book, Matthew refers to a number of Old Testament prophecies about the Messiah, and he presents a genealogy linking Jesus with the Davidic throne. Thus, he places Jesus in the context of Israel's history as the King of kings! He then charts Jesus' miracles, discourses, and parables. Moving beyond Israel to all of humanity, the book of Matthew concludes with the Great Commission (28:19–20).

Mark

Servant

Here we see an ark with a large M—a "M-ark." On the ark we find a waiter "serving an ant" to an anteater. "Serve ant" will remind you of the key word for the book of Mark, **servant**. In his brief and to-the-point gospel account, Mark portrays Christ as the Servant of God and focuses on His actions as the Servant of man. A well-known verse in the book of Mark says that Jesus did not come to be served, but to serve (10:45). Faithful to this theme throughout the book, Mark shows Jesus serving the disciples even after His resurrection (16:20).

Luke

Perfect Man

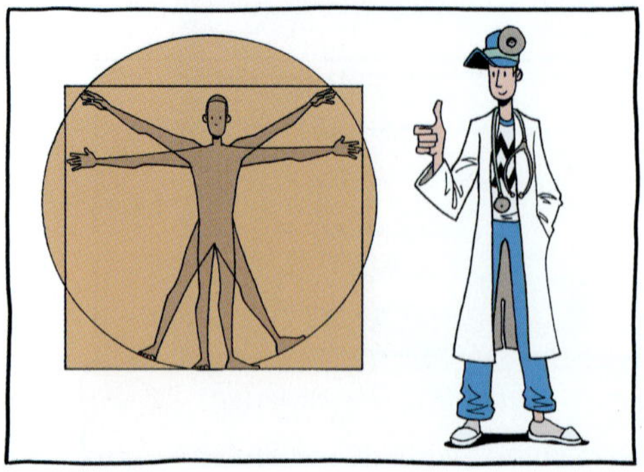

In this picture, our friend Wyatt plays a doctor looking (or "LUKE-ing") at an image inspired by Leonardo da Vinci's representation of the idealized human body. In the Gospel of Luke, Jesus is presented as the **Perfect Man** (also the key word) who is able to save any and all who trust in Him. Luke, a Gentile doctor, wrote his Gospel based on his own thorough investigation of the facts surrounding the life of Jesus. For example, Luke traces the genealogy of Jesus all the way back to Adam, the first man. Jesus Christ is depicted in this book as the Savior of all people, Jew and Gentile alike. Luke uses the term "Son of Man" to describe Jesus, who never sinned yet died for the sins of all mankind.

John

Son of God

This *J* is switched "on," and he's painting a picture. When you recall the Gospel of John, you'll think of "J-on" painting the "sun" of God. John shows us Jesus as the **Son of God**, the key word for this book. The apostle John records a more thematic and intimate account of Jesus' ministry, especially His interactions with the disciples. John's purpose in writing is to prove that Jesus is the Christ and that eternal life is found in Him (20:31). While the Gospels of Matthew, Mark, and Luke present Jesus in the fullness of His humanity, John shows us that Jesus is deity—God incarnate. He is the Light, the Truth, the Life, the Way, the Door, the Bread of Life, and the Water of Life. In fact, He is everything God is because He Himself is God.

Acts

Church

When you think of the book of Acts, you can remember it as the book of "Axe." The theme and key word of this book is building the **church**. Acts is volume two of Luke's record of the life and ministry of Jesus. After Jesus ascends into heaven, the central figures become Christ's apostles, who carry His gospel to all people. This book is structured around a key verse (1:8) in which Jesus instructs the apostles to go to Jerusalem and Judea (the homeland of the Jews), Samaria (neighboring countries), and even to the ends of the earth (all Gentile peoples). Acts records the growth of the church and the spread of the gospel to Asia and Europe, including Rome.

Romans

Paid in Full

This Roman soldier (notice the oars he carries, making him a "Row-man") is presented with the key word of the book of Romans: **paid in full.** When you think of Romans, remember that because of Jesus, our sin debt has been paid in full. This book was written by the apostle Paul and reveals both his heart and his intellect. Romans is the most systematic and profound presentation in the Bible of the righteousness of God. Paul shows us that because all people are sinners, God's righteousness requires their condemnation. But God—and only God—can provide, enact, and accept adequate payment to satisfy His own demands. Because our debt has been paid in full, Paul writes a worshipful doxology in which he proclaims the depth of the riches of the wisdom and knowledge of God (11:33–36).

1 Corinthians
Correcting the Saints

Here we see "One Corinthian" column using a megaphone to shout instructions and advice to a saint. He is **correcting the saint**, which is the key word for the book of 1 Corinthians. This book was written to the young church at Corinth by the apostle Paul. Corinth was a center of commercial confusion and cultural congestion. Immorality, doctrinal confusion, abuses of spiritual liberty—you name it, this young church was struggling with it. Paul displays a firm, loving hand as the apostle gives instruction to the church's leaders. His correction regarding righteousness and unity in the body will strengthen today's church too.

2 Corinthians
Anatomy of an Apostle

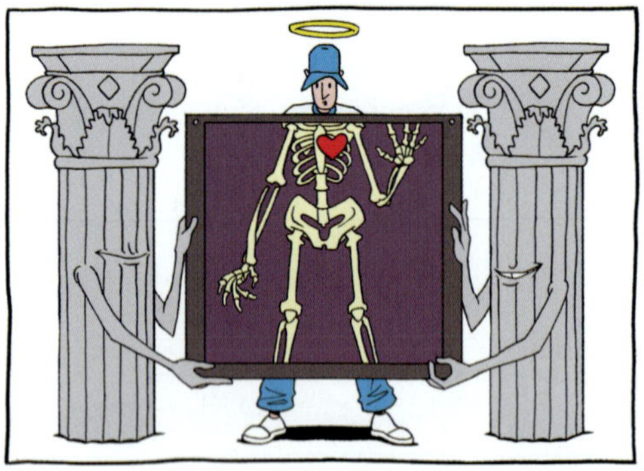

In this picture, we see "Two Corinthian" columns looking at an X-ray, or the **anatomy of an apostle**, the key word for the book of 2 Corinthians. After writing his first letter to the church at Corinth, Paul finds his apostleship and authority under attack. False teachers were accusing Paul of being selfish and acting without true authority from God. This emotional letter to the church at Corinth is Paul's defense of his apostleship and his appeal to the believers to continue to accept his God-given authority. He also asks them to give generously to the afflicted church in Jerusalem.

Galatians
Unshackled

This picture of an unchained seagull laying a shining egg can be described as "Gull Lay Shine," or Galatians. The shackles falling off the gull will remind you of the key word for the book of Galatians: **unshackled**. The fine line between the obligation to obey the law of God and the freedom to obey Him is at the heart of this letter written by the apostle Paul. It is the basic distinction between the Old and New Covenants that God has made with humanity. To be forgiven, does humanity still have to satisfy God's law? Or once we are forgiven—i.e., unshackled from the curse of the law—do we have the power and freedom in the Holy Spirit to please God? Here, Paul reestablishes the importance of life in the Spirit and urges the Galatians to walk in the Spirit rather than in the flesh (5:16).

This is an "E fishing" (Ephesians), and it has caught a bodybuilder, reminding you of the key word for the book of Ephesians: **body building**. The apostle Paul wrote this letter to build up the body of believers at Ephesus. For the believer, life is lived in two planes: the heavenly one, where we are seated with Christ positionally; and the earthly one, where we are in, but not of, the world. In this letter, Paul outlines both realities to the Christians at Ephesus. The book is divided into two parts of three chapters each. In the first section, Paul presents the reality of our spiritual riches in Christ, all based on God's grace (2:8–9). In the second section, believers are urged to walk in a manner worthy of the calling they have received (4:1).

Ephesians
Body Building

Picture this: a happy "Hmmm" bull flipping Ns. You've just learned the name of the book, Philippians (Flippin' Ns), and its key phrase, **happily humble**. The apostle Paul was happily humble as he wrote to the Philippian church from prison. If Jesus' church is going to endure in difficult times, its leaders must set a good example. Jesus suffered in an exemplary way, and in the book of Philippians, we find Paul experiencing joy even as he is chained in prison—a humbling experience indeed! Remaining joyful in adverse circumstances is the theme of this book, and Paul urges believers to focus on Christ, for He is life (1:21). He also urges believers not to be anxious but, rather, to live in peace and harmony with each other and have the mind of Christ regarding their suffering.

Philipians
Happily Humble

What happens when the vehicles of an Army commander and a fire chief run into each other? A big collision! You'll remember this "**commander in chief**" when you read the book of Colossians (from "Collisions"). This key word reminds us that Jesus is Commander in Chief of all creation. A complicated heresy concerning the person of Jesus had surfaced in Colossae, so the apostle Paul wrote a letter to the church clarifying exactly what Jesus did for us and what He is doing through us. His supremacy, which makes Him our Commander in Chief, requires our submission, an attitude unlikely to be manifested by anyone with a faulty view of Jesus and His deity. The doctrinal basis of being "in Christ" is followed by practical exhortations to live for Him.

Colossians
Commander in Chief

1 Thessalonians
Stay on Target

This thistle and onion are trying to do one thing: **stay on target**, which is the key word of the book of 1 Thessalonians ("One Thistle Onion"). The relationship between the apostle Paul and the believers at Thessalonica was like a father encouraging, comforting, and urging his children to live lives pleasing to God. The faith, steadfastness, service, and joy of these believers were reasons for commendation by Paul. And he urges them to stay on target. In order to alleviate fears that those who had died as believers would not participate in Christ's return, he clarifies matters concerning the Day of the Lord. He also sets their sanctification as a goal until Christ returns.

2 Thessalonians
Work While You Wait

Here you see "Two Thistles Onions" representing the book of 2 Thessalonians. Wyatt is shown perched on a scale and working while he "weighs." The key phrase for this book is **work while you wait**. After his first letter to the church at Thessalonica commended them for their faith and service, Paul's second letter to the Thessalonians is written in response to bad reports he has received since. False teachers have convinced some of the believers that the Day of the Lord has already occurred, which has led some to give in to idleness and laziness. Paul's tone of authority in this letter replaces his fatherly calm in the first letter. If anyone doesn't work, he says in 3:10, neither will they eat. In other words, "Work while you wait." He tells them what will transpire before Jesus returns and exhorts them to be patient and to turn away from disruptive elements in the church.

1 Timothy
Leadership Manual

Here's a species of moth you've never seen before—a "tie moth." This "One Tie Moth" (1 Timothy) is encouraging Wyatt to read his **leadership manual**, the key phrase for the book of 1 Timothy. This letter is a leadership manual from the apostle Paul to one of his protégés. As new churches were planted, the need for new leaders has become paramount. Knowing how to conduct oneself in the house of God (3:15) is Paul's goal for Timothy. This means not only developing his own life as a young leader but also appointing other godly leaders who will keep the church free of destructive doctrinal heresies. This practical letter has served as a leadership manual for myriad local churches ever since.

2 Timothy
Combat Manual

What are these "Two Tie Moths" up to? They're training a young "calm bat" in the art of spiritual warfare. Meanwhile, our friend Wyatt reads from a **combat manual**, the key phrase and theme of the apostle Paul's second letter to Timothy. This book was Paul's final letter before his death. Written to Timothy from a Roman prison, Paul urges him to be faithful and persevere, enduring hardship as a good soldier of Jesus (2:3–4). Warning Timothy against the coming apostasy in the church, Paul reminds him of the central place of God's Word. The Bible, he says, is inspired by the Spirit to equip believers for good works. Paul knows his own days are numbered and that God's Word must be Timothy's combat manual in the difficult days ahead.

Titus
Conduct Manual

This is the third of Paul's manuals to young church leaders. In this picture, we see a "con duck" taking a try at the "Tie Toss" (or Titus). He's getting tips from a **conduct manual**, the key phrase for this book. Another student of the apostle Paul, a young pastor named Titus has been given the task of organizing believers into a local church on the Mediterranean island of Crete. In light of the dubious moral reputation of "Cretans," this was not an enviable task. But it does explain the emphasis of the letter, a conduct manual of sorts. Church leaders (elders and deacons) must be of the highest integrity, above reproach in their character, loving leaders of their families, and able to preserve the spiritual purity of the church.

Philemon
Bondage to Brotherhood

This picture shows lemons walking in single file ("File Lemon" for Philemon) as they are set free from jail. They're going from **bondage to brotherhood**, which is the book's key phrase. Restitution by one who has done wrong and forgiveness by the one who was wronged are the themes of this book. In Rome, the apostle Paul has met and converted a young slave named Onesimus, who wronged his master Philemon by running away. Paul knows that Onesimus must return to Philemon and writes this brief letter urging Philemon to accept Onesimus as a brother in Christ. Not even speaking to the ethics of slavery itself, Paul shows that the bonds of Christ are stronger than those of human servitude, as evidenced by Onesimus's transition from bondage to brotherhood.

Hebrews
Milk to Meat

What is Wyatt doing here? He's pouring milk into what appears to be a coffeemaker, but the carafe is full of meat! It looks like "He Brews" from milk to meat. That's the theme and key phrase of this important New Testament book. Hebrews is about moving from **milk to meat**, or growing and maturing spiritually. The author of Hebrews seeks to dissuade Jewish Christians from reverting to Judaism as a way to avoid persecution for their new faith in Christ. He demonstrates how Christ is superior to all parts of their old religion. To be persecuted for Christ is better than returning to an empty religion. The author warns them against turning back and exhorts them to grow up spiritually, moving from drinking milk to eating the solid meat of sound doctrine in their quest for godliness. The message of this letter is for the church in every age.

James
Faith Gauge

In this picture, the *J* is "aiming." "J Aims" (James) is aiming for the **faith gauge**, the key phrase for the book of James. He's aiming to make his faith strong, as this letter written by James counsels believers to do. Written to Jewish Christians, this letter is one of the earliest penned in the young church. The author—probably Jesus' half-brother—focuses on "doing" faith. This is not a letter of theory; it's a faith gauge. It says that if a person's faith is not evidenced by good works, it is a dead faith. This sounds like Jesus talking to the Pharisees, doesn't it? A living faith is not defeated by trials, is no respecter of persons, is a mirror of God's Word, is a controller of the tongue, and displays heavenly wisdom. Above all, it waits patiently but actively for the Lord's return.

1 Peter
Pain With a Purpose

Here is "One Pea" with a "Tear" (for 1 Peter). But this pain comes with a porpoise. So the key phrase for 1 Peter is **pain with a purpose**. Written by the apostle Peter, this letter of encouragement to persecuted Jewish believers reminds them (and us) that suffering has a purpose in a believer's life. The proper response to suffering is the epistle's theme. Peter tells us not to be surprised when suffering comes. Instead, count it as a way of sharing in Christ's sufferings. And make sure your suffering is for the sake of righteousness, not the result of your unrighteousness. Believers are part of a royal priesthood, and our lives should reflect our royalty, even when we are suffering.

2 Peter
Poison in the Pew

Here are "Two Pea Tears" (for 2 Peter). They're weeping because there's **poison in the pew**, which is the book's key phrase. Peter's second letter conveys the message that, at times, false teachers can be found poisoning the church. And when defection, false teaching, and persecution come from within the body of Christ, a serious condition exists—poison in the pew. Peter warns that judgment awaits those who teach falsely and that believers must be on their guard so as not to be led into error by wicked teachers (3:17). The basis for truth is always the Scriptures, which have their origin in God, not in man, and therefore stand in authority over men (1:20–21).

1 John
Fellowship Barometer

Here, Wyatt is showing us "One Yawn" (1 John), and he's checking out a **fellowship barometer**, the key phrase. First John provides us a test of true fellowship—with God and with other believers. Written by the apostle John, this letter confronts Gnosticism, a then-emerging heretical belief that denied the reality of Christ and the truth of salvation through Him. John exposes the false teachers and assures believers that their salvation in Christ is true and secure. He says that sin matters so much to God that He has provided forgiveness and continual fellowship for us even when we do sin. His letter serves as a "fellowship barometer" for who is truly walking in the light, and who is not. Confession, fellowship, and love for believers summarize John's message.

2 John
Bolt the Door

Here we see "Two Yawn"—or the book of 2 John. And though these two are yawning, they're still alert enough to **bolt the door**, which is the key phrase. Second John points out that it's wise to stay spiritually alert to danger. First-century evangelists and teachers, traveling by foot to spread the gospel, would often stay in the homes of Christian families. But heretical teachers might also be hosted by unaware believers not wise enough to know the difference. Therefore, John writes to remind Christians that deceivers are about and that Christians should not welcome them or take them into their homes. In our day, false religious teachers have multiplied dramatically and often come in the name of Jesus. Thus, "bolt the door" remains wise counsel for the church.

3 John
Open the Door

Now we see "Three Yawn," or the book of 3 John. These three guys will help you remember the key phrase of 3 John, which is **open the door**. We are to open our homes to other believers in true hospitality. Gaius, a trusted friend of the apostle John, has acted hospitably in receiving and supporting teachers whom John sent to his church. John commends Gaius's love and faithfulness. But Diotrephes, who is apparently a false leader, is gossiping maliciously about John and refusing to welcome teachers John has sent. Diotrephes has gone so far as to throw out of the church anyone who shows hospitality to John's emissaries. John's admonition to Gaius is to continue in the right way, opening the door to good teachers. John also indirectly warns Diotrephes that anyone who does evil has not seen God (v. 11).

Jude
Fight for the Faith

Here, Wyatt is chewing on gum while giving his all in a **fight for the faith**. This is the key phrase for the little book of Jude ("Chewed")—fighting for the faith against spiritual enemies. Jude writes a passionate letter urging his readers to contend for the faith. He condemns as heretics outsiders who seem set on dividing the church. Jude promises that God has not been slow to judge false teachers in the past and will surely judge these evildoers as well. As a believer, you must protect yourself by building yourself up spiritually, praying in the Spirit, and remaining in God's love while waiting for Christ's return. Without judging, you must reach out to those who may be wavering in their faith. Snatch from the fire any who have fallen and show mercy to all.

Revelation
Coming Events

Our friend Wyatt, by pulling back the curtain of time, is enjoying a "Revelation" of **coming events**, the key phrase for this book. Toward the end of the first century, the apostle John wrote to encourage the churches to purify themselves and to stand firm against coming persecution. Believers were being threatened with death for their unwillingness to worship the Roman emperor. John warns that terrible days are ahead for the church and that believers must remain true until Jesus returns. Judgment will come from Him, and by the sword of His Word, all scales will be made to balance. John's beautiful imagery of the returning Lord and the New Jerusalem, our eternal home, is painted in words that give hope to the church, both then and now.